RESEARCH through PLAY

We express thanks to our families and the chapter authors for supporting us during a pandemic, to make this book a reality. To the practitioners, families and children who allowed their stories to be published in the name of research, we are eternally grateful!

RESEARCH
through
PLAY

Participatory Methods in Early Childhood

EDITED BY

LORNA ARNOTT
& KATE WALL

§SAGE

Los Angeles | London | New Delhi
Singapore | Washington DC | Melbourne

SAGE

Los Angeles | London | New Delhi
Singapore | Washington DC | Melbourne

SAGE Publications Ltd
1 Oliver's Yard
55 City Road
London EC1Y 1SP

SAGE Publications Inc.
2455 Teller Road
Thousand Oaks, California 91320

SAGE Publications India Pvt Ltd
B 1/I 1 Mohan Cooperative Industrial Area
Mathura Road
New Delhi 110 044

SAGE Publications Asia-Pacific Pte Ltd
3 Church Street
#10-04 Samsung Hub
Singapore 049483

Editor: Jude Bowen
Senior assistant editor: Cat McMullen
Production editor: Katherine Haw
Copyeditor: Tom Bedford
Proofreader: Sharon Cawood
Indexer: Charmian Parkin
Cover design: Wendy Scott
Typeset by: C&M Digitals (P) Ltd, Chennai, India

Library of Congress Control Number: 2021935780

British Library Cataloguing in Publication data

A catalogue record for this book is available
from the British Library

ISBN 978-1-5264-9355-2
ISBN 978-1-5264-9354-5 (pbk)

CONTENTS

ABOUT THE EDITORS AND CONTRIBUTORS

ABOUT THE EDITORS

Lorna Arnott is a Senior Lecturer and Director of Early Years in the School of Education, University of Strathclyde. Lorna's main area of interest is in children's early play experiences, particularly in relation to technologies, social and creative play. She also has a keen interest in research methodologies, with a specialist focus on consulting with children and methods derived from pedagogy. Lorna is the convener for the Digital Childhoods, Multimodality and STEM Special Interest Group as part of the European Early Childhood Educational Research Association, and is the Deputy Editor for the *International Journal of Early Years Education* and Assistant Editor for the *Journal of Early Childhood Research*.

Kate Wall is Professor of Education at the University of Strathclyde. A primary teacher by background, her work is characterised by enquiry-based partnership with children and practitioners of all ages and stages. She is interested in methodologies for gathering learner perspectives on experience, curriculum and metacognition, and is recognised for her work on how visual approaches can facilitate this kind of dialogue. Kate's work aims to generate knowledge of ethical practice for eliciting voice within a democratic community, and to do this, particularly with young children, she has needed to look to more creative methods and practices for supporting the level of participation and ensuring authentic voice.

ABOUT THE CONTRIBUTORS

Elisabetta Biffi is Associate Professor at the 'Riccardo Massa' Department of Human Sciences and Education – University of Milano-Bicocca. Her main research interests include childhood protection and children's rights, educator and teacher professional development, pedagogical documentation, narrative methods and arts-based methods for educational research.

Caralyn Blaisdell is an Early Years pedagogue, lecturer and researcher at Queen Margaret University. Her work explores, in various contexts, how children's participation rights under the UN Convention on the Rights of the Child (1989) are lived and experienced. Her current research focuses on emotional relations and participation rights.

Maddie Broad is an artist and musician with a Master's in Early Years Education. She explores things we can do here, now, together, and deals with possibility rather than certainty. This line of inquiry grew throughout art school and early years study, emerging now as a form of research through play.

Liz Chesworth is a lecturer in Early Childhood Education at the University of Sheffield. Her research focuses upon play cultures, curriculum-making and pedagogy with a particular focus upon responsive, contextually relevant approaches to working with young children and their families.

Jonathan Delafield-Butt is Professor of Child Development and Director of the Laboratory for Innovation in Autism at the University of Strathclyde. His multidisciplinary scholarship in education, psychology and neuroscience probes the origins of experience in human development and the role of agency and action in learning, development and health.

Sue Dockett is Emeritus Professor, Charles Sturt University in Albury, Australia and Director, Peridot Education. Sue remains actively involved in research which emphasises participatory rights-based research with children. Her publications reflect this emphasis in exploring children's expectations and experiences of transition to school, their engagement in play, and understandings of mathematics.

Pauline Duncan is a postdoctoral research associate at Moray House School of Education and Sport, University of Edinburgh. Her work explores the use of digital and creative methods to facilitate children's meaningful participation in education. Her writings have appeared in the *American Journal of Play*, *Early Years Educator* and the *Journal of Early Childhood Research*.

Marilyn Fleer is an Australian Research Council Laureate Fellow and Director of the Conceptual PlayLab at Monash University. She is the first Laureate in education to additionally be awarded The Kathleen Fitzpatrick Laureate Fellowship. Her research is focused on play, STEM learning, and human development.

Alma Fleet is Honorary Associate Professor at Macquarie University, Sydney, where she has taught undergraduate and postgraduate students and accepted leadership roles. Now involved in educational consultancies, she writes and researches across the early childhood landscape while advocating for the valuing of children's perspectives, teacher curiosity and agency, and workplaces endowed with curiosity and respect.

Elaine Hall is Professor of Legal Education Research at Northumbria University. Her research career has been directed towards the experience of teaching and learning from early years to old age, as curriculum-specific, metacognitive and professional practices. She is passionately engaged in play. To facilitate this, she is interested in the use of pedagogic and methodologic tools to support dialogue about lived experience and learning (metacognition) across contexts and learning communities.

Shannon Ludgate is the Deputy Course Leader for BA (Hons) Early Childhood Studies at Birmingham City University. Her research specialism is the use of educational technologies to support early childhood education and development, and she has a keen interest in using and developing innovative methods for gaining ethical consent when researching with young children.

Loreain Martinez-Lejarreta is an experienced Early Childhood Education teacher currently writing her PhD thesis at the University of Strathclyde. Her investigation involves exploring young children's critical thinking skills and dispositions in the context of detective play. She is especially interested in innovative research methods and pedagogy with young children.

Rhona Matheson is Chief Executive of Starcatchers, Scotland's national arts and early years organisation. Having worked in the arts and theatre for children for 20 years, Rhona is recognised as being an expert in the field of arts and early years, with a particular interest in work for babies.

Timothy J. McGowan is a graduate of the University of Oxford where he read History, and the University of Nottingham where he completed a Master's in Psychology. He is also a qualified teacher and Teach First ambassador. Timothy is completing his doctoral research on the temporal architecture of adult–infant interactions.

Jane Merewether is a research fellow at Edith Cowan University, Perth, Australia. Her research explores children's relations with the human and non-human world. Jane draws on 18 years as a teacher informed by the educational project of Reggio Emilia, as well as childhood studies, feminist new materialisms and environmental humanities.

Pekka Mertala is a former kindergarten teacher who currently works as an assistant professor of multiliteracies and digital literacies in the Faculty of Education and Psychology at the University of Jyväskylä, Finland.

Jane Murray is Associate Professor and Co-Director at the Centre for Education and Research, University of Northampton, UK. She has published extensively in the field of education, particularly in the areas of early childhood education and social inclusion. Jane is Editor of the *International Journal of Early Years Education*.

Cathy Nutbrown is Professor of Education at the University of Sheffield where she researches early childhood education and family literacy. Author of over 50 publications, including *Threads of Thinking* (2011) and *Early Childhood Educational Research* (2018), Cathy is also Editor in Chief of the *Journal of Early Childhood Research*.

Ioanna Palaiologou is a chartered psychologist with the British Psychological Society with a specialism in child development, cognition and learning theories. Her research interests focus on ethics, child development, the role of digital technologies and implications for pedagogy.

Heidi Sairanen is a researcher and a former kindergarten teacher. She wrote her doctoral thesis on relational agency in early years pedagogy. She serves on the advisory board of the Playful Learning Center situated at the University of Helsinki, Faculty of Educational Sciences.

Tríona Stokes is Lecturer in Drama Education at Maynooth University's Froebel Department of Primary and Early Childhood Education in Ireland. Formerly a primary school teacher, Tríona's research in recent years has focused on pretend play facilitation with young children, and arts education for early years.

Elizabeth Wood is Professor of Education at the University of Sheffield. Her current areas of research include leadership in early childhood education, digital/traditional play, critical policy analysis, curriculum and pedagogy in early childhood and primary education.

Franca Zuccoli is Associate Professor at the University of Milano-Bicocca, where she teaches Art Education and General Didactics. Her main research field is the relationship between school and museum and educational sections inside museums, focused on contemporary art.

PROLOGUE

LORNA ARNOTT AND KATE WALL,
UNIVERSITY OF STRATHCLYDE

This book offers a starting point for those who want to better understand the possibilities for innovative research methods that draw on the founding principles of early childhood pedagogy. The drive to involve children in research is becoming stronger as rights-based perspectives advocate for children's rights and ability to be involved in decision-making around matters that affect them (UN Commission on Human Rights, 1990). It is no longer acceptable to assume children are not capable of taking part (Lundy, 2007; Wall et al., 2019). While there are continuing debates about what this might look like in practice and the nuanced ethical considerations inherent in this stance (Alderson and Morrow, 2020; Mayne et al., 2018), the basic philosophy is that we should at least try, where possible, to make space for children's involvement.

Age is no longer an appropriate barometer for children's ability to be involved in research, and as such the notion that children under 8 – if we employ the internationally recognised age range for early childhood education – should be excluded because of the difficulty associated with the data collection, is now redundant. Nevertheless, consulting with children under 8 and involving them in research projects, particularly at the lower age range, is difficult and complex. Debates are ongoing about whether methods should be child-friendly, while others make the case that these age-appropriate methods perpetuate the divide between adult and child by highlighting difference (see discussions of ethical symmetry, in Christensen and Prout, 2002). In this book we do not pretend to solve these debates. Instead, we seek to present one particular conceptualisation of what research with children might entail. That conceptualisation is that any methods employed in research – any research, not just with children – should be appropriate to the pedagogy of that context. For early childhood, that pedagogy is play. It therefore makes sense to us that when working with young children and involving them in research, the methods should resemble play and playfulness to align with their natural lived experiences.

To better explain how this conceptualisation came to be in our minds, we offer the reflective narrative of our experience as researchers which has guided us towards editing this book.

OUR STORY: INSPIRATION AND POSSIBILITIES FOR PLAY

Lorna's story: Throughout my research career, from the beginning and that very first research project with young children, a focus on understanding children's perspectives seemed obvious and the most sensible approach in a study involving children. At the time, guided by Dr Christine Stephen as supervisor, a sector-leading scholar on early childhood pedagogy, the idea of consulting with children directly as research participants was planned without question (albeit always ethically and with great critical reflection). That is to say that I blindly embarked on this journey assuming it was standard practice. Why wouldn't we consult children and find appropriate methods to facilitate this engagement?

This laid the groundwork for devising methods for the project that were rooted in play. The methods chosen did not come from any methods textbook or previous study. Instead, with Stephen's support, the methods were imagined and designed from scratch from our knowledge of what children enjoyed doing and what everyday play might look like. They weren't overly sophisticated or complex, and if replicated today would probably be changed, as our knowledge of pedagogy has evolved. Yet they were always rooted in children's natural and everyday experiences in nursery. Of course, Clark and Moss' (2001) Mosaic Approach was, and still is, influential but it had not registered with me at the time that people might follow The Mosaic Approach as a model, engaging in walking tours and with magic carpet rides. Rather, I read The Mosaic Approach and it acted like a springboard which laid the foundation for what early childhood research could be in my mind. The Mosaic became a source of inspiration, creativity and possibilities in what play offered for research, but not necessarily a rigid structure to follow. That perspective, coupled with a real appreciation for a few other key sources at the time, including Christensen and James' (2008) Research with Children, led me to believe that devising methods from pedagogy was typical practice.

It wasn't until many years later, when my research bubble extended beyond the early years community and I met Kate Wall, that it became clear that these approaches, while not completely absent in research with children, were very much innovations in the broader research arena.

Kate's story: I was a primary teacher during the 1990s and started my research career in my own classroom. My PhD used a rather clunky questionnaire to ask the children in my class over two successive years what they thought of literacy under two different grouping arrangements. It didn't work very well, and since then I have sought more authentic ways to elicit the voice of children. In the younger age ranges or for those with additional support needs, this has often meant removing some of the barriers of literacy and numeracy, resulting in the development of visual approaches, something which was common sense to my teacher self, but felt new and risky in the research world. The notion of devising methods based on pedagogy (described by Wall, 2019, as pedagogically appropriate methods) became fundamental to the work being conducted on how to elicit children's voices in research and practice in the early years. My work on visual approaches to research, originating in my experience as a primary teacher, found useful leverage in the voice communities and this has cemented these connections (for example, Wall, 2017; Wall and Higgins, 2006).

I have continued to have strong affiliations to the teacher-researcher of my roots and as a result continue to collaborate with teachers and practitioners researching in their own settings, exploring ways to make this process pragmatic and not add to the ever-growing list of things to do. By linking pedagogy and research through the use of visual techniques (Wall, 2018) a productive space was found, supporting practitioner learning as an ethical prerogative connected to children's learning (Wall and Hall, 2016). A tightening of the feedback loops between practitioners' and children's learning has become facilitatory of new perspectives for eliciting children's voice and enabling authentic participation. This has manifested in the Look Who's Talking project and the production of eight factors for eliciting voice with children from birth to age 7 (Arnott and Wall, in press; Wall et al., 2019), which has also been translated into professional learning contexts (Wall, 2020).

Our story: In the last decade in particular, we have seen more creative methods for research emerging (Blaisdell et al., 2019; Cologon et al., 2019; Kara, 2015; Mayne et al., 2017), and with the development of non-traditional research paradigms like practitioner enquiry (Hall and Wall, 2019), a movement towards innovative research approaches has become increasingly likely. Yet, these approaches are still not the norm. This became abundantly clear over time, particularly when trying to support undergraduate students who were working on their dissertation research and continually struggled to source methods examples in the literature, which helps the undergraduate students to involve children directly in their practice-based research projects. Working in this way, in partnership with students, challenges the use of questionnaires, focus groups and interviews, and so we ask them to think creatively, drawing on their own practice to devise the methods. A key lecture at the start of their method training is always that they are already skilful researchers, already consulting with children, already interpreting meaning from play – they just call it pedagogy!

(Continued)

The notion that they should draw on their own pedagogy to design pedagogically appropriate methods (Wall, 2018, 2019), in this case related to play, seemed like a natural step in the process. Yet they have few guides to follow to help them visualise what this might look like in reality, when translating pedagogy into method, and they need literature that will do what Clark and Moss (2001) did for Arnott – to spark their own inspiration to be creative and see the possibilities for research through play. The decision was made to edit a book which laid out the principle factors that would help practitioners engage in enquiry while drawing on their key pedagogical ways of being – translating play into rich research methods.

THE STRUCTURE OF THE BOOK

We have gathered together an eclectic mix of innovative and world-leading authors to showcase the possibilities of play for research. The book is divided into four key Parts:

1. Founding Principles for Playful Research Approaches
2. Theoretical and Conceptual Frameworks for Playful Research
3. Adapting Play-Based Pedagogies as a Research Method
4. Research Resources from Early Childhood Education

The founding principles in Part 1 offer much-needed contextual information for any-one who is perhaps not familiar with play or research with young children. In the opening chapter, Wood and Chesworth contextualise this book in a rich, critically reflective narrative of what we mean by play, the debates and also challenges associated with adopting playful pedagogies in research. In the second chapter, Murray positions the book in an intentionally recognised conceptualisation of childhood and children's rights, and translates this narrative into a research context. The third chapter, by Dockett, concludes this Part by highlighting key ethical considerations inherent in messy and unpredictable research methods like play and with young children who are still developing their communication skills.

Part 2 takes us into a discussion of methodologies, paradigms and the complexity of interpreting data which is often inherently abstract, non-quantifiable and at times unruly. In Chapter 4, Wall, Arnott and Hall situate this work in a practitioner enquiry approach, reassuring you that the dual roles of researcher and practitioner and being an insider in the research is a key strength rather than a limitation or some challenge which reduces research rigour. Instead, the approach not only strengthens research data by adding rich-ness to the context, but also supports a process of professional learning which then feeds back into practice and into future research. In Chapter 5, Merewether and Fleet extend this process of researching within practice by drawing our attention to how key pedagogical tools, like pedagogical documentation, offer an avenue to rich, robust and authentic data with children. This Part is then concluded by Nutbrown's discussion in Chapter 6, where she sets out the process and complexity associated with playful research methods, arguing for a focus on faithfulness, integrity and trustworthiness.

The third Part is where play comes to life as the authors present case studies and research data about how play pedagogies translate into the focus of the research. Drawing on Dockett's encouragement to think ethically about research, Arnott, Martinez-Lejarreta, Wall, Blaisdell and Ludgate open the Part in Chapter 7 with innovative approaches to supporting children's informed consent. A critically reflective narrative is presented to demonstrate the successes and the challenges associated with the techniques chosen. This leads on to examples by Duncan in Chapter 8 about how drawing can be used playfully to understand children's perspectives. Importantly in this chapter, the final artistic output is not the most important factor, but rather a playful encounter during the drawing process adds richness to the data. Chapter 9 takes playful interaction to a new dimension as Arnott, McGowan and Delafield-Butt consider the art of understanding babies' perspectives by combining neuropsychological perspectives with early childhood pedagogy to better understand how observations of babies' play can be structured for meaningful interpretation and analysis. Key to this chapter is a focus on the contours of a narrative; a storying of the child's perspective. The focus on artistic representation and documentation which tell a story is also central in Chapter 10 where Biffi, Palaiologou and Zuccoli describe a process of combining pedagogical document and arts-informed methods to engage in playful data collection approaches as part of a highly conceptualised methodology. Chapter 11, by Fleer, grounds us back in the practical by showcasing how researchers can employ new technologies to gather, log and interpret play using an app. The chapter links us back to those methodological and conceptual chapters in Part 2 by stressing the importance of always interpreting the data gathered on the app from a suitable theoretical frame, in this case from cultural historical theory. The case studies are then concluded in Chapter 12, by Mertala, which brings us back almost full circle to Chapter 1 as he debates the definition of play and how that shapes his research design. He then showcases how he employs traditional analogue play to understand children's digital literacies.

Part 4 then stands as a reference point to support novice researchers, or researchers who aren't starting from a practice orientation, to understand what play might look like and how such a perspective can be facilitatory of research with young children. Within this Part we first include two examples of more established ongoing work: Rhona Matheson from Starcatchers, Scotland's national arts and early years organisation, provides three examples of play- and arts-based approaches for eliciting perspectives of babies and toddlers under 3, and Sairanen describes how in Finland a playful partnership approach has been used to explore and develop the learning environment to support transitions into school. We then also include two proposals for play-based projects to show how play can be embedded from the inception of the research: Stokes' research is exploring perspectives of play with the children and shows how she planned her project, using the Mosaic Approach (Clark and Moss, 2001), with full consideration of analysis and ethics, while Broad involves children as researchers of their own learning, astutely aligning the research with the pedagogy of the setting. The latter chapters offer a reference for those who might want to devise play-based or play-informed methods but need some inspiration of what play might look like. These act as a catalyst to designing pedagogically appropriate methods in early childhood.

OUR ETHOS

Play as a concept and practice is fundamentally debated in the literature, as described clearly in Chapter 1. We do not suggest that play holds all the answers or that it will offer a clean and unproblematic route to research. In many cases, employing play in research will likely add to the complexity in your decision-making and raise unexpected challenges. Yet play is meaningful for children, and so while pedagogy with children is unpredictable, it often leads to children flourishing in unexpected ways. We hope that play will allow research to also flourish in unexpected yet fruitful ways.

The chapters throughout this book do not represent a model or framework to follow. Instead, they are meant to offer inspiration to be creative and see the possibilities for research through play that are unique to your context. We hope they offer that springboard and give you the encouragement to explore a new path in your research. It may not always be successful, but that does not mean that there aren't opportunities for professional learning and reflection. Embracing the unknown and dedicating time to exploration in a flexible way is at the heart of children's play, and done thoughtfully and reflexively it can be at the heart of our research with children too.

REFERENCES

Alderson, P. and Morrow, V. (2020). *The Ethics of Research with Children and Young People: A Practical Handbook*. London: Sage.

Arnott, L. and Wall, K. (in press). *Theory and Practice of Voice in Early Childhood: An International Exploration*. London: Routledge.

Blaisdell, C., Arnott, L., Wall, K. and Robinson, C. (2019). Look Who's Talking: Using creative, playful arts-based methods in research with young children. *Journal of Early Childhood Research*, 17 (1): 14–31.

Christensen, P. and James, A. (Eds.) (2008). *Research with Children: Perspectives and Practices*. London: Routledge.

Christensen, P. and Prout, A. (2002). Working with ethical symmetry in social research with children. *Childhood*, 9 (4): 477–97.

Clark, A. and Moss, P. (2001). *Listening to Children: The Mosaic Approach.* London: National Children's Bureau.

Cologon, K., Cologon, T., Mevawalla, Z. and Niland, A. (2019). Generative listening: Using arts-based inquiry to investigate young children's perspectives of inclusion, exclusion and disability. *Journal of Early Childhood Research*, 17 (1): 54–69.

Hall, E. and Wall, K. (2019). *Research Methods for Understanding Professional Learning.* London: Bloomsbury.

Kara, H. (2015). *Creative Research Methods in the Social Sciences: A Practical Guide.* Bristol: Policy Press.

Lundy, L. (2007). 'Voice' is not enough: Conceptualising Article 12 of the United Nations Convention on the Rights of the Child. *British Educational Research Journal*, 33 (6): 927–42.

Mayne, F., Howitt, C. and Rennie, L. J. (2017). Using interactive nonfiction narrative to enhance competence in the informed consent process with 3-year-old children. *International Journal of Inclusive Education*, 21 (3): 299–315.

Mayne, F., Howitt, C. and Rennie, L. (2018). Rights, power and agency in early childhood research design: Developing a rights-based research ethics and participation planning framework. *Australasian Journal of Early Childhood*, 43 (3): 4–14.

UN Commission on Human Rights (1990). *Convention on the Rights of the Child* (E/CN.4/ RES/1990/74), 7 March. Available at: www.refworld.org/docid/3b00f03d30.html (accessed 5 September 2020).

Wall, K. (2017). Exploring the ethical issues related to visual methodology when including young children's voice in wider research samples. *International Journal of Inclusive Education*, 21 (3): 316–31.

Wall, K. (2018). Bridging the gap between methodology and pedagogy. *Scottish Education Review*, 50 (2): 3–22.

Wall, K. (2019). Pedagogic appropriateness: Judging quality in practitioner enquiry. BERA Blog. www.bera.ac.uk/blog/pedagogic-appropriateness-judging-quality-in-practitioner-enquiry

Wall, K. (2020). Productive parallels between young children's voice and practitioner voice. In *Encyclopedia of Teacher Education.* Singapore: Springer. Available at: https:// link.springer.com/referencework/10.1007/978-981-13-1179-6 (accessed 20 January 2021).

Wall, K. and Hall, E. (2016). Teachers as metacognitive role models. *European Journal of Teacher Education*, 39 (4): 403–18.

Wall, K. and Higgins, S. (2006). Facilitating and supporting talk with pupils about metacognition: A research and learning tool. *International Journal of Research and Methods in Education*, 29 (1): 39–53.

Wall, K., Cassidy, C., Robinson, C., Hall, E., Beaton, M., Kanyal, M. and Mitra, D. (2019). Look Who's Talking: Factors for considering the facilitation of very young children's voices. *Journal of Early Childhood Research*, 17 (4): 263–78.

PART 1

FOUNDING PRINCIPLES FOR PLAYFUL RESEARCH APPROACHES

1

FRAMING AND DEFINING
PLAY IN EARLY CHILDHOOD

ELIZABETH WOOD AND LIZ CHESWORTH

The task of framing and defining play underpins the remainder of this book in order to contextualise ethics, theories and methodologies for designing play-based research methods. The complexity of play forms and manifestations across the human lifecourse make play difficult to define, let alone to capture through research. Accordingly, we are not proposing that play can be defined, but we are arguing for clarity in articulating our own positions, as well as understanding those expressed in research, from contrasting theoretical and methodological perspectives. The choices we make in our research depend on our own histories, traditions, cultures, values and life experiences, and these in turn influence the theories and methods that we choose. What and who we look at is also influenced by cultures and contexts, which means that reflections on our own interpretations of play need to be sensitive to social and cultural diversities, such as class, ethnicities, languages, gender, sexual orientations and religious affiliations, with the possibility that there will be more than one explanation for children's play choices and activities. Moreover, how playful pedagogies are conceived will depend on the early childhood education policy frameworks in different countries, and their histories, cultures and values. This introductory chapter aims to:

- Outline contemporary debates;
- Clarify contrasting perspectives on framing and defining play;
- Consider the implications for curriculum and pedagogical approaches.

We define early childhood as birth to eight years, to reflect international variations in the age range for preschool and primary education, and the different types of settings that children of this age attend outside their homes – private, government-funded, voluntary and non-government organisations. The term 'practitioner' is used to encompass all adults who work with children in preschool settings, to reflect the range of qualifications and requirements in different countries. The term 'teacher' is used to denote adults who are qualified with a professionally recognised teacher training body, and work either in a preschool or primary school setting. The focus of this book is on qualitative enquiry and methods for working with children, and recognises that adults' roles incorporate playing, teaching, caring, researching and reflecting on their approaches and principles.

Given the ethical and participatory focus of the research approaches presented in this book, any definition of play should reflect children's perspectives and experiences. With these caveats in mind, much research is driven by adults' fascination with play, and the need to know more about what children do in their freely chosen activities, as well as the purposes those activities serve in children's learning and development, and in their peer cultures. Furthermore, the addition of 'educational play' has brought further challenges to framing and defining playful pedagogies because many national and international policy frameworks incorporate play as a process that is expected to produce specific learning outcomes. In other words, play has shifted away from being seen as the natural activity of childhood, defined by concepts of freedom – to choose, to roam, to express individual and group interests, and direct play for one's own purposes. Instead, play has been drawn into social, health and education policies in many countries to the extent that it is pulled in specific directions towards defined ends, sometimes with the means determined by adults. These contemporary contexts add to the complexity of researching play and using play-based or pedagogically appropriate research methods, because of the fuzzy boundaries between the researcher's and the children's play agendas.

In light of these complexities, where can we start when thinking about defining and framing play in order to design and carry out research?

The objectives for this chapter are:

1. To consider ways of defining and framing play.
2. To consider the significance of contexts for researching play and researching through play in education settings.
3. To understand three different modes of play as a means of framing research on playful pedagogies in different contexts.

WAYS OF DEFINING AND FRAMING PLAY

Although there are many ways of defining play and articulating its core characteristics and purposes, no single definition has been agreed upon (Wood, 2013). Sutton-Smith (1997: 4) takes an expansive overview of 'the great diversity of play phenomena', shown in the quote below, but argues that presenting these as a list has limitations because the boundaries between play forms and characteristics are never discrete:

> Mind or subjective play; solitary play; playful behaviours; informal social play; vicarious audience play; performance play; celebrations and festivals; contests, games and sports; risky or deep play. (Sutton-Smith, 1997: 4–5)

In each of these forms, play can be ambiguous. For example, children can structure social play with rules that are negotiated to set up and direct the play, the social hierarchies of who can lead or organise the play, and who can be included or excluded. Some play forms are spontaneous and involve the freedom to choose, and others, such as contests, games and sports, are highly structured with specific rules and rigorous training programmes for elite players. Because it is difficult to define play as observable activity, some researchers have proposed that it is a state of mind, a way of being, an orientation to life that involves not just the act of playing, but also being playful or being in a state of play (Sutton-Smith, 1997).

Given the struggle to define play, it is important to understand children's perspectives in the contexts of their play lives. Generally, children agree that play is freely chosen, takes place in their own spaces (indoors and outdoors, homes, communities and education settings) and takes place without adults. In relation to playful pedagogies, children may choose to involve adults in their play, but adults' presence and roles should be as co-players, on the children's terms and respectful of their purposes. Thus, children's intentions and meanings are central to designing play-based research methods. Howe (2016) focused on the meanings and values that children attributed to play/self-initiated activity, as they made the transition from the Early Years Foundation Stage (the curriculum framework for children from birth to 5) to Year 1 of the National Curriculum (age 5 to 6) in England. Using photographs, drawings and conversations, Howe identified that children value play/self-initiated activity as a means of exercising choice and autonomy, pursuing their own interests, building social relationships with peers, and for relaxation, enjoyment and reward. However, their experiences of play shifted in the transition to Year 1, as pedagogical approaches became more teacher-directed. This study highlights the impact of changing contexts, teachers' roles and curriculum demands on children, all of which are relevant in countries that have developed curriculum frameworks that link preschool with compulsory education.

The task of defining and framing play is complex because play is a contested concept that is used for different purposes in different contexts. Furthermore, play forms, tools and resources have changed over time, alongside children's material cultures, conceptions of childhood and how play is valued within different communities and societies. Digital or technological play has become widespread in recent years, and could be incorporated into any play forms and characteristics. The concepts of postdigital play (Marsh et al., 2019) and converged play (Wood et al., 2019) indicate no distinction between digital and traditional play because children move seamlessly across platforms and devices. However, as Wood et al. (2019) have argued, playful pedagogies that incorporate converged play are lagging behind children's engagement and competence with digital technologies. Therefore, stepping into the field of research on play demands that we are transparent about the theoretical and methodological lenses we are choosing, and for what purposes. In summary, the task of defining and framing play encompasses:

- Academic definitions based on research from contrasting disciplinary perspectives.
- Children's perspectives and experiences.
- How play is framed within curriculum guidance and policy frameworks.
- Adults' perspectives in different contexts.
- Cultural and contextual perspectives.

The diversity of play phenomena noted by Sutton-Smith (1997) has implications for researching play and the range of play-based methods that might be used. Play has been researched over time from contrasting disciplinary perspectives. From the early nineteenth century, philosophical views positioned play as the natural activity and occupation of childhood that has many benefits – cognitive, social, affective, psycho-motor as well as therapeutic, spiritual and existential. A universal view of play was applied to young children and animals in relation to different functions such as learning, development, rehearsal, imitation, acquisition of behaviours for survival and success, preparation for maturity/adulthood, and many more (Sutton-Smith, 1997). In the 20th century, the scientific study of children produced new theories of learning and development from psychology and developmental psychology. The addition of neuroscience and new research technologies generated further understanding of the development, structure and functions of the brain, its circuitry and architecture (Anderson and Reid, 2016). As the focus shifted from exploring what play is, to what play is good for, scientific research established its beneficial effects for learning, development and well-being, and its therapeutic value. These effects have been demonstrated in the developmental domains – cognitive, social, affective and psycho-motor – and in subject areas such as literacy, mathematics, science and technology.

Play is also associated with learning-relevant processes such as self-regulation, metacognition, memory, attention and problem-solving (Robson, 2010; Whitebread et al., 2012). As a result, scientific research has gradually influenced public policy in education, health and social care, based on claims about the universal benefits of play for children and families. Concepts from research about developmental ages and stages, categories and types of play, and various measures of the benefits of play, provided the scientific discourse of development proceeding in similar ways, but with some variations in the ages at which children progress through defined stages. However, developmental theories have been the focus of critique. In a historical review of research on children's play in an Australian indigenous context, Dender and Stagnitti note the limitations of this universal discourse, and challenge the deterministic view that all children play in the same or similar ways:

> It can be argued that play is situational, culturally contextual and socially constructed because play takes different forms in different cultures and some forms of play are discouraged or have a different emphasis in some cultural groups. (2015: 3)

Although Whitebread et al. (2012) acknowledge cultural variations in play, they document the progress from psychological perspectives to ECE curriculum frameworks, and the significant shift in the 20th century from demonstrating the value of play to informing education policies about its contribution to learning goals and outcomes. This shift also had implications for defining playful or play-based pedagogies, and for designing research methods.

Play is valued in many national early childhood curriculum frameworks (Roopnarine et al., 2018), often using normative and instrumental ways of defining and justifying play based on the concept of 'educational play'. In educational play, constructs such as play-based learning, curriculum and pedagogy are the foundations of practice, but have been interpreted in different ways in curriculum frameworks, and by practitioners. In a review of research on kindergarten teachers' concepts of play, Fesseha and Pyle (2016) propose that how play is defined depends on individual teachers' beliefs, how they use play and the roles they assume. Consistent with similar studies, they argue that while many kindergarten teachers support the use of play-based learning, how this is implemented lacks consistency and clarity (2016: 362). However, we argue that the focus on tensions between teachers' theories and practice obscures wider field-specific challenges for developing playful pedagogies, because competing influences are manifest in early childhood education settings. Early childhood policy frameworks influence provision for play, especially where the emphasis lies more towards adult-led rather than child-initiated play, and where adults set the learning goals that will achieve academic progression and school readiness (BERA-TACTYC, 2017). As Chesworth (2019: 5) has argued, these competing influences also draw attention to whose and what forms of knowledge are valued, and the problems of separating approved (curriculum) forms of knowledge and ways of knowing from children's interests and inquiries.

For all its status within early childhood education principles, theories and philosophies, providing evidence for the claims that are made about play remains problematic, specifically how play leads to specific goals and outcomes. In defining and framing play, we can see a pathway from understanding what play is, to what play does, to what outcomes play produces. As governments have increased policy attention and investment, the need to prove or demonstrate the educational effectiveness of play has intensified, which means that the relationship between playing and learning has been drawn into debates about appropriate or effective pedagogical approaches. Many early childhood curriculum frameworks determine what versions of play are acceptable in the pursuit of learning outcomes in order to create children who are 'school ready' at whatever age the transition to compulsory schooling takes place in different countries. Thus, from a policy perspective, curriculum discourses create and order what play is, what the playing child should be doing, and what play must produce. The desired practices and outcomes may value sameness rather than diversities, conformity rather than creativity, and may foreground adults' plans and purposes in ways that undervalue children's interests and choices.

Orderliness is reinforced in the transition to formal education in compulsory schooling where it is assumed that child-initiated play will be left behind, and children will benefit from 'formal' approaches, including adult-led activities and direct instruction. In contrast, Wood (2013) has argued that adults can plan for play to happen by providing resources, creating time and space for play, and responding to children's interests and inquiries. However, they cannot plan children's play because much of what happens, especially in social and pretend play, is spontaneous, fluid and in the moment.

Given these contemporary field-specific challenges, how can research capture the complexity and ambiguity of play (Sutton-Smith, 1997), and understand how play reflects curriculum goals and practitioners' pedagogical approaches? This question draws attention to the importance of designing research that is culturally and contextually informed, respects children's perspectives and experiences, and takes account of national policy frameworks as well as children's home and community experiences.

THE SIGNIFICANCE OF CULTURES AND CONTEXTS FOR RESEARCHING PLAY

Although much has been written about the relationship between play, learning and development, we do not know precisely what the connecting processes or mechanisms are. However, we do know that these processes are social, affective, cognitive, embodied, relational, material and multi-modal. Far from being the natural occupation of childhood, play is socially and symbolically complex in its different forms and manifestations. What children choose to do in and with their play is varied and often unpredictable, which presents many challenges to researchers. Chesworth (2016, 2018) shows how play reveals insights into children's interests and funds of knowledge[1] which include their home and family practices. Therefore, play is one of many ways in which children learn and develop, but its significance seems to lie in the distinctive contexts and characteristics that distinguish playfulness and playful activities from other forms of activity. Play in preschool and community settings also offers children opportunities for social and co-operative play with children of different ages, cultures and heritages (Broadhead, 2009; Chesworth, 2019), thereby providing distinctive contexts for researching through play.

There is broad agreement that play encourages exploration, experimentation and problem-solving, and enables children to follow their interests and inquiries. Over time, children's choices reveal important questions and processes of sustained inquiry, and the motivation to become more skilled and knowledgeable about their social, cultural and material worlds (Hedges and Cooper, 2016). However, learning is not just about acquiring and storing new knowledge or skills: many factors and processes coalesce in play, and the purposes vary according to who is playing, in what contexts, and with what materials, tools and resources. Therefore, it is difficult to identify what play leads to in terms of defined outcomes, because play is a mash-up of children's cultures and heritages, knowledge, skills and understanding, all of which contribute to the development of their play-based peer cultures and identities.

Sociological and anthropological research focuses on children's peer cultures, particularly their social relationships, rules, routines and meanings, and their interactions with their material cultures (Chesworth, 2018). Children are active in the co-construction and development of their play; learning through play incorporates learning about play, and what it means to be a player. Children's interests extend beyond curriculum goals, and incorporate relationships, morals and ethics; existential matters of life, death and dying; the natural world; the social world, safety and risk; technologies and popular culture; and developing their identities (Hedges and Cooper, 2016; Hill and Wood, 2019). In other words, play may be both a mirror that reflects children's social and personal interests and knowledge, and a motivating force for directing further learning.

Sociological and anthropological research indicates the importance of understanding play from children's perspectives, distinct from adults' perceptions and values. Such research typically involves deep ethnographic immersion, which may be as an adult participant in children's play lives, or a non-participant observer (Hill, 2015). Digital methods – cameras, videorecorders – may be used to capture events as they happen, and to stimulate discussions with children about their play, as well as with practitioners and family members (see Part 3, Chapters 7–12 for more examples). Choices have to be made about which children are the focus for research, and/or which specific areas (such as role play, small-world play, outdoor play). Following a child or children through their free-flow

---

[1]Accumulated knowledge and ways of being based on cultural and social experiences

play activities is fascinating but methodologically demanding in terms of observing and recording, and will always provide in-the-moment challenges to our ethical responsibilities towards participants.

For example, Chesworth (2016, 2018) used video recordings of play to explore the perspectives of children (age 4–5), parents and teachers in an early years classroom in England. Over an eight-month period, the video recordings acted as a provocation through which to explore the participants' perspectives as they selected episodes of play to watch and respond to during the researcher's visits to the classroom and to the children's homes. The children's responses to the recordings were enacted in multiple modes, requiring a research design that was responsive to the diverse and fluid ways in which they chose to participate. Allowing time and space for children to exercise choices regarding when, where and how they engaged in the research became a key consideration. Sometimes children gave 'running commentaries' as they viewed the recordings; on other occasions, these stimulated conversations with friends and family members. Children also used non-verbal modes of expression to communicate their responses. Therefore, whilst Chesworth's research highlights the possibilities afforded by digital methods, it also draws attention to the importance of respectful, responsive relationships between the researcher and the participating children (see Chapters 2, 3 and 4 for more). Such relationships are foundational to reflexive research which is attuned to the multiple modes and contexts in which children might choose to communicate their perspectives of play.

These contrasting theoretical and methodological orientations are significant in play research because it is important to understand the ways in which they structure a project and produce a particular discourse in which certain kinds of knowledge about play, and about children and childhood, are foregrounded. Therefore, our own position on framing and defining play is important in terms of the chosen focus, aims, methodology, methods and ethical orientations. The following section focuses on researching play in education settings and proposes three modes of play as a way of understanding playful pedagogies.

THREE MODES OF PLAY FOR FRAMING RESEARCH

As noted previously, embedding play in early childhood curriculum policies and frameworks has produced a distinctive form of 'educational play' within which the concept of playful pedagogies may be understood in different ways. However, educational play is not as straightforward as policy-makers assume. This means that implementing playful pedagogies creates challenges for practitioners/researchers, even where curriculum frameworks incorporate child-initiated and adult-led play. Exploring the interface between play and pedagogy, Wood (2014) identified three modes of play to indicate the choices that practitioners can make in order to respect children's choices and interests and meet learning goals in the curriculum.

MODE A: CHILD-INITIATED PLAY

Child-initiated play has distinctive qualities based on children's freedom to choose activities, resources and co-players, and opportunities to direct their play. Within education settings, there will always be some constraints on freedom (such as risk and safety, resources, space and time), but the freedom to choose creates potential for complex activities. Children reveal their emerging interests, needs, dispositions and patterns of learning, with interests becoming the springboard for child-led inquiries that may be sustained over time and in different contexts (Hedges, 2019). In Mode A, children's purposes and meanings are foregrounded, and incorporate their multimodal communicative practices.

The following episode, from Chesworth's (2015) research, focuses upon freely chosen play in an English early years classroom. Daniel, Peter and Tom, all 4 years old, have used wooden blocks to construct a spaceship. The following extract is from a conversation with Daniel and Peter whilst watching the video recording of the play:

CONVERSATION BETWEEN DANIEL AND PETER

Daniel: (*pauses the film, moves close to the screen*) Ah, well that was my game phone. And it can tell me messages about aliens and space monsters.

Peter: Game phone, Dan?

Daniel: (*nodding*) Yep. It was a brick that was my phone.

Peter: Ah yes, and you said there was a bomb heading for the spaceship. (*eyes wide, hands held up with fingers stretched*)

Daniel: Yes. It ... was ... going ... to ... crash. (*long pause, grave expression, turns to look at the researcher*) There was going to be a massive explosion. And then it went fast with bombers even chasing it. We turned it back around and went Bang! Bang! Bang! (*fists clenched, voice animated*) It went on a while and then the bombers, well they exploded. (*smiles*)

Peter: Exploded, yeah they exploded. Boom! (*very loud voice*)

The interests children explore in their play draw upon multiple funds of knowledge, and in this example Daniel's and Peter's shared familiarity with everyday technology was interwoven with their knowledge of plotlines from popular culture involving aliens, space monsters and explosions. The brick-that-was-a-phone could hence be ascribed with more-than-everyday properties from which Daniel was able to announce the imminent arrival of a bomb. This episode constituted a merging of everyday experiences, popular culture and humour in which the children's play embodied a multi-layered reconstruction of familiar cultural scripts. Daniel's and Peter's play highlights the potential complexity associated with freely chosen play that is not constrained by predetermined outcomes.

MODE B: ADULT-GUIDED PLAY

Adult-guided play can intersect with Modes A and C, and is described by Walsh et al. (2011) as 'playful structure' because the goals are responsive to children's interests, as demonstrated in Mode A, and reflect curriculum goals. The degree of structure may differ according to the goals within curriculum frameworks, including the immediate goals identified by practitioners, and the longer-term outcomes that they are expected to deliver or work towards. Mode B indicates the different ways in which the play–pedagogy interface can integrate children's and practitioners' purposes. Pedagogical interactions may include co-playing with children, guiding, facilitating, stepping in and stepping out of the play in ways that are responsive to children's requests, but do not direct or re-direct the play. These processes enable children to move from exploration and discovery – 'What does this do?' – to inquiry and knowledge creation – 'What can I do with this'?

The following excerpt is taken from Hill (2015), whose research focused on children's peer cultures, and how their interests were expressed in self-initiated play. Her methods included videotaped episodes of play, observations, and reflective conversations with the children (aged 5–6 years) and their parents. The children had been following shared interests in death and dying, and in this episode they reveal their fundamental interests and inquiries (Hedges and Cooper, 2016), their ongoing questions, as well as everyday and scientific knowledge.

THE DEAD NEWT

13th March. After Outdoor Learning at approx. 9.30am

Field notes from a conversation

The children begin each day playing outside in an area that includes access to a small garden with a pond. A group of children find a dead newt in the garden, and as they come in three children, Lucia (aged 4 years 11 months), Peter (aged 5 years 6 months) and Adam (aged 5 years 6 months), begin telling me about it at the same time, talking over each other excitedly. I stop them and ask how they know the newt was dead.

Lucia: It had its eyes open and I don't think it was sleeping.

Peter: People can die with their eyes open.

Lucia:	Sometimes they can die with their eyes closed or open.
Adam:	(indignantly) Or half open.
Lucia:	If they are dead they don't move.
Adam:	They go to heaven.
Peter:	People believe in it but that's where they stay alive, where the skeletons are.
Adam:	They die on earth and then they go to heaven where they started.
Peter:	I've got a book about digging up the past. The skeletons stay on earth and dirt goes on top.
Michelle:	So skeletons stay on earth?
Adam:	No. They go to heaven.

Source: Hill (2015: 159)

This episode prompts critical questions about how practitioners might respond to children's emerging scientific knowledge and inquiries. Sometimes it is appropriate to listen and note rather than intervene so that children's interests and inquiries can be followed up through group work and activities that are co-constructed between children and adults. However, this complex pedagogical approach is not always facilitated by curriculum frameworks with specific learning outcomes and a school-readiness agenda. Because practitioners may not have the time to observe and understand children's play, they may miss valuable learning opportunities. The more closely the adults' intentions are foregrounded, the less scope there is for play and playfulness, for children's purposes and meanings, and for pedagogical responsiveness.

MODE C: TECHNICIST/POLICY-DRIVEN

In Mode C, play is used to promote specific ways of learning in line with curriculum frameworks. Practitioners guide play activities in instrumental or directive ways, with adults' rather than children's goals and intentions in mind, and with little choice or flexibility. Mode C incorporates 'formal' pedagogical approaches, consistent with the expectations in some curriculum guidance documents. For example, in England, the expectation is that child-initiated approaches will be phased out in the Early Years Foundation Stage, with more teacher-led approaches being introduced to prepare children for formal learning in the National Curriculum. In Mode C play is not valued for its own sake, but for what it produces in terms of outcomes and the transition to formal learning.

In considering these three modes, it is important to understand their contrasting pedagogical orientations as a continuum. Hedges and Cooper (2016) argue that teachers are constantly making judgements about children's varied and often unpredictable interests and their implications for learning and curriculum. However, their freedom to act on those judgements may be constrained by a range of factors, including how play is positioned in the curriculum. Sometimes it is appropriate to teach children specific skills, for example playing a game with rules, or learning the skills to access and use digital technologies. Children may choose activities that are more like work because they enjoy using and applying their subject knowledge in ways that can be creative and playful. Children can also be directive in teaching each other skills or communicating knowledge in the context of play. In Modes B and C, practitioners can build on the significant content knowledge they have observed in Mode A, in ways that support progression in learning and respect children's ways of knowing and their diverse cultural knowledge. Responsive pedagogical approaches enable practitioners to move across adult-initiated and child-initiated activities in ways that:

- Build on children's interests and freely chosen activities.
- Connect interests with curriculum goals.
- Recognise and incorporate children's everyday working theories and their funds of knowledge into Modes B and C.
- Value children's ways of knowing and constructing sense and meaning from experience.

In light of these different pedagogical modes, it is also important for researchers to consider who the players are, what choices they are making in their play activities, and whose meanings and interpretations are being privileged in the analysis. Using reflective feedback from children, practitioners and family members can add depth to research, especially in culturally diverse communities where the subtlety of meanings may not be immediately visible. For example, 3-year-old Fatima is of Libyan heritage and has been attending a nursery setting in an English city for two years. Observations over a four-month period revealed that Fatima spent a lot of her time at nursery in the malleable materials area. We regularly noticed Fatima using her hands to pull, squeeze and flatten the Play-Doh. She also used rolling pins and cookie cutters to manipulate and make patterns in the dough. Fatima's keen interest in Play-Doh and other malleable materials could be interpreted as a repetitive behaviour from which she derived enjoyment in exploring familiar resources. However, reflective conversations with Fatima's mother enabled a deeper interpretation of the meaning of the activity in relation to Fatima's participation in household practices. Fatima's mother explained that she and her older sister frequently observe and assist with food preparation in the family kitchen. In particular, Fatima often helps to prepare the daily flatbread, a process that involves manipulating the dough in much the same way that we had watched her squeezing, flattening and rolling the playdough at nursery. Fatima's mother was therefore able to interpret her daughter's play interests in relation to everyday social and cultural practices. Such an interpretation highlights the potential for funds of knowledge to offer an alternative lens through which to interpret Mode A in freely chosen play and to inform teachers' decision-making in Modes B and C.

Although we have argued that defining and framing play remains a challenge, the diversity of play phenomena has implications for how to go about researching play. The examples presented in this chapter show that it is possible to take a microscopic view of one child, or a telescopic view of children playing socially in different contexts.

The following questions are useful in thinking about framing your own research:

1. What are the contexts in which children are playing, and how do contexts influence their choices, actions and decisions?
2. What are the pedagogical roles of teachers and adults in the setting?
3. How might the three modes of play influence the choices you make about research questions and methods when looking at play in preschool and school settings?
4. How have you considered the cultural appropriateness of framing and defining play, and of your choices of research methods?
5. What and who is included or excluded in your research, what can be communicated or spoken, and whose voices and silences come forth in play?

Whatever methods are chosen, they will provide a snapshot of play at a particular moment in time. Once captured, either through texts, digital images, or drawings, that moment is taken to present and represent something fundamental about play, and about the context – whether from children's or adults' perspectives. It is important not to see data as truths but as a cumulative construction of interpretations that present a cultural narrative in which different readings are possible and desirable (see Part 2, Chapters 4–6 for more). These ethical perspectives remind us that play is the private space within which children enact and experience their childhoods in unique and creative ways. In contrast, research on play will always seek to make children and their play known and knowable to adults, through adults' discourses, narratives, categories and measures. When looking at playful pedagogies, or educational play, critical reflection incorporates questions about what forms of order we impose on the fluid and apparently chaotic nature of play, and for what/whose purposes?

CONCLUSION

In the following chapters, you will engage with different ways of thinking about research on play and through play, using different methods and theories, all underpinned by close attention to ethics and reflection. By engaging with research on play, you will develop the skills to analyse the values, positions and assumptions that may (or may not) be conveyed by the authors. Although the task of defining and framing play remains a challenge, articulating your own choices is essential for setting the focus and boundaries of your research. You need to reflect critically on how you are positioned historically and culturally, and the version of play you privelege – whether romantic and idealised, critical and disruptive, or policy-compliant. As researchers we are always steeped in cultural and historical narratives, but reflexivity enables us to be mindful of what we are reproducing, legitimating or disrupting in our research (see Chapter 4 for more). Given that play is embedded in many policy frameworks and curriculum guidance documents, it is also important to be critical of what versions and forms of play are approved and how play has been drawn into different curriculum and pedagogical approaches as 'educational play'. The three modes of play can serve as a way of framing research questions about play and pedagogy in ECE settings. However, it is important to bear in mind that assumptions about ages and stages of play and about universal benefits and outcomes have limitations in complex and diverse socio-cultural contexts. Therefore, attention to diversities is significant for capturing the meanings, experiences and cultural knowledges that children bring to their play, and to appreciate their purposes and meanings.

REFERENCES

Anderson, M. and Reid, C. (2016). Theoretical insights from neuroscience in early childhood research. In A. Farrell, S. L. Kagan, E. Kay and M. Tisdall (Eds.), *The Sage Handbook of Early Childhood Research*. London: Sage. pp. 148–62.

BERA-TACTYC (2017). *Early Childhood Research Review 2003–2017*. Available at: www.bera.ac.uk/project/bera-tactyc-early-childhood-research-review-2003-2017 (accessed 19 January 2021).

Broadhead, P. (2009). Conflict resolution and children's behavior: Observing and understanding social and cooperative play in early years educational settings. *Early Years*, 29 (2): 105–18.

Chesworth, L. (2015). Multiple perspectives of play in a reception class: Exploring insider meanings. Unpublished PhD thesis, Leeds Beckett University, UK.

Chesworth, L. (2016). A funds of knowledge approach to examining play interests: Listening to children's and parents' perspectives. *International Journal of Early Years Education*, 24 (3): 294–308.

Chesworth, L. (2018). Embracing uncertainty in research with young children. *International Journal of Qualitative Studies in Education*, 31 (9): 851–62.

Chesworth, L. (2019). Theorising children's interests: Making connections and in-the-moment happenings. *Learning, Culture and Social Interaction*, 23 (100263): https://doi.org/10.1016/j.lcsi.2018.11.010.

Dender, A. M. and Stagnitti, K. (2015). Children's play in the Australian Indigenous context: The need for a contemporary view. *International Journal of Play*, 4 (1): 3–16.

Fesseha, E. and Pyle, A. (2016). Conceptualising play-based learning from kindergarten teachers' perspectives. *International Journal of Early Years Education*, 24 (3): 361–77.

Hedges, H. (2019). The 'fullness of life': Learner interests and educational experiences. *Learning, Culture and Social Interaction*, 23 (100258): https://doi.org/10.1016/j.lcsi.2018.11.005.

Hedges, H. and Cooper, M. (2016). Inquiring minds: Theorizing children's interests. *Journal of Curriculum Studies*, 48 (3): 303–22.

Hill, M. (2015). Dead forever: Young children building theories in a play-based classroom. Unpublished doctoral thesis, University of Sheffield, UK.

Hill, M. and Wood, E. (2019). 'Dead forever': An ethnographic study of young children's interests, funds of knowledge and working theories in free play. *Learning, Culture and Social Interaction*, 23: https://doi.org/10.1016/j.lcsi.2019.02.017.

Howe, S. (2016). What play means to us: Exploring children's perspectives on play in an English Year 1 classroom. *European Early Childhood Education Research Journal*, 24 (5): 748–59.

Marsh, J., Wood, E., Chesworth, L., Nisha, B., Nutbrown, B. and Olney, B. (2019). Makerspaces in early childhood education: Principles of pedagogy and practice. *Mind, Culture, and Activity*, 26 (3): 221–33.

Robson, S. (2010). Self-regulation and metacognition in young children's self-initiated play and reflective dialogue. *International Journal of Early Years Education*, 18 (3): 221–41.

Roopnarine, J. L., Patte, M., Johnson, J. E. and Kuschner, D. (Eds.) (2018). *International Perspectives on Children's Play*. Maidenhead: Open University Press.

Sutton-Smith, B. (1997). *The Ambiguity of Play*. Cambridge, MA: Harvard University Press.

Walsh, G., Sproule, L., McGuinness, C. and Trew, K. (2011). Playful structure: A novel image of early years pedagogy for primary school classrooms. *Early Years*, 31 (2): 107–19.

Whitebread, D., Basilio, M., Kuvalja, M. and Verma, M. (2012). *The Importance of Play: A Report on the Value of Children's Play with a Series of Policy Recommendations*. Available at: www.researchgate.net/publication/340137325_The_importance_of_play_A_report_on_the_value_of_children%27s_play_with_a_series_of_policy_recommendations (accessed 15 November 2020).

Wood, E. (2013). *Play, Learning and the Early Childhood Curriculum*. London: Sage.

Wood, E. (2014). The play–pedagogy interface in contemporary debates. In E. Brooker, M. Blaise and S. Edwards (Eds.), *The Sage Handbook of Play and Learning*. London: Sage. pp. 145–56.

Wood, E., Nuttall, J., Edwards, S. and Grieshaber, S. (2019). Young children's digital play in early childhood settings: Curriculum, pedagogy and teachers' knowledge. In O. Erstad, R. Flewitt, B. Kümmerling-Meibauer and I. Pereira (Eds.), *Routledge Handbook of Digital Literacies in Early Childhood*. New York and Abingdon: Routledge. pp. 214–26.

2

YOUNG CHILDREN'S PLAY, VOICES AND RIGHTS IN RESEARCH

JANE MURRAY

In the previous chapter, Wood and Chesworth laid out a discussion about the complexity of play in early childhood research, in terms of exploring play and what the multiplicity of play definitions may mean for those researching through play. Building on these complex definitions of play, the current chapter extends this thinking into the rights-based framework, allowing us to see the role of children involved as researchers and active participants in research projects, where ideas are developed with and through play-based experiences. This chapter exemplifies:

- Children's right to be heard;
- How being heard may be realised by drawing on established frameworks for play to better understand children's motives, intentions and capabilities.

Early childhood education and care practice is shaped increasingly by policy (Rebello Britto et al., 2013). During the past 20 years, national governments have produced early years frameworks for their countries where previously there were none (Australian Government Department for Education, 2009; Department of Basic Education, 2015; Qualifications and Curriculum Authority and the Department for Education and

Employment, 2000). Equally, recent international policy has included the World Health Organization's *Nurturing Care Framework* (2018) which focuses on an integrated holistic approach to early childhood, the 2015 *Sustainable Development Goals* which target pre-primary education for major focus until 2030 (United Nations, 2015) and the Organisation for Economic Cooperation and Development's (OECD) *International Early Learning and Child Well-Being Study* (2019) which frames specific – albeit contested – expectations for young children's development (Moss et al., 2016). The explosion of national and global early childhood policy is driven by persuasive evidence for the importance of the early years for lifetime outcomes (Shonkoff and Richter, 2013). Strong policy is informed by evidence, so research that produces evidence can be powerful (Bridges et al., 2009).

Research may be regarded as a right (Appadurai, 2006), whether research engagement is as researcher, participant or research user. The exponential rise of research-informed early childhood policy indicates that infants and young children are increasingly becoming research users. However, they still tend to be marginalised as researchers and research participants. Adults can find it difficult to recognise the non-verbal languages that infants and young children use to express their views (Lansdown, 2010), so policy-makers and the academy tend to disregard the agenda, thoughts, actions and meanings that citizens aged 0–8 years present as researchers or research participants when these do not conform to the academy's preferred ways of working and communicating (Murray, 2017). Consequently, children's right to have their views considered and taken seriously 'in all matters affecting them', as set out in the United Nations Convention on the Rights of the Child (UNCRC), is not respected as fully as might be the case if policy-makers and adult researchers could learn to understand children's 'autonomous world(s)' (Hardman, 1973: 95; Murray et al., 2019; Office of the High Commissioner for Human Rights (OHCHR), 1989: Article 12).

A principle way that children express their views and voices is through their play (Lansdown, 2010). The UNCRC articulates children's rights to play (Article 31) and freedom of expression (Article 13) (OHCHR, 1989), yet adults find children's play and children's 'voice' challenging to define and understand (Brooks and Murray, 2018; Murray and Devecchi, 2016). Moyles (2014) describes play as being 'analogous to try-ing to seize bubbles' (p. 16), though there have been many well-documented attempts to define, characterise and frame children's play. These include, for example, 'freely chosen, personally directed, intrinsically motivated behaviour that actively engages the child' (National Playing Fields Association (NPFA), Children's Play Council (CPC) and Playlink, 2000: 6), a definition that will appear again within this chapter. Play is described as political, voluntary, spontaneous, meaningful, attuned to the player's mood, symbolic, joyful, involving, active, exciting and humorous (Kernan, 2007; Ryan, 2005), games with rules, ludic and epistemic (Hutt, 1979) and solitary, parallel, associa-tive, social and cooperative (Broadhead, 2004; Parten, 1932). Equally, 'children's voice' is defined and characterised variably. Often, no account is taken of 'children's voice' in matters that affect children (Singer, 2014). Even when the term 'children's voice' is used, it can be tokenistic (Whitty and Wisby, 2007) and the term 'children's voice' suggests that children are one homogeneous collective. Conversely, the plural 'children's voices' acknowledges that children express their thinking as individuals (Bakhtin, 1963), affording respect for children's participation rights, and their 'identity, agency and empowerment' (Maybin, 2013: 383; Whitty and Wisby, 2007). I have, therefore, argued elsewhere for the use of the term 'children's voices', defined as: 'views of children that are actively heard and valued as substantive contributions to decisions affecting the children's lives' (Brooks and Murray, 2018: 145).

Taking into account these challenges and opportunities, this chapter draws on established play categories (Broadhead, 2004; Hutt et al., 1989; Parten, 1932) and the *Young Children As Researchers* (YCAR) project (Murray, 2017) to exemplify ways that adults may understand children's voices and play in research, whether children are positioned as research participants or researchers. The content of the chapter is drawn from rigorous empirical research, so it provides robust evidence for practitioners, policy-makers and researchers to apply in the contexts where they work, in order that young children's play, voices and rights in research might be recognised more widely.

YOUNG CHILDREN IN RESEARCH

The Young Children as Researchers (YCAR) project (Murray, 2017) was a participatory study for which a qualitative 'jigsaw methodology' was adopted to co-research with children aged 4–8 years (n = 138), their parents, practitioners and professional researchers to conceptualise ways in which young children are researchers and may be considered to be researchers. Prior to the YCAR project, some recognition had emerged that children can be researchers and co-researchers (Clark and Moss, 2011; Fielding, 2001), but that work tended to focus on older children and young people who were trained according to the academy's research protocols (Kellett, 2005; O'Kane, 2008). The YCAR project captured and inductively analysed data that demonstrated congruence between (i) young children's own self-chosen, self-directed everyday activities at home and school, and (ii) four research behaviours that professional researchers considered 'most important' out of 39 research behaviours they identified for the study: finding solutions, basing decisions on evidence, conceptualisation and exploration (Murray, 2017: 27). Data were constructed in accordance with the ethical requirements of the institution where the research was based and elicited 68 epistemological categories (Table 2.1). The epistemological categories were constructs the young children in the YCAR project used to build their knowledge: provocations that enabled young children to adopt research behaviours.

Conversely, 12 epistemological barriers were identified that inhibited young children's research behaviours (Table 2.2). YCAR findings revealed that young children aged 4–8 years in the study were sophisticated thinkers and competent rights holders with expertise in their own lives (James and James, 2008; Langsted, 1994; OHCHR, 1989; Papert, 1980). The YCAR study therefore established a warrant for recognising young children as researchers on the academy's terms, particularly in matters affecting them.

Neither children's play nor children's voices were primary considerations for the YCAR study, for which the principle aim was to conceptualise ways in which young children are researchers and may be considered to be researchers. However, the data captured and analysed for the YCAR study revealed many examples of children's play – 'freely chosen, personally directed, intrinsically motivated behaviour that actively engages the child' (NPFA, CPC and Playlink, 2000) – and children's voices – 'views of children that are actively heard and valued as substantive contributions to decisions affecting the children's lives' (Brooks and Murray, 2018: 145). The merging of documented play experiences alongside a search for meaning-making can allow researchers to better understand children's voices and their right to be heard. Some of those examples are set out in the sections that follow.

Table 2.1   YCAR epistemological categories (adapted from Murray, 2017, 2020)

Research Behaviour: Base Decisions on Evidence	Research Behaviour: Conceptualisation	Research Behaviour: Find a Solution	Research Behaviour: Exploration
Extrapolates	Recalling instructions	Is an able reader	Patterned behaviour
Applies mental model	Linking prior knowledge to new application	Wants to preserve what s/he is doing	Experiment
Applies prior experience	Synthesising concepts	Finds practical use for solution	Social encounter
Acts on adult opinion	Thinking tangentially	Applies rule to create solution	Develops own agenda
Values peer perspectives	Thinking through a problem by applying concepts	Finds own solution	Interested in context
Enacts personal preference	Identifying an anomaly	Devises practical method to create solution	Cause and effect
Has senses provide evidence for action	Creating an imagined space/persona	Creates a problem to solve	Focused on task
Applies 'Humean' reason	Developing own idea[s] from external stimulus	Uses theory of mind	Shows interest in materials
Thinks strategically	Inventing a process/method	Employs others to help with finding a solution	Seeking

Research Behaviour: Base Decisions on Evidence	Research Behaviour: Conceptualisation	Research Behaviour: Find a Solution	Research Behaviour: Exploration
Trial and error	Conceptualising after adult stops conceptualisation	Shares solution	Curious
Meta-cognition	Following adult's direction to conceptualise	Resolves another person's problem	
Basing decisions on evidence is research	Working with others to conceptualise	Is focused on something of personal interest	
Sampling issue	Making decision/s based on own criteria	Has time and freedom to explore, investigate, experiment with something of personal interest	
Methodological issue	Autonomously deciding what needs to be done and doing it	Self-regulates	
	Creating a problem	Uses inductive reasoning	
	Creating a new use for object/s	Uses deductive reasoning	
	Making links – analogy	Explores properties	
	Planning	Is excited by finding solution	
	Being engaged in symbolic representation	Is motivated by finding solution	
	Having language support thinking	Perseveres to resolve problem	
	Using imagination		
	Being involved in pursuing a train of thought		
	Predicting		
	Applying anthropomorphism		

Table 2.2   YCAR epistemological barriers (adapted from Murray, 2017)

Reproducing knowledge s/he already had

Solution not shared with or witnessed by others

Solution not shared with or witnessed by others (unconfirmed)

Denied opportunity to share solution

Responding to adult's semi-open questions

Responding to adult's closed questions

Following adult's direction

Believes s/he has failed

Unmotivated

Has become disinterested

Gives up

Solution unconfirmed

YOUNG CHILDREN AS RESEARCHERS AND HUTT'S TAXONOMY OF PLAY

This section considers how findings that emerged from the YCAR project compare with Hutt's play taxonomy (1979), which comprised 'games with rules', 'ludic behaviour' and 'epistemic behaviour'. In terms of methodology, this begins to offer an overview of how observational data can be transformed and better understood through play.

GAMES WITH RULES

In Hutt's taxonomy of play (1979), games with rules include cooperative or competitive games and games of chance or skill (p. 115). Gemma (aged 5) participated in the YCAR study at school and at home. She and her family captured data about her research behaviours at home and the researcher visited on agreed days to review the data with the family. During one of the researcher's visits, Gemma showed how she identified a problem and **found a solution**, one of the four 'most important' research behaviours (Murray, 2017). She talked about a game with a Velcro ball and numbered target that she had developed further below.

GEMMA'S GAME WITH RULES (ADAPTED FROM MURRAY, 2017)

Gemma: 'I was playing with that ball and that thing and I was writing down my scores … That's making the score. I did that ball in the thing that the ball sticks on.'

Gemma's mother: 'So you made a chart? For the target with a sticky ball you threw.'

Gemma (pointing to the chart she had created – Figure 2.1): 'Yes – they're all the scores that I got.'

Here, when playing a game with a Velcro ball for which she had to hit a numbered target – a game of skill (Hutt, 1979) – Gemma identified that she needed to create a chart to record her scores (Figure 2.1) in order to demonstrate and record her skill. Her planning, development of strategy and resources, and evaluation of her activity resonated with established definitions of problem-setting and problem-solving (DeLoache et al., 1998). Equally, Gemma exhibited agency by posing *and* resolving her own problem in this context that seemed genuinely meaningful to her (Lowrie, 2002).

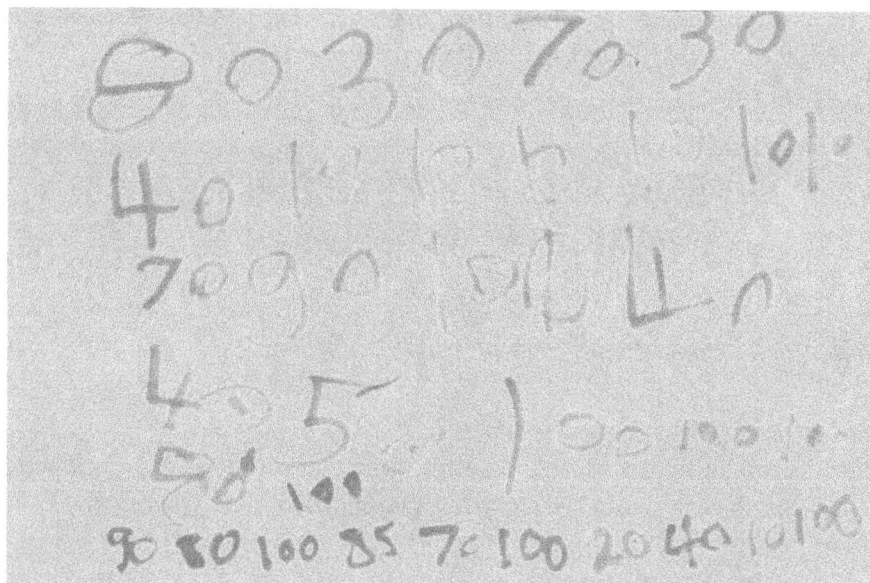

Figure 2.1   Games with rules: Gemma keeps score (adapted from Murray, 2017).

LUDIC BEHAVIOUR

Hutt (1979) identifies two types of ludic behaviour: symbolic play and repetitive play. The YCAR data revealed children engaging in symbolic representation, a sub-category of Hutt's symbolic play that is also indicative of **conceptualisation**, one of the YCAR study's four 'most important' research behaviours (Murray, 2017), and of cognitive mastery (Bruner, 1966; Vygotsky, 1976). Like Gemma, Annie (aged 7) participated in the YCAR study at school and at home. In her bedroom at home one day, Annie (aged 7) and her mother captured video footage of her fiddling with bear ornaments on the windowsill and they talked about them (below).

DYAD: ANNIE AND HER MOTHER (ADAPTED FROM MURRAY, 2017)

Annie:	'They're usually in twos.'
Annie's mother:	'Why do they need to be in twos?'
Annie:	'I was – it's just I saw them and thought ...'

Later, the researcher visited Annie and her parents at home, and they watched and discussed the video content Annie's mother had captured (below).

DYAD: ANNIE AND THE RESEARCHER (ADAPTED FROM MURRAY, 2017)

Researcher: 'Why do they have to be in twos?'

Annie: 'Because they're dance partners!'

Here, Annie combines past experiences with mental activity to engage in a posteriori conceptualisation (Scruton, 2001). The video was captured during a period when the BBC television programme about ballroom dancing – *Strictly Come Dancing* – was broadcast, and to Annie the bear ornaments symbolised 'dance partners'. Annie engaged in a form of symbolic play – socio-dramatic and thematic fantasy play – demonstrating 'the ability to separate meaning from object' (Manning-Morton and Thorp, 2003: 75), and she created her own meaning concerning the bear ornaments (Cobb-Moore et al., 2010). Bruner (1966) identifies symbolic representation as 'a system … governed by rules or laws forming and transforming propositions' (p. 45). Annie ruled that her bear ornaments had to be in pairs, symbolising a desire for order and her understanding of a mathematical concept and of a social convention.

EPISTEMIC BEHAVIOUR

Hutt's taxonomy of play features three types of epistemic behaviour: problem-solving, exploration and productive behaviour (comprising materials and acquisition of skills). Two of Hutt's epistemic behaviours are the same as two of the four 'most important' research behaviours identified in the YCAR study: problem-solving (finding a solution) and exploration (Murray, 2017). Isaacs (1944) observed that the 'factor of epistemic interest and inquiry … is in every respect the same in the child as in the adult' (p. 322), while Cagliari et al. (2016: 307) describe young children as being 'innate carriers of … an "epistemological curiosity" for researching into meanings'. Children in the YCAR study 'showed interest in materials', which was a sub-category of the 'important' research behaviour of exploration in the YCAR data. This fits with Hutt's sub-category of epistemic behaviour concerned with being 'productive (with) materials'. India (aged 5) was in a reception class in a large primary school – Beech Setting – when she participated in the YCAR project (below).

INDIA EXPLORES (ADAPTED FROM MURRAY, 2017)

One day in her school's under-cover outdoor area, the teachers had placed on the floor side-by-side two large cylinders made of black plastic (2m x 0.5m), which were off-cuts from industrial water pipes. India walked to the cylinders with her friend. She rolled a cylinder forwards while on top of it on her tummy and, with her friend, created one long 'tube'. She and her friend crawled inside one cylinder each and rolled the cylinders at the same pace as one another several times, to and fro, for almost 12 minutes.

During this experience, India explored objects while engaging in functional, realistic object play (Bergen and Fromberg, 2006). She interacted with the cylinders inductively, constructing and problem-solving (Piaget, 1945); when she travelled over and through the cylinders, her actions indicated that she was asking herself 'What can and does it do?' (Abbott and Langston, 2005: 153). She studied, examined and investigated the cylinders, became familiar with them by testing and experimenting with them and 'travelled over (and) through a particular space for the purposes of discovery': these actions align with Stebbins' (2001) definition of exploration in social sciences research (p. 2).

Everyday objects can enhance young children's cognitive mastery (DeLoache, 1989; Karpov, 2005; Nelissen and Tomic, 1996). Elements of India's cylinder play, such as creating one long 'tube' from the two cylinders, indicate mental modelling, which is 'analogous to the structure of the corresponding state of affairs in the world' (Craik, 1943; Johnson-Laird, 1983: 156).

Importantly, analysing data from a play perspective presents an opportunity to identify key overlaps between children's natural ability to play and their skills to engage in higher-order thinking and decision-making congruent with research behaviours. Therefore, rather than viewing children as less competent research participants than young people and adults, we should reflect on children's innate capabilities to explore to understand how these can be applied in a research context. This is not a perfect science and continual reflection on the child's role and ability to engage in research behaviours is required, as demonstrated in the next section.

YOUNG CHILDREN AS RESEARCHERS AND SOCIAL PLAY

In the section that follows, YCAR findings are discussed in conjunction with findings from Parten's (1932) and Broadhead's (2004) studies concerning social play. Parten's study – 'Social participation among pre-school children' – was based on observations of pre-school children in the United States, from which she identified three categories of social play – 'non-social activity', 'parallel play' and 'social play' (comprising 'associative play' and 'cooperative play'). Broadhead (2004) framed these categories slightly differently for her Social Play Continuum which she structured according to the terms 'associative domain', 'social domain', 'highly social domain' and 'cooperative domain'. In the YCAR study data, a set of epistemological categories that were specifically grouped as 'social domains' emerged (Table 2.3), but different levels of social play were evident across a wide range of epistemological categories in the study.

Table 2.3   YCAR social domains as epistemological categories (adapted from Murray, 2017)

Research Behaviours	Epistemological Categories
Base decisions on evidence	Acts on adult opinion Values peer perspectives
Conceptualisation	Conceptualises after adult stops conceptualisation Follows adult's direction to conceptualise Works with others to conceptualise
Find a solution	Uses theory of mind Employs others to help with finding a solution Shares solution Resolves another person's problem
Exploration	Has a social encounter

Among the 12 epistemological barriers that were identified in the YCAR study, six 'social domains' inhibited young children's research behaviours (Table 2.4). They diminished or denied children opportunities to engage in research behaviours.

Table 2.4   YCAR social domains as epistemological barriers (adapted from Murray, 2017)

Epistemological Barriers
Solution not shared with or witnessed by others
Solution not shared with or witnessed by others (unconfirmed)
Denied opportunity to share solution
Responding to adult's semi-open questions
Responding to adult's closed questions
Following adult's direction

NON-SOCIAL ACTIVITY

Parten framed non-social activity as activity for which young children appear 'unoccupied' or engaged in 'onlooker behaviour (or) solitary play' (Xu, 2010: 490). Pedro (aged 4) participated in the YCAR study at school. He attended the reception class unit at Cherry Setting. In the vignette that follows, Pedro engaged in solitary play, though not 'onlooker behaviour', and he was not 'unoccupied' (Xu, 2010: 490).

PEDRO STUDIES THE ROCK
(ADAPTED FROM MURRAY, 2017, 2020)

One morning, during free-flow play, Pedro chose to go to the Safari role-play area in the outdoor area for Cherry Setting where a large mound of earth had been left by builders the previous week at the request of the practitioner. First, Pedro collected a pair of binoculars, then he used them to look at pictures of animals placed earlier by a practitioner on the fence that surrounded the outdoor area. Pedro then lowered the binoculars to survey a rock within the mound of earth. He lifted the rock and studied it closely through the binoculars.

During this activity, Pedro engaged alone while demonstrating two features of research activity identified in the YCAR study: exploration, one of the 'important' research behaviours, and experimentation, an epistemological category. He indicated his intention to look through the binoculars by going deliberately to collect them first; Robson (1993) suggests that a 'central feature (of an experiment) is that you need to know what you are doing before you do it' (p. 78). He engaged in exploratory behaviour used in research (Stebbins, 2001): he tested his binoculars by looking at the animal pictures, then he travelled to the rock and studied, examined, tested and investigated it by observing its physical properties through the binoculars. This was a procedure that Pedro developed himself to examine how to use binoculars to test the physical properties of the rock; he extended the procedure in incremental stages, indicating that he was engaged in 'experimental reasoning concerning matter of fact and existence' (Hume, 1748: 123). Pedro applied Creswell's (2008) key characteristics of experiments to his activity: by using his binoculars to examine different objects, Pedro assigned random objects to the group of objects he observed. He controlled variables by always using his binoculars to observe the objects and he manipulated treatment conditions by observing the rock on the ground then lifting it towards his binoculars.

Pedro's activity was play – 'freely chosen, personally directed, intrinsically motivated behaviour that actively engages the child' (NPFA, CPC and Playlink, 2000) – and his engagement provided some evidence of his 'voice': his wishes to engage in the play were valued (Brooks and Murray, 2018: 145).

PARALLEL PLAY / ASSOCIATIVE DOMAIN

In Parten's definition of parallel play, 'children play side-by-side with similar materials, but do not talk about the play activity' (Xu, 2010: 490). Broadhead (2004: 41) includes parallel play as a feature of her 'associative domain', for which children may also look towards their peers, watch or imitate play, or offer objects which are not accepted. However, Broadhead's associative domain is not the same as Parten's (1932) associative play for which 'children engage in separate activities but interact with each other about the activity' (Xu, 2010: 490). Nora (aged 5) and Sadie (aged 5) participated in the YCAR study in the reception class unit at their school – Cherry Setting (below).

NORA AND SADIE (ADAPTED FROM MURRAY, 2017)

One day, during a free-flow play session in Cherry Setting, Nora and Sadie chose to play with the 'Chilly Polar Regions' small-world play (SWP) activity which featured small-world polar animals, a helicopter, a ship and people on a table top covered with white and blue fabric to represent snow and water. Nora tried to put a SWP lifebelt over a SWP person's head so the SWP person could wear it. She tried to push it over the person's head; it would not go on. Nora took it off and tried again and it still would not go on. She repeated this sequence three times. After more than two minutes, Nora pushed the lifebelt onto the SWP person and then put him in the boat.

Here, Nora was engaged in parallel play. She and Sadie were both playing with the small-world play animals, but although Nora played side-by-side with Sadie, she did not talk with Sadie about the play activity (Xu, 2010: 490). However, Nora was able to find a solution because she had time and freedom to explore, investigate and experiment with something of personal interest – one of the YCAR epistemological categories and evidence of her 'voice' being heard and valued (Brooks and Murray, 2018: 145). She was also engaged in play: 'freely chosen, personally directed, intrinsically motivated behaviour that actively engages the child' (NPFA, CPC and Playlink, 2000). Nora explored whether the lifebelt could be pushed over the 'person's' head, by examining it for 'diagnostic purposes' (Stebbins, 2001: 2). In her actions, she adopted elements of scientific investigation: question, hypothesis, experiment (Penn State LeHigh Valley, 2016). She questioned, then hypothesised, that she would be able to put the lifebelt on the person. She experimented by testing her hypothesis: controlling the variables, restricting them to herself, the SWP lifebelt and SWP person, and manipulating the treatment conditions by exerting increasing pressure in repeated tests. The solution was found: the lifebelt went on the person and Nora was able to continue her small-world play (Creswell, 2008). Nora pursued her play autonomously: she planned according to a goal and operated consciously and voluntarily to enact her goal (Heidegger, 1962; Lyotard, 1992; Merleau-Ponty, 2002: 481), without time constraints imposed by her teacher (Markström and Halldèn, 2009).

SOCIAL INTERACTION / SOCIAL, HIGHLY SOCIAL AND COOPERATIVE DOMAINS

According to Parten (1932), social interaction between preschoolers includes two forms of play: (i) associative play, and (ii) cooperative play. As indicated above, Parten's (1932) associative play includes interactions between children about activities which they are engaging in separately. This is congruent with Broadhead's 'social' and 'highly social' domains (2004). In Broadhead's social domain, children typically smile, laugh, make eye contact, give and receive objects as questions and give answers. In her highly social domain, children offer and accept objects, share eye contact, laugh and engage in dialogue which may centre on activity (Broadhead, 2004).

Parten's cooperative play features children acting together towards a common goal such as a project or a make-believe theme (Xu, 2010: 490). It resonates with Broadhead's 'cooperative domain' (2004), for which children offer and accept objects from each other to extend their play theme, engage in sustained dialogue focused on their activity together and demonstrate shared understanding of mutual goals. Within the scope of this chapter, there is not space to include YCAR examples for all these sub-categories; the vignette that follows exemplifies both Parten's cooperative play and Broadhead's cooperative domain.

PEDRO AND FRIENDS ON SAFARI (ADAPTED FROM MURRAY, 2017)

One day during free-flow play in Cherry Setting, Pedro (aged 5) chose to go outside. The children in the setting had limited access to the field, controlled by eight coloured bands: only those children who wore a band could play on the field. The field had been set up as a safari park following a setting visit the previous week to a safari park. Pedro approached one of his friends, then another, and said each time: 'Come and play' and they went with him. Pedro put on an elephant mask and his two friends did the same. He got a chair and moved it to other chairs in a row and he said to his friends: 'I'm going to wait'. Pedro sat down on a chair facing the field where other children were playing and his two friends joined him. Pedro and his two friends sat with elephant masks on, watching children playing in the field and waiting their turn to play in the 'safari park'. After several minutes, other children moved from the field and Pedro and his friends went onto the field to play.

Here, Pedro and his friends engaged in play – 'freely chosen, personally directed, intrinsically motivated behaviour that actively engages the child' (NPFA, CPC and Playlink, 2000), and although their choice was limited by the coloured bands protocol, they were able to make the decision to wait and play as they wanted to in the end, suggesting their 'voices' were heard and valued (Brooks and Murray, 2018: 145). Pedro also engaged in the 'important' research behaviour of conceptualisation by adopting the epistemological category 'planning'. He developed a concept: the 'clearly specified idea' that he wanted to play elephants outside with his friends, 'deriving from a particular model' that was the previous week's visit to the safari park (Silverman, 2006: 400). Because of the setting's rule that only eight children could play on the grass, Pedro and his friends had to wait until other children had finished their game. While he waited, Pedro prepared for his game by gathering friends, securing an elephant mask and ensuring he was in a prime position to see when his opportunity arose to play on the field. Pedro's plan involved him identifying a goal and a strategy for pursuing and realising it and he valued the idea of playing elephants with his friends on the field so much that he was prepared to wait. Pedro's planning indicated that he was agentic (Alkire and Deneulin, 2009).

In this section, it becomes clear that children's competency with social play is a driving factor in shaping their ability to engage in 'research behaviours'. In this case, children's ability to engage as research participants is less about age and more to do with unique individual characteristics and preferences for play, as well as the adult's ability to interpret meaning from those play preferences.

CONCLUSION

This chapter has considered young children's play, voices and rights in the context of research. Citizens younger than 8 years tend to be marginalised from research, because adults can find it difficult to recognise the non-verbal languages that they use to express their views (Lansdown, 2010; Murray, 2017). 'Too often children's voices are not heard or not heeded' (Singer, 2014: 381), many adults do not understand children's play (Moyles, 2014) and after more than three decades of the UNCRC, there remains 'significant work still to do' to secure universal affordance of children's rights, particularly the rights of children younger than 8 years (Murray et al., 2019). Yet everyone could have a right to research if we were to acknowledge that 'children's thoughts and social behaviours may not be totally incomprehensible to adults, so long as we do not try to interpret them in adult terms' (Appadurai, 2006; Hardman, 1973: 95).

This chapter has exemplified some ways that adults can understand children's voices and children's play in research by drawing parallels between the Young Children as Researchers (YCAR) project (Murray, 2017) and established play categories (Broadhead, 2004; Hutt et al., 1989; Parten, 1932). In doing so, the chapter makes a small contribution to the 'significant work' still to do to secure children's rights to play (Article 31), to freedom of expression (Article 13) and to their views being considered and taken seriously 'in all matters affecting them' (Murray et al., 2019; OHCHR, 1989).

As early childhood education and care practice continues to be shaped increasingly by national and international policy informed by research evidence (Bridges et al., 2009; Rebello Britto et al., 2013), young children's contributions to research 'in all matters affecting them', become ever more important for securing their right to have their views considered and taken seriously (OHCHR, 1989: Article 12). For children's views to be included authentically in research, adults must try harder to understand children's play and children's voices in their myriad forms. Indeed, children's play and children's voices are not only major aspects of young children's 'autonomous world(s)'; they are also children's rights (Hardman, 1973: 95; OHCHR, 1989: Articles 13 and 31).

REFERENCES

Abbott, L. and Langston, A. (2005). *Birth to Three Matters*. Maidenhead: Open University Press.

Alkire, S. and Deneulin, S. (2009). The human development and capability approach. In S. Deneulin and L. Shahani (Eds.), *An Introduction to the Human Development and Capability Approach*. London: Earthscan. pp. 22–48.

Appadurai, A. (2006). The right to research. *Globalisation, Societies and Education*, 4 (2): 167–77.

Australian Government Department for Education (2009). *Being, Belonging and Becoming: The Early Years Learning Framework for Australia*. Available at: https://docs. education.gov.au/documents/belonging-being-becoming-early-years-learning-framework-australia (accessed 15 November 2020).

Bakhtin, M. M. (1963). *Problems of Dostoevsky's Poetics*. Moscow: Khudozhestvennaja Literatura.

Bergen, D. and Fromberg, D. (Eds.) (2006). *Play from Birth to Twelve*. London: Routledge.

Bridges, D., Smeyers, P. and Smith, R. (Eds.) (2009). *Evidence-Based Education Policy: What Evidence, What Basis? Whose Policy?* Chichester: Wiley Blackwell.

Broadhead, P. (2004). *Early Years Play and Learning*. London: RoutledgeFalmer.

Brooks, E. and Murray, J. (2018). Ready, steady, learn: School readiness and children's voices in English early childhood settings. *Education 3–13*, 46 (2): 143–56.

Bruner, J. S. (1966). *Toward a Theory of Instruction*. Cambridge, MA: Harvard University Press.

Cagliari, P., Castagnetti, M., Giudici, C., Rinaldi, C., Vecchi, V. and Moss, P. (Eds.) (2016). *Loris Malaguzzi and the Schools of Reggio Emilia: A Selection of his Writings and Speeches, 1945–1993*. Abingdon: Routledge.

Clark, A. and Moss, P. (2011). *Listening to Young Children* (2nd edn). London: National Children's Bureau.

Cobb-Moore, C., Danby, S. and Farrell, A. (2010). Locking the unlockable: Children's invocation of pretence to define and manage place. *Childhood*, 17 (3): 376–95.

Craik, K. (1943). *The Nature of Explanation.* Cambridge: Cambridge University Press.

Creswell, J. (2008). *Educational Research.* Upper Saddle River, NJ: Pearson.

DeLoache, J. S. (1989). The development of representation in young children. *Advances in Child Development and Behavior*, 22: 1–40.

DeLoache, J. S., Miller, K. F. and Pierroutsakos, S. L. (1998). Reasoning and problem solving. In D. Kuhn and R. Siegler (Eds.), *Handbook of Child Psychology* (5th edn, Vol. 2). New York: Wiley. pp. 801–50.

Department of Basic Education (2015). *The South African National Curriculum Framework for Children from Birth to Four: Comprehensive Version.* Pretoria: Department of Basic Education.

Fielding, M. (2001). Students as radical agents of change. *Journal of Educational Change*, 2 (2): 123–41.

Hardman, S. J. (1973). Can there be an anthropology of children? *Journal of the Anthropology Society of Oxford*, 4 (1): 85–99.

Heidegger, M. (1962). *Being and Time.* New York: HarperCollins.

Hume, D. (1748). An enquiry concerning human understanding. In T. Beauchamp (Ed.) (2000), *David Hume: An Enquiry Concerning Human Understanding.* Oxford: Oxford University Press. pp. 5–123.

Hutt, C. (1979). Play in the under 5s: Form, development and function. In J. G. Howell (Ed.), *Modern Perspectives in the Psychiatry of Infancy.* The Hague: Bruner/Maazel. pp. 94–141.

Hutt, S. J., Tyler, S., Hutt, C. and Christopherson, H. (1989). *Play, Exploration and Learning.* London: Routledge.

Isaacs, N. (1944). Children's 'why' questions. In S. Isaacs (Ed.), *Intellectual Growth in Young Children.* London: Routledge. pp. 291–354.

James, A. and James, A. (2008). *Key Concepts in Childhood Studies.* London: Sage.

Johnson-Laird, P. N. (1983). *Mental Models: Towards a Cognitive Science of Language, Inference and Consciousness.* Cambridge: Cambridge University Press.

Karpov, Y. V. (2005). *The Neo-Vygotskian Approach to Child Development.* Cambridge: Cambridge University Press.

Kellett, M. (2005). *How to Develop Children as Researchers.* London: Sage.

Kernan, M. (2007). *Play as a Context for Early Learning and Development: A Research Paper.* Dublin: National Council for Curriculum and Assessment.

Langsted, O. (1994). Looking at quality from the child's perspective. In P. Moss and A. Pence (Eds.), *Valuing Quality in Early Childhood Services: New Approaches to Defining Quality.* London: Paul Chapman. pp. 28–42.

Lansdown, G. (2010). The realisation of children's participation rights. In B. Percy-Smith and N. Thomas (Eds.), *A Handbook of Children and Young People's Participation.* Abingdon: Routledge. pp. 11–23.

Lowrie, T. (2002). Designing a framework for problem posing: Young children generating open-ended tasks. *Contemporary Issues in Early Childhood*, 3 (3): 354–64.

Lyotard, J.-F. (1992). *Phenomenology*. Paris: Presses Universitaires de France.

Manning-Morton, J. and Thorp, J. (2003). *Key Times for Play*. Maidenhead: Open University Press and McGraw-Hill Education.

Markström, A. and Halldèn, G. (2009). Children's strategies for agency in preschool. *Children in Society*, 23 (2): 112–22.

Maybin, J. (2013). Towards a sociocultural understanding of children's voice. *Language and Education*, 27 (5): 383–97.

Merleau-Ponty, M. (2002). *Phenomenology of Perception*. London: Routledge.

Moss, P., Dahlberg, G., Grieshaber, S., Mantovani, S., May, H., Pence, A., Rayna, S., Swadener, B. B. and Vandenbroeck, M. (2016). The Organisation for Economic Co-Operation and Development's International Early Learning Study: Opening for debate and contestation. *Contemporary Issues in Early Childhood*, 17 (3): 343–51.

Moyles, J. (2014). Starting with play: Taking play seriously. In J. Moyles (Ed.), *The Excellence of Play*. Maidenhead: McGraw-Hill Education and Open University Press. pp. 14–24.

Murray, J. (2017). *Building Knowledge in Early Childhood Education: Young Children Are Researchers*. Abingdon: Routledge.

Murray, J. (2020). How do children build knowledge in early childhood education? Susan Isaacs, 'Young Children Are Researchers' and what happens next. *Early Child Development and Care*. doi: 10.1080/03004430.2020.1854242.

Murray, J. and Devecchi, C. (2016). The Hantown Street Play Project. *International Journal of Play*, 5 (2): 196–211.

Murray, J., Swadener, B. B. and Smith, K. (Eds.) (2019). *The Routledge International Handbook of Young Children's Rights*. Abingdon: Routledge.

National Playing Fields Association (NPFA), Children's Play Council (CPC) and Playlink (2000). *Best Play: What Play Provision Should Do for Children*. London: National Playing Fields Association.

Nelissen J. M. C. and Tomic, W. (1996). *Representation and Cognition*. Heerlen: Open University.

Office of the High Commissioner for Human Rights (OHCHR) (1989). *The United Nations Convention on the Rights of the Child*. Available at: www.ohchr.org/Documents/ProfessionalInterest/crc.pdf (accessed 15 November 2020).

O'Kane, C. (2008). The development of participatory techniques. In P. Christensen and A. James (Eds.), *Research with Children*. London: Routledge. pp. 125–55.

Organisation for Economic Cooperation and Development (OECD) (2019). *International Early Learning and Child Well-Being Study*. Available at: www.oecd.org/education/school/international-early-learning-and-child-well-being-study.htm (accessed 15 November 2020).

Papert, S. (1980). *Mindstorms: Children, Computers and Powerful Ideas*. New York: Basic Books.

Parten, M. B. (1932). Social participation among pre-school children. *Journal of Abnormal and Social Psychology*, 27: 243–69.

Penn State LeHigh Valley (2016). *Biology 110 Laboratory Independent Research Project.* Available at: www2.lv.psu.edu/jxm57/irp/sci_inv1.html (accessed 15 November 2020).

Piaget, J. (1945). *Play, Dreams, and Imitation in Childhood.* New York: Norton.

Qualifications and Curriculum Authority (QCA) and the Department for Education and Employment (DfEE) (2000). *Curriculum Guidance for the Foundation Stage.* London: Qualifications and Curriculum Authority.

Rebello Britto, P., Engle, P. and Super. C. (2013). *Handbook of Early Childhood Development Research and its Impact on Global Policy.* Oxford: Oxford University Press.

Robson, C. (1993). *Real World Research.* Oxford: Blackwell.

Ryan, S. (2005). Freedom to choose. In N. Yelland (Ed.), *Critical Issues in Early Childhood Education.* Maidenhead: Open University Press. pp. 99–114.

Scruton, R. (2001). *Kant.* Oxford: Oxford University Press.

Shonkoff, J. and Richter, L. (2013). The powerful reach of early childhood development: A science based foundation for sound investment. In P. R. Britto, P. Engel and C. Super (Eds.), *Handbook of Early Childhood Development Research and its Impact on Global Policy.* Oxford: Oxford University Press. pp. 24–34.

Silverman, D. (2006). *Interpreting Qualitative Data* (3rd edn). London: Sage.

Singer, A. (2014). Voices heard and unheard: A Scandinavian perspective. *Journal of Social Welfare and Family Law*, 36 (4): 381–91.

Stebbins, R. A. (2001). *Exploratory Research in the Social Sciences.* Thousand Oaks, CA: Sage.

United Nations (2015). *Sustainable Development Goal 4.* Available at: https://sustainable development.un.org/sdg4 (accessed 15 November 2020).

Vygotsky, L. S. (1976). Play and its role in the mental development of the child. *Soviet Psychology*, 5: 6–18.

Whitty, G. and Wisby, E. (2007). Whose voice? An exploration of the current policy interest in pupil involvement in school decision-making. *International Studies in Sociology of Education*, 17 (3): 303–19.

World Health Organisation (2018). *Nurturing Care Framework.* Available at: https://apps. who.int/iris/bitstream/handle/10665/272603/9789241514064-eng.pdf?ua=1 (accessed 15 November 2020).

Xu, Y. (2010). Children's social play sequence: Parten's classic theory revisited. *Early Child Development and Care*, 180 (4): 489–98.

3

ETHICAL CONSIDERATIONS: PLAY FOR FUN AND PLAY FOR DATA COLLECTION

SUE DOCKETT

Play is a common feature of young children's experiences. Educators often assume that children do not differentiate between play and learning (Pramling Samuelsson and Asplund Carlsson, 2008). Is the same assumption made about play and research? Do children make distinctions between general play and play that generates research data? Does it matter? If so, how do adult researchers make this distinction and how is this communicated to the participating children? The aim of this chapter is to explore ethical considerations as children engage with research grounded in play-based methodologies. Such research may focus on investigating the phenomenon of children's play or utilise play as a method for exploring some other aspect of their experiences.

The previous two chapters have introduced the concept of play and how it may feature in research approaches with young children. One thing that was clear across Chapters 1 and 2 was that play is complex and multifaceted, and therefore so too is research which encompasses play. This brings with it related challenges in terms of research ethics, not least because play should be a mechanism to support communication and expression, rather than a draw to participate in research because

(Continued)

children perceive it to be 'fun'. In light of this, the current chapter moves us forward in the discussion by considering the ethical implications of play-based research with young children. This chapter will investigate:

- Children's rights-based research;
- Ethical considerations in research with children;
- Participatory methods;
- Building the capacity of duty-bearers;
- Play as data;
- Ethical research and play.

CHILDREN'S RIGHTS-BASED RESEARCH

This chapter is based on the framework of children's rights-based research (Beazley et al., 2011; Lundy and McEvoy, 2012). Children's rights-based research brings together the discourses of sociology of childhood (Christensen and James, 2017) and children's rights (Freeman, 2009). Within this rights-based framework, children are accorded their right to have their views heard and listened to in ways that respect their agency and competence.

The basis for children's rights-based research derives from the Convention on the Rights of the Child (CRC) (UN Commission on Human Rights, 1990) – even though this document does not explicitly reference research with children. Despite this, the Articles of the CRC, together with the human rights principles which accord dignity and respect to all people, provide a powerful frame to guide ethical research with children. This can be seen in a wide range of recent research (see Groundwater-Smith et al., 2015, for an overview) that promotes children's participation (Article 12) in ways that allow them to express their views freely (Article 13). Children's rights-based research also promotes the best interests of the child (Article 3); includes provision for children's access to information (Article 17); provides opportunities for appropriate direction and guidance to support children's exercise of their rights (Article 5); and ensures protection from exploitation (Article 36). As well as generating research consistent with children's rights, this approach build's children's capabilities to understand and exercise their rights as well as the capabilities of those who engage with children to comply with and promote children's rights (Lundy and McEvoy, 2012). The principles of children's rights-based research are reflected in the charter developed by the international project entitled Ethical Research Involving Children (ERIC) (Graham et al., 2013), which urges researchers to adopt the following commitments:

- Ethics in research involving children is everyone's responsibility.
- Respecting the dignity of children is core to ethical research.

- Research involving children must be just and equitable.
- Ethical research benefits children.
- Children should never be harmed by their participation in research.
- Research must always obtain children's informed and ongoing consent.
- Ethical research involves ongoing reflection.

Each of these commitments has implications for ethical research involving *all* children: these commitments are not age-defined. That is, they do not only apply to children above or of a specific age. Rather, all children – even the very youngest – are entitled to the same ethical commitments when involved in research. The essence of this position derives from the principle of ethical symmetry – that is, that the relationship between researcher and researched should be the same for all (Christensen and Prout, 2002).

Ethical symmetry argues that the same ethical principles apply to all – adults and children – and that the starting point for research should acknowledge the everyday lives of participants, their competencies, interests, values and local 'cultures of communication' (Christensen and Prout, 2002: 483). In other words, approaches to research need to be responsive to the potential participants and their cultures and contexts, rather than based on assumptions about any of these elements. For example, this stance argues that methods described as child-friendly are neither necessary nor appropriate when based primarily on assumptions about children's age, interests or competence. Rather, choices about method are best guided by the participants themselves and the contexts in which they interact.

One conclusion to draw from this position is that play reflects children's interests and capabilities and promotes dialogic practice about what matters to them. As such, it can provide a rich context and a possible method for the exploration of children's everyday lives and experiences. However, even in a context that seems as 'natural' as play, ethical considerations must be addressed.

In practice, adopting the stance of ethical symmetry involves ensuring that: children are accorded the same rights in research as adults; the methods chosen are responsive to those involved; there is engagement with the contexts in which children interact; and reflection of the differences, as well as commonalities, across children's experiences, interactions and meanings is promoted. These issues are highlighted in the following discussion.

Conducting children's rights-based research can be both challenging and exciting. Engaging with young children requires flexibility, responsiveness and reflexivity (see Chapter 4), as well as the capacity to expect the unexpected. Ethical issues are often at the forefront of research with young children, as institutional ethics boards, organisations and gatekeepers exercise caution in approving research with those – such as children – who are considered vulnerable. Researchers engaged in children's rights-based research need to be aware of procedural requirements and conscious of the everyday ethics that underpin decisions taken and the implications of these. This involves ongoing reflection on ethical issues and the promotion of genuinely participatory methods that are appropriate to the research issue. Further, children's rights-based research extends to building the capacity of those considered duty-bearers – that is, those responsible for ensuring that children are afforded opportunities to exercise their rights (Lundy and McEvoy, 2012).

ETHICAL CONSIDERATIONS IN RESEARCH WITH CHILDREN

Research that respects the rights of children must be in line with relevant ethics standards, such as those of institutional ethics boards or organisational codes of practice. It must also reflect the principles of the CRC. This means that children are entitled to be informed about the research before they agree (or not) to be involved and supported as they form their own views about research participation over the course of the study. Research should ensure that children are not exploited and that their best interests are at the heart of the research.

THE IMAGE OF CHILD

Underpinning any research with young children is the theoretical position adopted by the researcher. This position influences the researcher's image of the child, which in turn impacts on the nature of the research. For example, are children considered to be subjects or objects of research (Woodhead and Faulkner, 2008)? What form of engagement is presupposed by the research? Are children positioned as agents, co-researchers or participants? Are they offered opportunities to be reflexive participants (Christensen and James, 2017)?

It is easy for researchers to make assumptions about children based on factors such as age, gender, and geographical, political or social location. Researchers themselves need to be critically reflexive as they examine and question their own expectations. Children's rights-based research is informed by both a rights framework and a sociological framework that recognise children's competence. This guides researchers to consider children's strengths – what they can do, rather than what they cannot do – and locates at the heart of the research children's perspectives rather than adult expectations or assumptions.

BEING INFORMED

When young children are involved in research, it can be tempting to assume that the research occurs without them being aware. It can be argued that educators engage in research every day as they observe and record children's interactions and use these to plan educational experiences, and that observational research can simply be an extension of this. For example, is being a 'focus child' participating in research? While educators may assume that their actions are unobtrusive, Helen's comments in the example below suggest that this is not necessarily so. Further, without appropriate explanation of what the adult is doing and why, what is observed may not accurately reflect the child's experiences.

BEING THE FOCUS CHILD

On the way home from childcare, Helen announced to her mother that she was Lorraine's 'focus child' this week. 'How do you know?', asked her mother. 'She was following me, and I could see her writing in her book. So I asked her why she was watching me. She said I was her focus child'. 'What does that mean?', asked her mother. 'It means she watches me and writes down what I do'. 'How do you feel about that?' 'It's OK, everyone gets a turn. [*thinks for a while*] Maybe I just have to be really, really good this week'.

Respecting children's rights in research suggests that prior to observing children's actions and interactions, they have the right to be informed about the research in ways that make sense to them, and that they have the right to make an informed choice about participation. This includes rights to decline to participate, to withdraw from the research at any point, and rights to privacy and confidentiality.

Providing appropriate information to children may occur through ongoing conversations, the reading of written information or the use of images (Figure 3.1).

To know more about play, I would like to observe you playing. This might involve watching you and writing down what you are doing and saying. I might ask you to have conversations with me. And you are invited to talk to me any time, too.

Figure 3.1 Part of an information sheet for young children

© Carmen Huser (text 2018: 388) and Renate Alf (illustrations 2013, 2016). Reproduced with permission.

Children's entitlement to support to help form their views may mean that they need some time to think about their involvement, that they ask further questions, engage in discussions and/or seek advice from people they trust.

SEEKING CONSENT

Once information has been provided and children have the time and opportunity to discuss it, they may be invited to indicate their willingness to be involved through recording their name or symbol on a form (Figure 3.2).

However, these formats are unlikely to be suitable for use when seeking the consent of very young children. Neither are they guarantees that children have understood the complexities of the proposed research or that they agree to continued participation or non-participation (Palaiologou, 2014). Rather, they represent a child's decision at a moment in time.

What then can be done to inform younger children of the research and support them as they make decisions about participation? Several studies note the difficulties of assessing whether very young children have made informed decisions, while also noting that attending to their expressions, actions and signals can provide some indications of their preferences, often referred to as assent rather than consent (see Cree et al., 2002 and Tisdall, 2018 for elaboration of these concepts). As one example, Pálmadóttir and Einarsdóttir (2016: 727) note how Anna, a 1-year-old girl, used both language and actions as she shook her head and said 'No, no, no!' as the researcher used a video camera. Salamon (2015: 1023) recounts interactions with 9-month-old Timmy who initiated and maintained very close contact as he climbed upon her, rested against her and repeatedly vocalised towards her. Key to these examples are the relationships that surround the interactions, with Salamon (2015: 1024) noting that 'the relationship we had developed afforded him [Timmy] particular opportunities to participate in the research as an agentic "co-researcher"'.

We have asked your parents if it is ok if we talk to you and they have said yes. Now we want to know if you would like to talk to us about what you like about your town?

If you would like to talk to us please write your name just here.

Figure 3.2   One part of the form seeking preschool children's consent

Opportunities for young children to participate in research and to demonstrate their willingness (or not) to continue their participation occur as they interact with and relate to the researcher. Christensen (2010: 146) emphasises the importance of such relationships in promoting 'attentive listening and looking' whereby 'the researcher enacts (and performs) real interest in understanding children's experiences ... it is such communicative qualities that are the keys to engaging children (as well as adults) in research'.

These relationships also provide the context for children's consent to be revisited and renegotiated as the project continues. Process consent – where researchers provide ongoing opportunities for children to make decisions about participation (Einarsdóttir, 2007; Flewitt, 2005), including the option of withdrawing from the research – continues through to the conclusion of data generation and beyond to considerations of how and to whom the research is reported and disseminated. The latter assumes increased importance when visual data are involved, as the reproduction and display of images present challenges related to ownership of the data, the anonymity of participants and the permanency of images, particularly when published on the internet (Dockett et al., 2017). See Chapter 7 for some more examples of how consent may be negotiated with children in pedagogically appropriate or play-based ways, and for the challenges associated with these approaches.

ROLE OF THE ADULT/RESEARCHER

Building relationships that promote communication between the researcher and the participating children is important. Several researchers note the value of using children's communicative forms as a means of engaging with children (Christensen, 2010; Corsaro, 2003; Pálmadóttir and Einarsdóttir, 2016). For example, engaging with children as they play could create a space for communication and the construction of shared meaning, based on understandings of both verbal and non-verbal interactions. But what role should the adult take? Should the adult seek to be a player, just as the child is a player? Should the adult adopt the same role as other educators in the setting? As illustrated in the following example, there can be challenges when adults seek to enter play on the same terms as children.

ADULT ROLE

Naomi (student teacher) was eager to start researching play in the preschool. Upon noticing the children playing a game of chase and catch, she asked if she could join in. The children agreed. After some time, Naomi herself was caught by some of the children and taken back to 'home'. Two of the children took a nearby skipping rope and proceeded to wrap it around her. In only a few minutes, Naomi found herself effectively tied to a post, unable to free her hands. The children left her and proceeded to catch other children.

Children tend to 'see through' adults' attempts to 'be' children. At the same time, researchers are often wary of adopting the same role as educators such as setting or enforcing rules and solving conflicts among children, as in the following example. One alternative is to adopt the role of 'other' adult; someone who seeks to interact in play and is interested in understanding children's worlds and experiences but who is clearly not a child player and not an educator (Christensen, 2010). The 'other' adult can also be described as adopting a 'least' adult role (Mandell, 1988), where the aim is to promote joint engagement in activities such as play as a means of reducing some of the social distance between children and adults, demonstrating interest in, and valuing of, children's social worlds.

AREN'T YOU A TEACHER?

While talking with Elly as she played in the sandpit, Mack approached with an angry look on his face. 'Jason took my bucket. Can you get it back for me?', he asked. 'That's unfortunate', I said, 'What do you think might be best to do?' 'You can get it back for me'. When I did not make any move, he looked at me, 'Aren't you a teacher?' When I replied 'No', he shook his head and walked away to approach a 'real' teacher.

PARTICIPATORY METHODS

Much of the recent research involving young children has focused on the use of participatory methods, both to engage children in the research itself and as an effort to facilitate children's expression of their views. Indeed, 'the world of methods has become so fascinating and now offers such opportunity for innovation that we sometimes lose sight of *why we choose* particular methods and, more importantly, *how we use them*' (Bessell, 2009: 17).

While developing and using methods that facilitate children's participation is central to children's rights-based research, the principle of ethical symmetry reminds us that methods themselves do not make research rights-based. Indeed, it is possible to use methods that seem to promote participation in ways that instead promote adult direction and control, as in the example below. This example serves as a reminder that the attitude – including the theoretical stance and image of the child – assumed by the researcher, rather than the method adopted, is central to participatory research.

CHILD GUIDED OR TEACHER GUIDED?

A group of preschool children have recently visited the school nearby. Many of these children will attend that school next year. The preschool teacher has set up a range of school-related props including some school uniforms, lunch boxes, drink bottles, blank paper and pencils in pencil cases. A whiteboard and markers are adjacent to these props. Several children are drawn to the area and don the uniforms. Joey stands at the white-board and directs the other children to draw, using a stern voice. The other children ignore him, and he raises his voice. Melissa – the teacher who accompanied the children on the school visit – observes the play. After a few minutes, she interrupts Joey to say, 'That's not what happened, Joey.' To those who have been ignoring Joey, Melissa says 'You need to play properly, or these things will have to go away'.

In some contexts, the drive to produce ever-more innovative methods is akin to building a box of tricks to entice children's participation. Christensen (2010: 146) puts it this way: 'The researcher, like the magician in the marketplace, urgently feels the need to entice, entertain and intrigue their audience. They do this by bringing their box of tools and tricks'. While many innovative methods may encourage children's participation, Dockett and Perry (2007: 50) note that 'there is often tension between developing interesting methods to engage children, while at the same time avoiding a gimmick approach'. In this sense, a gimmick is defined as something that is not serious, serving to attract attention, rather than having any real value. The (fictional) activity described below could be considered a gimmick. It serves to attract children's interest and attention but there is lit-tle effort to engage in the co-construction of meaning with children, and the connection between the 'data' contributed to the research topic seems limited. The activity may be an engaging and playful experience with many positive interactions. However, it does not reflect the principles of children's rights-based research.

A GIMMICK

As part of a project exploring play preferences, children are invited to write about or draw their favourite play activity on paper. With the assistance of adults or peers, these are made into paper planes and, sometimes after many attempts, flown into a net hanging in the corner of the classroom. Many children are eager to make many planes and often offer only a cursory scribble on the paper in order to make and fly the planes. Those planes that make it into the net stay there for several days until the researcher retrieves them for analysis. Over several days, the children remain eager to make paper planes. There is no discussion with the researcher of what is on the paper.

There are many participatory methods that aim to acknowledge children's diverse ways of communicating and participating in research, as well as their preferences (many of which are articulated in Part 3, Chapters 7–12). Recognising this diversity, many studies involving young children offer a range of methods from which children can choose. These may include drawing, photovoice, videos, child-led tours, dance, role play, model-making, diaries, storytelling and using puppets, among many other possibilities. However, it is important that the choice of methods is guided by efforts to promote children as active participants in research, where they can tell their stories and share their experiences as they engage with researchers in meaningful ways. The notion of a 'gimmick' or even methods so enticing that they 'trick' children into participation (Einarsdóttir, 2007) is not compatible with images of children as competent rights holders, nor is it compatible with the image of respectful, interested and engaged researchers. Genuinely participatory research methods provide opportunities for children to engage in many phases of the research; they recognise children's preferences for engaging; and help to promote children's developing capabilities.

The label of 'child-friendly' is often applied to methods used in research with young children. Underpinning this label can be an image of children that highlights their perceived limitations, rather than a focus on their competence and strengths. It is indeed the case that any methods employed are likely to appeal to children when they are interesting and fun. However, methods best suited to investigating issues of interest to children should not necessarily be perceived as 'childish' or less rigorous in planning, implementation and analysis than other methods (Beazley et al., 2011). Rather than advocating for 'child-friendly' methods, the principle of ethical symmetry promotes methods that are relevant for the participants and their contexts (Christensen and Prout, 2002).

BUILDING THE CAPACITY OF DUTY-BEARERS

Many adults engage with children in participatory research contexts. For example, in early childhood settings children interact with parents and other family members, educators and other professionals. Children's rights-based research has the potential to remind each of these people of children's rights, their competence, and the value of understanding their perspectives and experiences. Not only does this contribute to developing understandings of children's rights, but also to recognition of the obligations of adults to respect and promote children's rights.

IT'S ONLY PLAY

As they participated in a project exploring their play preferences, some children chose to share their play experiences on posters they constructed jointly with educators.

These were displayed in the foyer of the childcare centre. On viewing the poster and reading a child's description of constructing a rocket ship, one parent expressed her surprise at the complexity of the task. She commented, 'I thought they were just playing'. Another parent complained to educators that her child had not made a poster. The educator explained that her son had decided that he did not want to share his experience and that staff at the centre had respected his choice.

PLAY AS DATA

Young children's play has been the focus of a great deal of research. In some instances, investigations have addressed play as the subject of research (for example, Huser, 2018; Pyle and Alaca, 2018), and in other instances, play has been employed as a participatory method (for example, Kalkman and Clark, 2017). Part of the rationale for the research focus on play is that it is something that is familiar for children and a context guided by child initiation and choice. Yet play also presents some challenges for researchers. While it is possible to compile a list of the common characteristics, play remains a unique and individualised experience: what constitutes play for one child may not be considered play by another. How then do researchers ensure that they recognise the individuality of children and their play, while also acknowledging commonalities across play?

Play is also familiar to educators. Much of educators' pedagogical documentation recognises the value of children's play and promotes play as a context for social engagement, recognition of children's rights and the co-construction of meaning. Each of these is also a contributor to children's rights-based research. Perhaps it is not surprising then that some forms of pedagogical documentation have also been used in research. For example, both Learning Stories (Carr and Lee, 2012) and the Mosaic Approach (Clark, 2017) have served as methods in participatory research. However, Waller and Bitou (2011) caution that while these approaches 'have the ability to inform research through the depth and range of data elicited from and interpreted by children' (p. 15), they can also 'replicate the teacher–pupil dynamic of power' (p. 17). A similar point has been made by Gallacher and Gallagher (2008: 506), who argue that the uncritical use of such tools can reinforce the power differentials between adults and children, and reduce, rather than increase, the likelihood of 'children's participation on the basis of active, informed decisions'.

ETHICAL RESEARCH AND PLAY

Play and rights-based research can be complementary: children's play can provide the focus for rights-based research and rights-based research can employ play as a method.

However, the coexistence of play and rights-based research does not necessarily ensure this complementarity. Consideration of ethical spaces for researching play has the potential to address this. Drawing on Palaiologou's (2014) description of ethical spaces, Huser (2018) outlines three overlapping ethical spaces for researching with children: physical; socio-emotional; and creative. Within each of these spaces, the concepts of privacy, agency and relationships are enacted. Using this framework, ethical approaches to researching children's play require researcher reflexivity in responding to questions such as:

- What image of the child guides the research?
- How is information about the research shared with children on an ongoing basis?
- What possibilities do the children have to give consent within a timeframe they set for themselves?
- How can children physically self-regulate proximity and distance to the researcher?
- Does the space provide opportunities for children to address topics they wish to withhold from others, such as peers or educators?
- How do researchers facilitate children's own decision-making about how to participate?
- What efforts do researchers make to become familiar with children's modes of communication and expressive forms?
- How does the research support children's peer cultures?
- What strategies are used to respect children's silence?
- How can feelings of obligation be uncovered and challenged?

(Adapted from Huser, 2018: 327–30)

CONCLUSION

This chapter explored the principles of children's rights-based research in the context of researching children's play. It outlined ethical considerations related to the provision of information, seeking children's consent and the role of the adult/ researcher in play-based research. Advocating the principle of ethical symmetry, it argues that appropriate participatory methods require connection to the competencies, interests, values and contexts of potential participants, rather than being based on developmental assumptions. Children's rights-based research is underpinned by an image of the child as a competent rights holder and by recognition of the obligations of adults to respect and promote children's rights. Exploration of ethical spaces for researching play has the potential to enhance understandings of these obligations and enactments.

REFERENCES

Alf, R. (2013). *The Purest Kindergarten 2*. Oldenburg: Lappan Publishing House.

Alf, R. (2016). *Educators in Their Best!* Freiburg: Herder.

Beazley, H., Bessell, S., Ennew, J. and Waterson, R. (2011). How are human rights of children related to research methodology? In A. Invernizzi and J. Williams (Eds.), *The Human Rights of Children: From Visions to Implementation*. London: Taylor & Francis. pp. 159–78.

Bessell, S. (2009). Research with children: Thinking about method and methodology. In ARACY and the NSW Commission for Children. *Involving Children and Young People in Research*. Sydney: ARACY and the NSW Commission for Children. pp. 17–27.

Carr, M. and Lee, W. (2012). *Learning Stories: Constructing Learner Identities in Early Education*. London: Sage.

Christensen, P. (2010). Ethnographic encounters with children. In D. Hartas (Ed.), *Educational Research and Inquiry: Qualitative and Quantitative Approaches*. London: Bloomsbury. pp. 145–57.

Christensen, P. and James, A. (2017). *Research with Children: Perspectives and Practices*. London: Routledge.

Christensen, P. and Prout, A. (2002). Working with ethical symmetry in social research with children. *Childhood*, 9 (4): 477–97.

Clark, A. (2017). *Listening to Children: A Guide to Understanding and Using the Mosaic Approach*. London: Jessica Kingsley.

Corsaro, W. (2003). *We're Friends, Right? Inside Kids' Culture*. Washington, DC: Joseph Henry Press.

Cree, V., Kay, H. and Tisdall, K. (2002). Research with children: Sharing the dilemmas. *Child & Family Social Work*, 7 (1): 47–56.

Dockett, S. and Perry, B. (2007). Trusting children's accounts in research. *Journal of Early Childhood Research*, 5 (1): 47–63.

Dockett, S. and Perry, B. (2011). Building a Child Friendly City. Unpublished project report, Charles Sturt University, Australia.

Dockett, S., Einarsdóttir, J. and Perry, B. (2017). Photo elicitation: Reflecting on multiple sites of meaning. *International Journal of Early Years Education*, 25 (3): 225–40.

Einarsdóttir, J. (2007). Research with children: Methodological and ethical challenges. *European Early Childhood Education Research Journal*, 15 (2): 197–221.

Flewitt, R. (2005). Conducting research with young children: Some ethical issues. *Early Childhood Development and Care*, 175 (6): 553–65.

Freeman, M. (2009). Children's rights as human rights: Reading the UNCRC. In J. Qvortrup, W. A. Corsaro and M. S. Honig (Eds.), *The Palgrave Handbook of Childhood Studies*. London: Palgrave Macmillan. pp. 377–93.

Gallacher, L.-A. and Gallagher, M. (2008). Methodological immaturity in childhood research? Thinking through 'participatory methods'. *Childhood*, 15 (4): 499–516.

Graham, A. P., Powell, M. A., Anderson, D., Fitzgerald, R. and Taylor, N. (2013). *Ethical Research Involving Children*. Florence: UNICEF Office of Research Innocenti.

Groundwater-Smith, S., Dockett, S. and Bottrell, D. (2015). *Participatory Research with Children and Young People*. London: Sage.

Huser, C. (2018). Children's Perspectives of Play and their Research Participation. Unpublished doctoral thesis, Charles Sturt University, Australia. Available at: https://researchoutput.csu.edu.au/en/publications/childrens-perspectives-of-play-and-their-research-participation (accessed 15 November 2020).

Kalkman, K. and Clark, A. (2017). 'Here we like playing princesses' – newcomer migrant children's transitions within day care: Exploring role play as an indication of suitability and home and belonging. *European Early Childhood Education Research Journal*, 25 (2): 292–304.

Lundy, L. and McEvoy, L. (2012). Childhood, the United Nations Convention on the Rights of the Child, and research: What constitutes a 'rights-based' approach? In M. Freeman (Ed.), *Law and Childhood Studies: Current Legal Issues (Vol. 14)*. Oxford: Oxford University Press. pp. 75–91.

Mandell, N. (1988). The least-adult role in studying children. *Journal of Contemporary Ethnography*, 16 (4): 433–67.

Palaiologou, I. (2014). 'Do we hear what children want to say?' Ethical praxis when choosing research tools with children under five. *Early Child Development and Care*, 184 (5): 689–705.

Pálmadóttir, H. and Einarsdóttir, J. (2016). Video observations of children's perspectives on their lived experiences: Challenges in the relations between the researcher and children. *European Early Childhood Education Research Journal*, 24 (5): 721–33.

Pramling Samuelsson, I. and Asplund Carlsson, M. (2008). The playing learning child: Towards a pedagogy of early childhood. *Scandinavian Journal of Educational Research*, 52 (6): 623–41.

Pyle, A. and Alaca, B. (2018). Kindergarten children's perspectives on play and learning. *Early Child Development and Care*, 188 (8): 1063–75.

Salamon, A. (2015). Ethical symmetry in participatory research with infants. *Early Child Development and Care*, 185 (6): 1016–30.

Tisdall, E. K. M. (2018). Applying human rights to children's participation in research. In M. Twomey and C. Carroll (Eds.), *Seen and Heard: Exploring Participation, Engagement and Voice for Children with Disabilities*. Bern: Peter Lang.

UN Commission on Human Rights (1990). *Convention on the Rights of the Child* (E/CN.4/RES/1990/74), 7 March. Available at: www.refworld.org/docid/3b00f03d30.html (accessed 5 September 2020).

Waller, T. and Bitou, A. (2011). Research with children: Three challenges for participatory research in early childhood. *European Early Childhood Education Research Journal*, 19 (1): 5–20.

Woodhead, M. and Faulkner, D. (2008). Subjects, objects or participants? Dilemmas of psychological research with children. In P. Christensen and A. James (Eds.), *Research with Children: Perspectives and Practices*. New York: Routledge/Taylor & Francis. pp. 10–39.

PART 2

THEORETICAL AND CONCEPTUAL FRAMEWORKS FOR PLAYFUL RESEARCH

4

PRACTITIONER ENQUIRY: A REFLEXIVE RESEARCH METHOD FOR PLAYFUL PEDAGOGY

KATE WALL, LORNA ARNOTT AND ELAINE HALL

In this chapter we are going to explore the productive learning associations we see between a practitioner enquiry approach to professional learning and playful pedagogy in the early years. In doing so, we hope to show a complementary and facilitatory relationship that is evident in learning, tools and techniques used for research and dispositions that result for children and practitioners as researchers or participants in research projects. We will make clear the underlying assumptions of practitioner enquiry and what the implications of engaging in enquiry are in regards to an orientation towards play. The basic premise behind this perspective is that practitioners in early childhood settings are already skilled researchers, unearthing and interpreting the intricacies in children's play. This chapter suggests that it is important to harness those skills in order to explore children's perspectives through play. In particular, we will focus on:

- The ways in which early childhood practices can support an approach to research that facilitates meaning and interpretation of data in playful spaces for learning;
- Using real-life examples from early years settings to exemplify the discussion and ground this approach in practice;
- Giving guidance about the use of enquiry-based tools which have often been used to support professional learning.

A practitioner enquiry approach to professional learning in education has become increasingly likely as practitioners are encouraged to engage in and with research (Cordingley, 2013) as part of their professional learning. In Scotland, the new National Professional Learning Model (Education Scotland, 2018: Figure 4.1) has the concept of research engagement embedded within it, including a range of structures and prompts, formal and informal, to facilitate this engagement. Importantly, at the centre of the model is the relationship between learner and education professional, as such emphasising the need to focus professional learning on learner need (Timperley, 2008). For us what it also does is encourage parallels between the learning of children and young people and professional learning, and therefore it supports productive connections in the pedagogy used (Wall and Hall, 2016). These associations mean we can draw on the founding principles of playful pedagogies to inform our research approaches with children from birth to 8 years old.

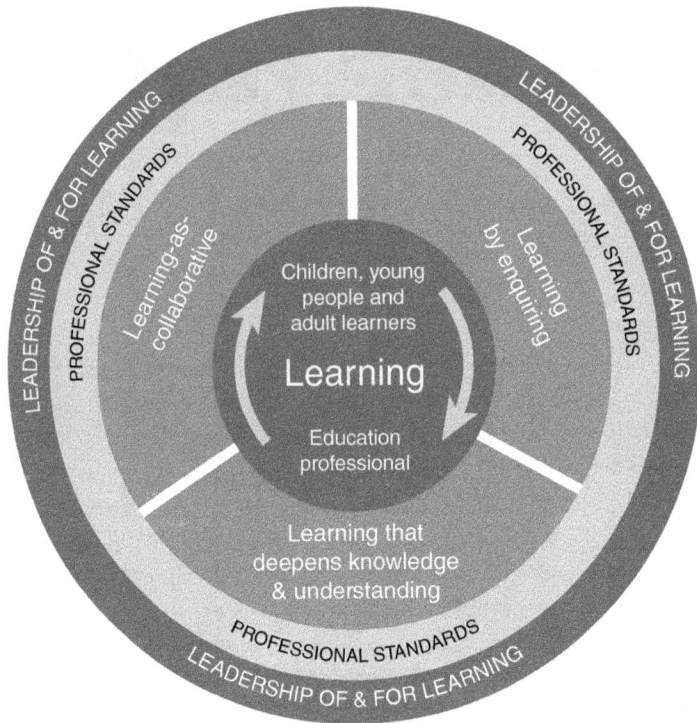

Figure 4.1   Scottish Professional Learning Model (Education Scotland, 2018)

© Crown copyright 2020

WHAT IS PRACTITIONER ENQUIRY?

In 1916, Dewey first discussed the importance of teachers engaging in pedagogic enquiry to fully understand processes and outcomes in their classrooms. We see two dominant standpoints on practitioner enquiry, with a potential lack of transfer between the two resulting in a lack of opportunity for sustainability (Wall, 2018). On the one hand, we have practitioner enquiry as stance. Originating in the work of researchers such as Cochrane-Smith and Lytle (2009), this position suggests practitioner enquiry is an epistemological stance, a way of understanding the world and how it is made up, arguably a way of being that is tied up with views of democratic purpose and social justice. The other view is practitioner enquiry as project. This is far better publicised, easier to grasp, and as such is probably more dominant in the profession's consciousness. Here practitioner enquiry tends to be driven by structures and organisations. Menter et al. (2010) defined enquiry as a strategic finding out, a shared process of investigation that can be explained or defended. This is an orientation much more directly associated with research, via the language of strategic enquiry. Often perceived as being more achievable in its boundedness and immediate tangibility, one of the challenges is that each 'project' is positioned as being separate and finite. While there is nothing to prevent enquiries becoming cumulative and connecting to career-long professional learning (Reeves and Drew, 2013), this cumulative process is not 'designed in': with the focus on the project outcomes, what happens to the enquirer when the module finishes or the organisation moves on?

Within both 'types' of practitioner enquiry, there is an assumption that the approach will lead to an engagement with research as a means to generate answers to pertinent questions of practice (Nias and Groundwater-Smith, 1988). This could be research-informed and/or involve a research process undertaken by practitioners (Cordingley, 2015; Hall, 2009). Completing a systematic review on the topic, Dagenais et al. (2012) found that practitioners with an inquiry standpoint were more likely to have positive views on research and therefore were more likely to use it to inform their practice. However, beyond those already in the enquiry camp, some practitioners are turned away from practitioner enquiry because of the use of 'research': the term itself forming an obstacle. Those practitioners who do not already have an enquiry identity have to perform some kind of translation to achieve a degree of fit with this uncomfortable term (Hall, 2018). In our work with practitioners, we have seen forms of translation along a continuum: from 'importing lab-coats' to 'duelling banjos'. In the first, teachers reify research and researchers as 'other and better' and import a set of research assumptions, tools and analysis methods wholly inappropriate for the context in which they work. In the second, teachers still consider research as 'other' but write it off as alien, irrelevant and, in the worst cases, threatening to practice. Thus, often with the best of intentions, the 'project' can become an add-on and the process of enquiry, rather than being a way to find out something useful, becomes meaningless or disconnected from the practice it set out to explore. As is often the case, a meaningful and organic translation sits somewhere between the extremes: chosen by the practitioner, mediated by the research support team.

We therefore work from the position that encouraging research-informed practice requires a reimagining of what research in early childhood entails, which should be born out of pedagogy which is suitable for the context. Rather than indoctrinating early childhood practitioners into the formal research world associated with academia, academic research must evolve to recognise the strengths of our practitioners as skilled investigators. For most practitioners in early childhood and for the purposes of this book, those investigations are rooted in children's play experiences.

WHY ENQUIRE?

Practitioners are constantly asking questions which could arise from pressing problems – the learner, stuck and frustrated, right in front of you – or from the growing awareness of a pattern in the classroom – the 'tried and tested' has gone stale for learners and practitioner alike. Problem-solving and exploratory questions – the *How can I fix this?* and the *What's going on?* – are part of the practitioner's innate enquiry process. The core values of early years are about real-time adaptation to the learners in the context of broader and more concrete developmental goals; a balancing act of relational skills, scaffolding, awareness of complexity and willingness to try, fail and try again. Our belief is that practitioners are like Dorothy in the Wizard of Oz: she had everything she wanted already and the tools and potential to make the everyday an adventure. Practitioner enquiry therefore has the potential to turn 'research work' into an 'absorbing game' (Lawrence, 1994).

It is important to recognise that practitioner enquiry is one of many lenses offered under the umbrella of social science research (Hall and Wall, 2019). Its strength, and also its challenge, is the close connection between practice and research as the practitioner researcher takes an embedded and influential position integral to what is under investigation. This means that scientific models of research are difficult, if not impossible, to implement. The scientist in a white lab coat having minimal impact on the context and process under investigation is not easily transferable to the practitioner researcher. Rather than lament this lack of detachment, however, we should embrace the strengths of practitioner researcher positioning: the unique insight, the access to perspectives, evidence and experience that might otherwise not be considered and the closeness to action with regard to iterative development and understanding. We need to value and privilege our knowledge of the pedagogic process, of the context and the children and young people in our care, to value our 'insider' knowledge as being fundamental to a practitioner enquiry approach.

We need, therefore, to think about the different purposes for which practitioner enquiry might be applied and how different understandings of research might be used, and we hope that by linking to play, in terms of the dominant pedagogy of the phase and in regards to the nature of professional learning recommended, we encourage a productive synergy for both. Practitioners can build a bridge that starts in pedagogy and connects to methodology (Wall, 2018): an opportunity to merge skill sets. Rather than seeing research as something additional, it can be something useful, integral and indeed, essential, in our practitioner repertoire to address the needs of our children. A refocus is needed on what research is trying to do when undertaken by a practitioner to explore their practice. If the intent is inherently pedagogical then tools and processes should be evaluated against what is pedagogically appropriate in that setting. Are we trying to measure, to scaffold learning, to change perspectives, to generate new ways to interact (Lofthouse and Hall, 2014)? Which tool or which way of using a tool will best support this? To what extent does play help or hinder this process?

BRIDGING RESEARCH AND PEDAGOGY

When researching real life, we have to accept complexity. It is not possible to transfer a practitioner and class into a research laboratory to create experimental conditions without altering the naturalistic processes evident in a playroom: even if we could, this would not iron out the complexities of what each individual brings into the lab from their previous experiences. With each starting point, there is likely to be a range of possible factors which might be explored and a number of measures that could be used (Baumfield et al., 2012). The place that any enquiry starts from can only be a best guess: there are always unexpected and unknown factors which impact on the situation we are exploring. This means that the enquirer needs to work through a number of choices in deciding on the most appropriate question for their study. These choices depend on what makes most sense (to the individual researcher and to the context), what is practical within the organisation (some changes might be impossible to measure, some voices might need creative approaches to be heard and some data might be overwhelming to collect) and who the audience is for the research (will your audience be more convinced by stories, graphs or a combination of the two?). There is no right or wrong pathway through this process, but you must be clear about the decisions that you have made and why (see Chapter 6 for more on this decision-making process). A colleague reading our work needs to understand the link we've made between the outcome and the measure, so we need to present our thinking in a transparent way, acknowledging the variables that might be an influence.

Practitioner enquiry becomes more realistic when we see the productive connections it has with normal practice (Wall and Hall, 2017) – when it is not something else to fit onto the long list of things to do and the outcomes feel useful in helping to progress practice. Fundamentally we see the enquiry cycle as having a good fit onto the plan-do-review cycle that is core to how we teach and how we implement our practice (Hall and Wall, 2019: Figure 4.2). In this way we are fulfilling Stenhouse's (1981) blueprint of 'systematic enquiry made public'. We are not recommending research in every lesson or all the time. Indeed, one of the critiques we would level at the project stance or practitioner enquiry approach is that it seems to imply an on/off model of enquiry; rather, it would seem more pragmatic to think about a dialling up or down of the research element depending on the motivation of the enquirer and the qualities required of an answer to any particular enquiry question.

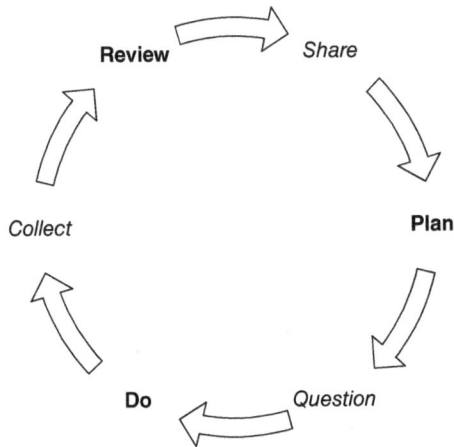

Figure 4.2   Practitioner enquiry as building on the process of plan-do-review

Source: Hall, E. and Wall, K. (2019). *Research Methods for Understanding Professional Learning*. London: Bloomsbury Academic. p. 11. Reproduced with permission of the publisher.

To ensure this model of 'turning up and down' the research dial within practitioner enquiry is manageable, it needs to be flexible depending on the nature of the enquiry question, and the answer required, as well as on the context in which it is being undertaken and the personal epistemologies of the person undertaking the enquiry (what evidence convinces you?). Therefore, it is helpful to look for bridges and associations. This is difficult in a system dominated by the language of evaluation, measurement and intervention as promoted in the Global Education Reform Movement (GERM) agenda (for example, Sahlberg, 2016). The move towards standardised testing and the 'what works' agenda (Biesta, 2007; Katsipataki and Higgins, 2016) in many systems around the world means that the common discourse of research most practitioners are familiar with is not sensible or even possible within a practitioner enquiry frame. These are research terms that are more positivist in their epistemology, and as such imply a position of distance between the researcher and the researched to avoid bias, increase reliability and encourage generalisability. If you are researching your own practice, as we have implied early in this chapter, then you are immersed in the context and integral to the very thing that you are exploring; to try to be true to a viewpoint that fundamentally requires something alternative leads to an unsatisfying and uneasy marriage. Instead, you must embrace your position as an insider in the context, and reflect on the associated complexities that go along with that by engaging in a critically reflexive approach.

When bridging to play-based pedagogies, the enquiry process has to be iterative, open-ended and inclusive of different voices, just as play can be. One lesson we have learned is that it is incredibly challenging to marry the free child-led nature of play with your own research or teaching agenda (see Blaisdell et al., 2019; Pyle and Danniels, 2017) and therefore flexibility and time to explore possibilities become central. Just as planning for play is planning for endless possibilities (Gripton, 2013), so too is practitioner enquiry in play-based contexts.

This really raises big questions about your position as researcher and player. Who are you in this instance of play and in the research? Are you setting the narrative and the roles, the boundaries of the play in terms of included and excluded objects and spaces? Such a form of play might be investigated using more problem-solving tools, measuring beginnings and ends or tracking development against some kind of map or plan, such as Parten's Social Participation Model (1932), Broadhead's Social Play Continuum (2004), Hutt's Taxonomy of Play (1979) or any variation of this as set out by Marsh et al. (2016). Or are you following the narrative set by other players? For this, you might find exploratory approaches useful so that you can understand how the players conceptualise narrative, roles, objects and spaces. Here you see more open-ended pedagogical tools that support this expansive data collection such as Learning Stories (Carr and Lee, 2019) or Pedagogical Documentation (see Chapters 5 and 10).

The interesting element here is interdependency between your role as player and researcher whereby you assume different roles in both. You may engage in adult-initiated play and possibly therefore more researcher-directed data collection tools, or you may engage in child-led play and therefore more exploratory and unstructured data collection tools. Or you may develop a combination of both. A child-led play approach can draw heavily on well-established pedagogical documentation tools, which double up not only as a record of the play experience for practice but also as a key entry in your data set. The perception that all research must require some formal development of 'academic style' research methods and tools often hinders practitioners researching their own practice and play. Yet, to be in keeping with the pedagogy of the setting, tools for recording learning in everyday practice are no less rigorous than other forms of research, and in some cases, such as with pedagogical documentation discussed in Chapter 5, they can add extra depth to the narrative.

The model of play-based learning as presented by Wood (2010: Figure 4.3) shows the interrelationship between teaching and learning, but we would suggest that a practitioner enquiry approach will have added value in bringing these aspects closer together while also emphasising the importance of the practitioners' learning: learning that happens not just alongside the children, but in a dynamic relationship. As such, it has to be flexible enough to fit with different kinds of play, walk a fine line between structured and unstructured play, and be adaptable to unexpected provocations that might come from the child or the practitioner.

The tools used need to reflect the context, in this case a playful one, generating evidence and insight that allow the practitioner to engage with the children's learning and facilitate a:

> dynamic process that occur[s] within play, because of the unique ways play creates imaginative, relational and interactive spaces, and enables children [and practitioners] to develop and express their cultures and identity. (Wood, 2010: 12)

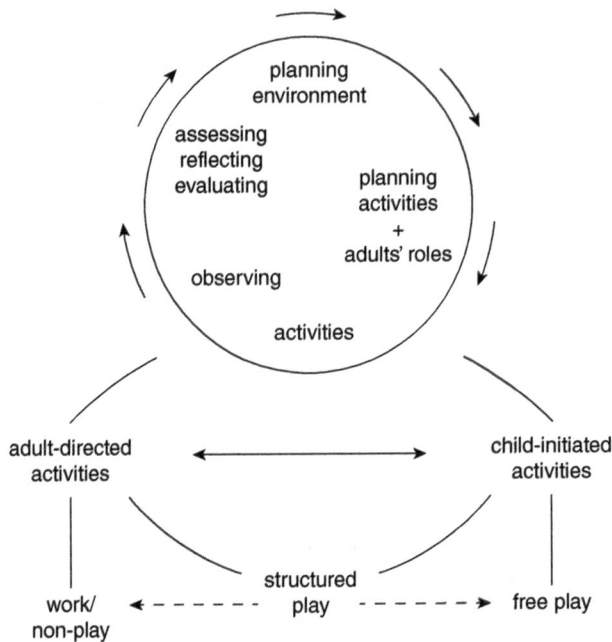

Figure 4.3   A model of integrated play-based pedagogical approaches

Source: Wood, E. (2010) Developing integrated pedagogical approaches to play and learning. In P. Broadhead, J. Howard and E. Wood (Eds.), *Play and Learning in the Early Years: From Research to Practice*. London: Sage. p. 21. Reproduced with permission of the publisher.

PROFESSIONAL LEARNING THROUGH PLAYFUL ENQUIRY

In our work, we have found that an enquiry focus on improving learning has significant potential for productive professional development. Learning is at the heart of what we, as education professionals, do and as such it is difficult for a community member, whether adult or child, to not admit some vested interest. Of course, to facilitate reflection on learning participants need to be asked in the right way and be given appropriate language with which to express themselves (two factors obviously more pertinent when including children, but relevant for all age ranges; Wall, 2012). However, if this is done appropriately then because participants are being asked to engage with the learning process, to think about thinking, they will move into the metacognitive realm: thinking about [their] thinking (Flavell, 1977, 1979). Indeed, play has been shown to incorporate sophisticated cognitive and metacognitive processes (Siraj and Asani, 2014; Whitebread and O'Sullivan, 2012) and so using a play-based pedagogy to underpin enquiry is likely to maintain, if not reinforce, the metacognitive benefits.

In an enquiry scenario that focuses on learning, it is a relatively simple thing to focus on the child; their learning is a fundamental preoccupation, successful or not, of much formal and informal education. For practitioners, it is more complex and has multiple strands. They have their view of the children's learning progression and the influence their learning practice has on this. But they also have their own learning, whether as part of professional development or in their personal lives, to reflect on. This could be their learning in action or on action (Schön, 2017). We have noticed that, for the practitioners, an enquiry that focuses on child learning tends to draw together these elements of their own learning, producing a mirroring effect between their classroom practice and their own learning trajectories, both professional and personal, supporting this idea of a metacognitive role model (Wall and Hall, 2016). Just as Vygotsky talked about play being a mirror to the child's development (see Chapter 11), the process of enquiry into practice supports the practitioner's own learning.

We believe that where enquiry is located alongside a playful pedagogy, this same tightening of feedback loops between children's and practitioners' learning can be apparent. The characteristics of play and those we propose to underpin enquiry complement and facilitate productive parallels in practice. This is a mutually reinforcing process, as the closer the ties, the more likely we are to see innovative practice and open, negotiated spaces for learning and research-informed practice. It is our understanding that professionals orientated towards enquiry and playful learning are likely to have questioning dispositions that encourage a willingness to play with key ideas. They are open-ended in their view of learning, accepting of different kinds of learning (for children and themselves) and are supportive, indeed encouraging, of learning initiated by others, especially the children themselves.

EXAMPLES OF PLAY-BASED ENQUIRY TOOLS

To exemplify the interaction described above, we will give two examples from partner schools/early years settings. In each we include a brief description of the tool and how it was used. The latter is important because effective tools can be used in more than one way and have increased pedagogic value due to this versatility; however, care should be taken not to overuse these tools as the impact is likely to diminish. We will also suggest the nature of the students' and practitioners' learning as a result of the tools' use and how this relates to our typology, and explore how the two were supported in mutual development.

LEAF LANE INFANT SCHOOL: AN ENQUIRY TO CONNECT HOME AND SCHOOL LEARNING

This project aimed to develop learning skills for pupils and their families across a nursery and infant school setting (3–7 years) with around 200 children on roll. All staff in the school and nursery were engaged in aspects of the enquiry and therefore the associated professional learning, with regular sharing sessions organised across the school year. The project focused on the role of the wider school community, out of school hours learning and family and community learning in supporting young children's views of learning and themselves as learners. It arose because findings from a previous enquiry in the school had shown that reflecting on learning improved learning and performance. This enquiry wanted to build on that to include the child's family. It was decided that the children would take home a learner log book to keep a record of all achievements both in and out of school. Pre-prepared certificates were developed to ensure this wasn't 'hard work' for parents or practitioners and time was put aside on a Friday afternoon for children to complete their books. However, children were encouraged to value experiences from both home and school as learning opportunities and, as the children began to own their books and to create the responses they wanted, the initial scaffold prepared resources became less useful. Through reflecting on what they had learnt from each experience, everyone was able to instil a readiness for future learning opportunities. The log books as an enquiry tool were left sufficiently open for the children and families to personalise and take ownership of what they contained and how they were presented. This meant an inclusive lens through which to view diverse learning experiences. For the children, families and teachers, this openness resulted in a richer view of learning that framed more satisfying conversations about learning progress and achievement, and as a result a shared vision of partnership around the child's learning trajectory emerged.

COUNTRY NURSERY AND FAMILY CENTRE: DEVELOPING THE OUTDOOR ENVIRONMENT

Practitioners at this early years centre for children from birth to 5 years old were interested in opening up more of the learning space outside the building to facilitate effective play-based learning indoors and out. In particular, they wanted to move elements of the art area outside and explore how to get all children involved in the resulting learning. To explore the way that space was used before, during and after the changes, motion capture filming was used.

This tool supported a relatively playful (the children found it hilarious) and economic (the camera could be discretely set up to record from the corner of the room for a whole session) way of gaining insight into the use of space. The resulting video had the advantage of being relatively quick to view, but also, due to the fast pace, it enabled quick impressions of space use without being inhibited by too much detail. For example, it enabled staff and children to note the impact of a second door to the outdoor space being opened and how this changed the footfall through the art area; how having an adult working within the art area increased the likelihood of children using the space; and how some individuals might spend a long time in the area, while others just passed through. The analysis of the video was done in partnership with the children, allowing a free-ranging dialogue about what they saw and why. This enabled the next steps in development and evaluation to be done in consultation with the children and arguably increased the likelihood of success through this negotiated process.

CONCLUSION

Throughout this chapter, we have attempted to demonstrate that research in play-based contexts is not only needed but is also a route towards practitioners' own professional learning and development. Adopting a practitioner enquiry approach which is highly reflexive – always considerate and interpretative – provides a platform for our highly skilled workforce to translate their abilities to unearth and interpret meaning from play into rigorous research data. We suggest that the approach does not need to be highly academic, yet it does not offer any less rigour in the process. Instead, it offers an alternative insight for research about and through play: an insight which is rich in narrative, exploratory in nature and pedagogy-developing in practice.

REFERENCES

Baumfield, V., Hall, E. and Wall, K. (2012). *Action Research in the Education: Learning through Practitioner Enquiry* (2nd edn). London: Sage.

Biesta, G. (2007). Why 'what works' won't work: Evidence-based practice and the democratic deficit in educational research. *Educational Theory*, 57 (1): 1–22.

Blaisdell, C., Arnott, L., Wall, K. and Robinson, C. (2019). Look Who's Talking: Using creative, playful arts-based methods in research with young children. *Journal of Early Childhood Research*, 17 (1): 14–31.

Broadhead, P. (2004). *Early Years Play and Learning: Developing Social Skills and Cooperation.* Hove: Psychology Press.

Carr, M. and Lee, W. (2019). *Learning Stories in Practice.* London: Sage.

Cochrane-Smith, M. and Lytle, S. L. (2009). *Inquiry as Stance: Practitioner Research for the Next Generation.* London: Teachers College Press.

Cordingley, P. (2013). *The Contribution of Research to Teachers' Professional Learning and Development: Research and Teacher Education – The BERA-RSA Inquiry.* London: British Educational Research Association.

Cordingley, P. (2015). The contribution of research to teachers' professional learning and development. *Oxford Review of Education*, 41 (2): 234–52.

Dagenais, C., Lysenko, L., Abrami, P. C., Bernard, R. M., Ramde, J. and Janosz, M. (2012). Use of research-based information by school practitioners and determinants of use: A review of empirical research. *Evidence & Policy: A Journal of Research, Debate and Practice*, 8 (3): 285–309.

Dewey, J. (1916). *Democracy and Education.* Carbondale, IL: Southern Illinois University Press.

Education Scotland (2018). *The National Model for Professional Learning.* Available at: www.scelframework.com/about/the-model-of-professional-learning (accessed 15 November 2020).

Flavell, J. H. (1977). *Cognitive Development.* Upper Saddle River, NJ: Prentice Hall.

Flavell, J. H. (1979). Metacognition and cognitive monitoring: A new area of cognitive developmental inquiry. *Cognitive Development*, 34 (10): 906–11.

Gripton, C. (2013). Planning for endless possibilities. In A. Woods (Ed.), *Child Initiated Play and Learning: Planning for Possibilities in the Early Years, 8–19.* London: David Fulton.

Hall, E. (2009). Engaging in and engaging with research: Teacher inquiry and development. *Teachers and Teaching: Theory and Practice*, 15 (6): 669–82.

Hall, E. (2018). Grasping the nettle of doctorateness: A framework for thinking critically about curriculum design. *Studies in Continuing Education*, 41 (2): 157–72.

Hall, E. and Wall, K. (2019). *Research Methods for Understanding Professional Learning.* London: Bloomsbury Academic.

Hutt, C. (1979). Play in the under 5s: Form, development and function. In J. G. Howell (Ed.), *Modern Perspectives in the Psychiatry of Infancy.* The Hague: Bruner/Maazel. pp. 94–141.

Katsipataki, M. and Higgins, S. (2016). What works or what's worked? Evidence from education in the United Kingdom. *Procedia, Social and Behavioral Sciences*, 217: 903–9.

Lawrence, D. H. (1994). *The Complete Poems of D. H. Lawrence.* Ware: Wordsworth Editions.

Lofthouse, R. and Hall, E. (2014). Developing practices in teachers' professional dialogue in England: Using coaching dimensions as an epistemic tool. *Professional Development in Education*, 40 (5): 758–78.

Marsh, J., Plowman, L., Yamada-Rice, D., Bishop, J. and Scott, F. (2016). Digital play: A new classification, *Early Years*, 36 (3): 242–53.

Menter, I., Elliott, D., Hulme, M. and Lewin, J. (2010). *Literature Review on Teacher Education in the Twenty-First Century*. Edinburgh: The Scottish Government.

Nias, J. and Groundwater-Smith, S. (Eds.) (1988). *The Enquiring Teacher: Supporting and Sustaining Teacher Research*. London: Routledge.

Parten, M. B. (1932). Social participation among pre-school children. *The Journal of Abnormal and Social Psychology*, 27 (3): 243–69.

Pyle, A. and Danniels, E. (2017). A continuum of play-based learning: The role of the teacher in play-based pedagogy and the fear of hijacking play. *Early Education and Development*, 28 (3): 274–89.

Reeves, J. and Drew, V. (2013). A productive relationship? Testing the connections between professional learning and practitioner research. *Scottish Educational Review*, 45 (2): 36–49.

Sahlberg, P. (2016). The global educational reform movement and its impact on schooling. In K. Mundy, A. Green, B. Lingard and A. Verger (Eds.), *The Handbook of Global Education Policy*. Oxford: Wiley-Blackwell. pp. 128–44.

Schön, D. A. (2017). *The Reflective Practitioner: How Professionals Think in Action*. Abingdon: Routledge.

Siraj, I. and Asani, R. (2014). The role of sustained shared thinking, play and metacognition in young children's learning. In S. Robson and S. Flannery Quinn (Eds.), *The Routledge International Handbook of Young Children's Thinking and Understanding*. London: Routledge.

Stenhouse, L. (1981). What counts as research? *British Journal of Educational Studies*, 29 (2): 103–14.

Timperley, H. S. (2008). *Teacher Professional Learning and Development*. Geneva: The International Bureau of Education.

Wall, K. (2012). 'It wasn't too easy, which is good if you want to learn': An exploration of pupil participation and learning to learn. *The Curriculum Journal*, 23 (3): 283–305.

Wall, K. (2018). *Think Piece: Practitioner Enquiry*. Available at: www.gtcs.org.uk/web/FILES/research/practitioner-enquiry-think-piece-kate-wall.pdf (accessed 15 November 2020).

Wall, K. and Hall, E. (2016). Teachers as metacognitive role models. *European Journal of Teacher Education*, 39 (4): 403–18.

Wall, K. and Hall, E. (2017). The teacher in teacher-practitioner research: Three principles of inquiry. In P. Boyd and A. Szplit (Eds.), *International Perspectives: Teachers and Teacher Educators Learning through Enquiry*. Krakow: Wydawnictwo Attyka. pp. 35–62.

Whitebread, D. and O'Sullivan, L. (2012). Preschool children's social pretend play: Supporting the development of metacommunication, metacognition and self-regulation. *International Journal of Play*, 1 (2): 197–213.

Wood, E. (2010). Developing integrated pedagogical approaches to play and learning. In P. Broadhead, J. Howard and E. Wood (Eds.), *Play and Learning in the Early Years: From Research to Practice*. London: Sage.

5

PEDAGOGICAL DOCUMENTATION AS A THINKING COMPANION

JANE MEREWETHER AND ALMA FLEET

In Part 1, this book outlined some of the foundational principles that are important when adopting play as part of your research repertoire. Then, the opening chapter in this Part (Chapter 4) provided an introduction to practitioner enquiry and reflexivity as a key participatory methodology to underpin work which draws on pedagogically inspired research methods. The current chapter extends this focus on practice and pedagogy to offer a conceptual framework which can facilitate play for research – pedagogical documentation. This chapter will:

- Introduce the reader to pedagogical documentation as a useful research companion;
- Clarify the nature of co-researching with children through playful and participatory methodologies;
- Discuss how pedagogical documentation has the potential to create spaces for thinking collaboratively about and through play;
- Invite readers to apply this way of being with children to their own work.

PEDAGOGICAL DOCUMENTATION

This chapter proposes that the processes of pedagogical documentation provide a rich context for documenting, interpreting and making play visible. Pedagogical documentation is a participatory way of researching *with* children rather than *on* them. The chapter draws on insights from our long engagement with the acclaimed educational project of Reggio Emilia in Italy. Alma first visited the schools and infant-toddler centres in 1994 and has been writing about the potential of pedagogical documentation ever since (see, for example, Fleet et al., 2006, 2012). Jane began using pedagogical documentation as an early childhood teacher following a visit to Reggio Emilia in 2001, then took these strategies into her postgraduate research. In this chapter, we discuss our use of pedagogical documentation as both 'teachers' and 'researchers' in play-based contexts. We propose ways these strategies might be used to collaborate with children as co-researchers in potentially playful ways. In this discussion, we are not claiming to be comprehensive about this way of being, this set of processes, this approach to researching and pedagogical thinking. The intent is to introduce ideas for those less familiar with pedagogical documentation as a form of participatory research, and to affirm those who have been working in this way.

The term 'pedagogical documentation' refers to the process of inquiry undertaken as an everyday practice by educators in the preschools and infant-toddler centres in the educational project of Reggio Emilia (Edwards et al., 2012; Fleet et al., 2017; Giamminuti, 2013; Giudici et al., 2001). Pedagogical documentation has been a feature of the 'Reggio Approach' since the project's inception after World War II and is driven by an image of both teachers and children as researchers and co-constructors of knowledge (Dahlberg et al., 2013; Rinaldi, 2006). Examples of people building on that thinking appear not only in Italy (Biffi, 2019) but also across Scandinavia (e.g. Bjervås and Rosendahl, 2017), and as interpreted in Canada (Pacini-Ketchabaw et al., 2015). According to Dahlberg et al. (2013: 154), pedagogical documentation is 'about trying to see and understand what is going on in the pedagogical work and what the child is capable of without any predetermined framework'. It is one of a range of playful approaches to research being explored in this book.

It is important to note that although 'seeing thoughtfully' is a key strategy of pedagogical documentation, it must not be confused with the 'child observation' used in developmental psychology in which development is monitored against categories such as developmental norms or 'objectives'. Pedagogical documentation is not a collection of documents intended to demonstrate the 'truth' or present facts; nor is it a collection of documents to be reflected on only at the end of an educational experience (Rinaldi, 2006). Instead, it supports the ongoing search for meaning that characterises pedagogical practice in the schools of Reggio Emilia (Rinaldi, 2006). It is a process as much as a product, and involves listening to children with openness and 'sensitivity to the patterns that connect' (p. 49), taking account of 'what the children are saying and doing, the work of the children, and how the pedagogue relates to the children and their work' (Dahlberg et al., 2013: 156). Pedagogical documentation involves multimodal and multi-perspectival strategies for making learning visible and includes, but is not limited to, fieldnotes, photographs, video/audio recordings and transcriptions of conversations.

WHY DOCUMENT WITH AND THROUGH PLAY?

There is considerable literature on the benefits of play and of play-based education (Lester and Russell, 2010; O'Keefe et al., 2016; Wood, 2014). Nonetheless, in contexts dominated by discourses of accountability, standardised testing, and measurable outcomes, the role of play in educational settings has become increasingly contentious (Barblett et al., 2016; Gunnarsdottir, 2014) (see Chapter 1 for more). Similarly, research approaches that are less formal may arouse suspicion as being less reliable than their conventional counterparts. Educators who aspire to play-based approaches can find themselves in a position where parents, colleagues, administrators and even children themselves are sceptical of the learning potential of play (Barblett et al., 2016; Breathnach et al., 2017). While not dismissing the value of learning through play, Grieshaber and McArdle (2010) point out that we cannot assume play is educative and call educators to 'look more deeply at what is being learned, and how that learning is occurring' (p. 1). Thus, given the contested space that many early childhood educators find themselves in, it is imperative that educators and researchers make visible the learning that happens in play. We argue that the participatory strategies associated with pedagogical documentation are a way to do this.

Moreover, as educators around the world have found, the processes of pedagogical documentation generate insights into children's imagination, knowledge, interests, dispositions and thinking, and are thus a powerful form of professional learning (Fleet and Harcourt, 2018; Pacini-Ketchabaw et al., 2015). These thoughtfully enabled and analysed approaches might be considered playful in themselves; they can make visible taken-for-granted ways of thinking and working and have the potential to lead educators and others, including children, to think differently about play. Pedagogical documentation, then, can offer an important site of resistance to standardised/formulaic approaches to early childhood curriculum and research. It offers a space of dialogue and has the potential to open up an 'ethic of resistance' (Lenz Taguchi, 2008) whereby early childhood educators can challenge and interrogate commonly held beliefs about play as part of their daily practice. Given the extent of the complexities and tensions surrounding play, pedagogical documentation offers a way to 'stay with the trouble' (Haraway, 2016), rather than ignore or normalise values and beliefs about play. We now turn to the richness that can emerge when play, research and pedagogical documentation intersect.

CONTEXT

What is happening in the 'researching with and through play' space? While the topic is too broad to be explored in depth here (and the reader will be informed by other chapters in this publication), we offer a few examples of the ways in which researchers engage this topic. An invitation to muse about multiple ways of using playful research methodologies opens myriad possibilities. Here, we consider the role of pedagogical documentation, hoping to highlight multiple voices that can be heard in this arena.

To begin, as the United Nations Convention on the Rights of the Child (UN Commission on Human Rights, 1990) reminds us of the centrality of respectfully involving children in decisions that affect them. Certainly, growing our understandings about the nature of play includes the gathering of children's perspectives, in whatever ways seem appropriate for the research question. So, our task becomes one of learning more about the meaning of 'play' for children, its 'constitution' (i.e. what are we talking about?) and the interpretations of playful behaviours, philosophies and practices by adults. To this end, we have analysed three sources of information: (i) an encyclopedia/handbook entry (Fleet and Harcourt, 2018); (ii) a special issue on 'participatory pedagogies' in the *European Early Childhood Education Research Journal*; and (iii) a volume in an edited book series (Alcock and Stobbs, 2019).

Fleet and Harcourt's (2018) contribution to the *International Handbook of Early Childhood Education* argues for children to be seen as co-researchers who contribute to decisions about data collection, analysis and findings. The special issue of the *European Early Childhood Education Research Journal* (Volume 27, Issue 3, 2019) highlights the nature and benefits of participatory pedagogies; these articles help identify current approaches to researching with children. For example, de Sousa (2019) presents her work on pedagogical documentation in Portugal: 'The search for children's voice and agency'. Framed by the 'Pedagogy-in-Participation approach' developed by the Childhood Association (Formosinho and Oliviera-Formosinho, 2016) and referencing Vygotsky (1978), this author's thinking is supported through narratives of children's perspectives. These 'key moments' reveal:

> an educator with genuine interest to discover and know the child's natural orientation towards the exploration of herself, the objects, the relationships, the knowledge ... the systematization of documenting allows [us] to give evidence to and value children's doing, feeling and telling, thus fostering possibilities of participation and learning. (de Sousa, 2019: 378)

This choice of pedagogical documentation as a research tool reflects the teacher's philosophy and the valuing of participatory practice in supporting a daily research agenda.

Another article in this collection (Cruz, 2019) which is also inspired by Formosinho and Oliviera-Formosinho, comes from Brazil. Drawing on material that 'listened to children', from the youngest in nursery groups to the 4- and 5-year-olds in public preschools, the focus was children's perceptions of their educational experiences. Regretfully, Cruz (2019) concludes that in Brazilian contexts, children have limited rights to play, due to the prevalence of transmissive pedagogies. Her data includes transcripts of children's conversations, often made while drawing their experiences. In conclusion, she offers 'a reminder that listening to children's voices is a premise of democracy. Children should participate actively in the decisions that affect them, something that is impossible in a daily routine marked by authoritarianism' (2019: 417).

For an example of another research approach, consider the formal experimental model used by Lichene (2019) with a group (n = 21) of 4-year-olds in Liguria, Italy, using audio and video recordings to help understand ways in which children approached and explored materials, particularly within science education. Observations took place weekly for an hour in a laboratory classroom. Informed by Dewey (1938), and building on the construct of 'promoting from within' (Bondioli, 2008), this research found that the greatest gains in engagement and understanding took place when play experiences offered space, materials and time for exploration as well as valuing adult participation in 'ending conversations'. In this case, 'The role of the adult in these situations is to support dialogue, exchange and encourage the group to express themselves and say what they think about the issue discussed, encouraging them to recount experiences' (Lichene, 2019: 404).

Finally, a very large Spanish study (Muela et al., 2019), which was informed by Pascal and Bertram (2009) and the Mosaic Approach (Clark, 2010, 2017), reported on children's perceptions of their outdoor play environments: 'The primary aim of this study was to show how the quality of outdoor environments can be improved through a participatory intervention involving children, parents and teachers' (Muela et al., 2019: 393). This research valued multiple stakeholders. The study included 1001 children who attended seven different preschools in the Basque country. A key element was commitment that action would be taken on the basis of these perceptions.

The range of research approaches in this special journal issue can be considered alongside other research. In a collection of 12 chapters relating to *Rethinking Play as Pedagogy* (Alcock and Stobbs, 2019), reported research approaches range from narrative explorations to policy reviews. Students of 'Play' would note that the authors report on work in nine countries, with concerns including 'Facilitating after-school play in school grounds' (Mannello et al., 2019), 'Playing with digital drawing' (Robertson, 2019), and 'Playing in and through the musical worlds of children' (Barrett, 2019). This diversity reminds us of the breadth of possibilities open to those interested in researching children's experience of and participation in play and the contexts in which that play occurs. Questions of appropriateness relate to the nature of questions asked, the purpose of the research, perhaps the goals of a funding body or the curiosity motivating a particular research team. For our current purposes, we return attention to pedagogical documentation.

SOME CAUTIONS

Before proceeding, we stress that pedagogical documentation does not exist in a value-free vacuum. It is a political act and is never proposed as innocent activity; in fact, as Dahlberg et al. (2013: 164) caution, it can be dangerous:

> As a critical means of resisting the power/knowledge nexus, pedagogical documentation is a dangerous enterprise ... if we are not alert, documentation may become a practice for exercising, not resisting, control and power. Considering these risks, we always have to pose questions concerning what right we have to interpret and document children's doings and what is ethically legitimate.

Furthermore, Grieshaber and McArdle (2010) point out that although documenting children's play can bring the advantages already mentioned, the act of recording may interrupt the play. Pressure to produce glossy and detailed documentation can place enormous strain on teachers and may 'reinforce a trend to commodify children's art as product' (p. 48). So, although pedagogical documentation offers much promise for researching play in teaching and research, the ethical motivations of our work must remain paramount (see Chapter 3 for more).

GETTING STARTED

What do we mean by stating that you can document research through pedagogical documentation? Let's clarify key definitions. What do we mean by 'research' in this context? And in fact, what do we mean by pedagogical documentation? To address the second part, we are not referring simply to collections of photographs or reports of events, though these may contribute to the thinking processes that are inherent in documenting pedagogically. We are referring particularly to a philosophical way of working alongside children, an ongoing process of being present which is captured in analysed pieces of pedagogical thoughtfulness, a source of reflection that opens up the unexpected rather than being limited by first impressions or predetermined outcomes.

Whether you are primarily a researcher or primarily an educator (and of course, these roles can overlap/coexist), approaching the work of pedagogical documentation demands an attitude of curiosity, or as Reggio educator Vea Vecchi (2001) puts it, a 'curiosity to understand' (p. 158). An attitude of inquiry, then, is the first step in pedagogical documentation (and guidance on how this might be facilitated can be found in Chapter 4). But we cannot possibly investigate everything we are curious about; researchers must make choices about what to investigate. Thus, the second step is to decide what to document. Possibilities are endless but will be informed by your context. In our work in play-based contexts in the early years, we have found it helpful to frame inquiries with questions. In Jane's classroom practice, research questions included (amongst others): What do children know about numbers? How do children use colour to perform gender? What is the relationship between children and birds? How are children reproducing dominant discourses about 'good' and 'bad'? In her doctoral research, Jane was guided by the question: How do children encounter outdoor spaces in their early learning setting? The questions you ask might be informed by curriculum requirements, something you have heard a child say, a reaction to an event, or something you are curious about.

If these are your first attempts at pedagogical documentation for practice or research, we suggest you start with something small. Perhaps you could begin by documenting how a few children play in one area of a setting, or how children use a particular object in play.

THE POSSIBILITY OF A STICK (PART 1)

Often, it is ordinary and unexpected moments that generate starting points. A child's remark or an unplanned event might provide a spark for further investigation. In the work that informs the current chapter, Jane recalls how a proposed whole-school ban on children picking up sticks led her to document children's everyday use of sticks in their play and the project The Possibility of a Stick was born. Photographing children using sticks and talking to children about their use made the humble stick visible, bringing attention to the key role of sticks in children's play. The act of documentation drew attention to sticks and led to a play-full project that included making a stick alphabet and using sticks to make words (Figure 5.1). Subsequently, the proposed ban on picking up sticks was not implemented.

Figure 5.1 'It's a Y'!

THE MULTIPLICITY OF PEDAGOGICAL DOCUMENTATION

Pedagogical documentation is both multimodal and multi-perspectival; multimodal in that it deploys *multiple* ways of listening to children (Rinaldi, 2006) and multi-perspectival as it is dependent on not only listening to children but also to adults (e.g. teachers, parents, community members). The process of pedagogical documentation is never linear; rather, strategies overlap and are ultimately entangled as each strategy always involves others.

To help illustrate, we share several multimodal strategies for listening that we have used in our work, none of which are used in isolation (Fleet, 2017; Merewether, 2017, 2018; Merewether and Fleet, 2014). These strategies allow children to represent their thinking and knowledge in ways playing to their strengths.

SEEING THOUGHTFULLY

While 'observing children' may be seen as central to our work, that phrase implies observation in a clinical, almost medical sense, a 'standing back' or peering through a microscope. We prefer to avoid the term 'observation' in this context and think instead of 'seeing thoughtfully' which may occur from sharing in children's play, but definitely involves 'being present' with children, sharing space, walking alongside and learning together. This is a way of thinking which requires the capacity to be unsettled, to seek understanding rather than simply reporting behaviour. It often means pausing to think about what is unfolding rather than rushing into routines. Just this week there was a delicious moment when Alma was visiting a childcare centre and was able to share pure joy when a toddler arrived to find a familiar (not yet crawling) infant beaming up at him to clap a welcome. Learning to 'see welcome' in the nursery is as much a valuable educator behaviour as keeping track of meals and sleep-times! Such mini-events can become part of an analysed photo-collage that shares the concept with adults who are not sure what it is that an educator sees when looking at morning arrival behaviours. Note that photos on their own are not enough; pedagogical documentation is not simply scrapbooking! To be *pedagogical*, there needs to be visible evidence of critical reflection, of analytical recording of 'why it matters', of what makes this very little interchange noteworthy. It also suggests that the educator is mindful of evolving relationships, and alert to seeing repeated actions that suggest patterns of behaviour to be shared with other adults.

This mindset foregrounds ethical behaviour, a recognition that children have rights – to privacy, to share in decision-making that affects them and so on – rather than being studied like rare tropical insects. Ethical decisions require children's agreement to be part of the activities and environments we provide, albeit with the recognition that adults are responsible for health and safety, negotiating tearful goodbyes from family in the morning and so on. Beyond the baby years, it can also mean seeking their permission to share their images in workshops and other gatherings, and acknowledging that 'no' means 'no' in this space, as well as in the more familiar context. Families and carers have similar rights; it also needs to be clear as to whether identifiable images are being shared only 'in-house' or in a larger forum.

CONVERSATIONS

In this work, we do not rely on interviews or questionnaires, which in our experience are not effective with very young children who may be pre-verbal or come from diverse language backgrounds. Nonetheless, informal conversations with children, which take place while we are playing, singing, drawing with or alongside children are very useful. With our research questions in mind, we chat to (or sing with!) children, being careful to be conversational. This often means being prepared to talk about all sorts of other things as well: a sore finger, Auntie's holiday and last night's dinner are just some of many 'off-topic' conversations we have had. We may audio-record these conversations, or write down responses relevant to our research in our notebooks. Pedagogical documentation involves multiple ways of recording.

PHOTOGRAPHY

We have found child-led photography to be a very effective 'language' to offer children in our research. Children often see this as an opportunity to play where the camera becomes a non-verbal 'gathering' device for their thinking and ideas. For example, Jane asked children what they thought was 'good' outdoors, and they very playfully used photography to show her (Merewether and Fleet, 2014). We have also found that children use cameras in playful ways as a means of establishing relationships with others, human and non-human. We also use cameras ourselves as a form of note-taking, finding it a quick and easy way to record what is happening while children are playing, especially when we too are involved in the play. Other ways of seeing thoughtfully can be explored in Part 3 of this book, Chapters 7–12.

MULTIPLE PERSPECTIVES

Carla Rinaldi (2006: 67) suggests that schools should be 'first and foremost, a context of *multiple listening* (emphasis added) ... involving the teachers but also the group of children and each child, all of whom can listen to others and listen to themselves.' Therefore, unlike some kinds of research where the researcher is a solitary and 'objective' observer, pedagogical documentation is a site of multiple listening and dialogue involving varied perspectives. This requires researchers to make the research visible to children and adults as it unfolds, not just at the end; this way, children and adults can respond to what emerges. In our work, we have used various online and digital documentation logs, presentations, displays, conversations and journals for this purpose; further examples are available in Fleet and Harcourt (2018).

INTERPRETATION (THE ANALYSIS OR 'SO WHAT?')

A stumbling block in this work is the tendency to report action/behaviour rather than taking an attitude of curious sharing and co-investigation. Instead, we value a collective process of knowledge construction where each fragment (noticed/collected/shared) is part of ongoing cyclical thinking, planning and valuing daily experience.

Another stumbling block is the problem of what to do with the ideas arising and material collected; as there is often an unclear endpoint, this is problematic. Stepping back from the daily rush and analysing what is being seen/heard/experienced is a key part of this process. Choosing a carefully considered invitational title is often a useful strategy to focus others' attention. In Jane's example, reporting that children 'like to play with sticks' would not have been enough to develop a shared understanding able to inform pedagogy and influence a policy decision. Consider the following excerpts from her documentation.

THE POSSIBILITY OF A STICK (PART 2)

Figure 5.2 'We are playing teachers'

Figure 5.3 'I am stirring pink chocolate'

Figure 5.4 'Pointing to our map'

> In the final documentation of The Possibility of a Stick, Jane's analysis of the play included a defence of 'the field' (the area of investigation). In one section she wrote:
>
> Children find an endless array of uses for the sticks in the outdoor area. In the hands of children, sticks become bats, fishing rods, pointers, stirrers, and swords, and much, much more. They are used for building, decorating, sculpting, digging and drawing. In fact, they may be the ultimate open-ended toy. Sticks cultivate children's imagination and creativity and are a vehicle for exploration, invention and discovery. Sticks are easy to come by and best of all, they cost nothing!

The lens being used influences the nature of the analysis. Jane was keen to demonstrate how stick play supports children's learning across the curriculum. A focus on children's theories of 'stickness' could have been another possibility for analysis. Depending on purpose, a teacher might wonder if there is a gender factor – 'Do girls and boys play differently with sticks?' A new materialist perspective might ask, 'How are sticks part of the school environment?' From a STEM point of view, the investigation might ask about the experimental hypothesising of budding scientists. All of these possibilities are potentially rich. The interpretation need not be long-winded, but it needs to be more than a report, and certainly more than a collection of 'happy snaps'! In any case, the issue of 'safe play' and 'respectful behaviour' would be considered alongside the opportunities of stick play; investigations unfold alongside attention to forging relationships, pursuing intellectual curiosity, developing creativity, and supporting safe yet engaging environments. The pedagogical documentation includes each of these elements to the extent that the context enables and supports this work.

CONCLUSION

As implied in this overview, no approach will be suited to all situations. Thinking about pedagogical documentation in relation to playfulness and researching through and with play is always a work in progress. There can, however, be key principles associated with this arena. For the moment, we might consider these to be the centrality of:

- Valuing children's perspectives (see Chapter 2).
- Ethical decision-making (see Chapter 3).
- Giving time and space to ideas that matter/have substance (see Chapter 4).

(Continued)

- Diverse approaches to noticing/collecting/managing relevant material (see Part 3).
- Shared thinking about emergent possibilities.
- Varied presentation formats that invite engagement.

Such an approach to research, whether by the on-site teacher or collaborating researcher, aims to generate new knowledge about play (rather than seeking to confirm preconceived categories or what is already known) and to deepen our understanding of the children with whom we are sharing our lives.

REFERENCES

Alcock, S. and Stobbs, N. (Eds.) (2019). *Rethinking Play as Pedagogy*. London: Routledge.

Barblett, L., Knaus, M. and Barratt-Pugh, C. (2016). The pushes and pulls of pedagogy in the early years: Competing knowledges and the erosion of play-based learning. *Australasian Journal of Early Childhood*, 41 (4): 36–43.

Barrett, M. S. (2019). Playing in and through the musical worlds of children. In S. Alcock and N. Stobbs (Eds.), *Rethinking Play as Pedagogy*. London: Routledge. pp. 33–46.

Biffi, E. (2019). Pedagogical documentation as 'agora': Why it may be viewed as a form of citizenship for children, parents and communities. In S. Alcock and N. Stobbs (Eds.), *Rethinking Play as Pedagogy*. London: Routledge. pp. 139–52.

Bjervås, L. and Rosendahl, G. (2017). Pedagogical documentation and pedagogical choices. In A. Fleet, C. Patterson and J. Robertson (Eds.), *Pedagogical Documentation in Early Years Practice: Seeing through Multiple Perspectives*. London: Sage. pp. 27–39.

Bondioli, A. (2008). Promuovere esperienze di educazione e formazione per bambini e adulti. In R. Zerbato (Ed.), *Infanzia: Tempi di Vita, Tempi di Relazione*. Azzano S. Paolo, Bergamo: Edizioni Junior. pp. 177–82.

Breathnach, H., Danby, S. and O'Gorman, L. (2017). 'Are you working or playing?' Investigating young children's perspectives of classroom activities. *International Journal of Early Years Education*, 25 (4): 439–54.

Clark, A. (2010). *Transforming Children's Spaces*. New York: Routledge.

Clark, A. (2017). *Listening to Young Children* (3rd edn). London: Jessica Kingsley.

Cruz, S. H. V. (2019). Brazilian research into children's perspectives on their educational experience: Participation and play at risk. *European Early Childhood Education Research Journal*, 27 (3): 409–19.

Dahlberg, G., Moss, P. and Pence, A. (2013). *Beyond Quality in Early Childhood Education and Care: Languages of Evaluation* (3rd edn). London: Routledge.

de Sousa, J. (2019). Pedagogical documentation: The search for children's voice and agency. *European Early Childhood Education Research Journal*, 27 (3): 371–84.

Dewey, J. (1938). *Logic: The Theory of Inquiry*. New York: Henry Holt.

Edwards, C., Gandini, L. and Forman, G. (Eds.) (2012). *The Hundred Languages of Children: The Reggio Emilia Experience in Transformation* (3rd edn). Santa Barbara, CA: Praeger.

Fleet, A. (2017). The landscape of pedagogical documentation. In A. Fleet, C. Patterson and J. Robertson (Eds.), *Pedagogical Documentation in Early Years Practice: Seeing Through Multiple Perspectives*. London: Sage. pp. 11–26.

Fleet, A. and Harcourt, D. with colleagues (2018). (Co)-researching with children. In M. Fleer and B. van Oers (Eds.), *International Handbook of Early Childhood Education* (Vol. 1). Amsterdam: Springer. pp. 165–202.

Fleet, A., Patterson, C. and Robertson, J. (2006). *Insights: Behind Early Childhood Pedagogical Documentation*. Mt Victoria: Pademelon.

Fleet, A., Patterson, C. and Robertson, J. (Eds.) (2012). *Conversations: Behind Early Childhood Pedagogical Documentation*. Mt Victoria: Pademelon.

Fleet, A., Patterson, C. and Robertson, J. (Eds.) (2017). *Pedagogical Documentation in Early Years Practice: Seeing Through Multiple Perspectives*. London: Sage.

Formosinho, J. and Oliviera-Formosinho, J. (2016). The search for a holistic approach to evaluation. In J. Oliviera-Formosinho and C. Pascal (Eds.), *Assessment and Evaluation for Transformation in Early Childhood*. London: Routledge. pp. 93–106.

Giamminuti, S. (2013). *Dancing with Reggio Emilia: Metaphors for Quality*. Mt Victoria: Pademelon Press.

Giudici, C., Rinaldi, C. and Krechevsky, M. (2001). *Making Learning Visible: Children as Individual and Group Learners*. Cambridge, MA: Harvard Graduate School, Project Zero.

Grieshaber, S. and McArdle, F. (2010). *The Trouble with Play*. Maidenhead: OUP/McGraw-Hill.

Gunnarsdottir, B. (2014). From play to school: Are core values of ECEC in Iceland being undermined by 'schoolification'? *International Journal of Early Years Education*, 22 (3): 242–50.

Haraway, D. (2016). *Staying with the Trouble*. Durham, NC: Duke University Press.

Lenz Taguchi, H. (2008). An 'ethics of resistance' challenges taken-for-granted ideas in early childhood education. *International Journal of Educational Research*, 47 (5): 270–82.

Lester, S. and Russell, W. (2010). *Children's Right to Play: An Examination of the Importance of Play in the Lives of Children Worldwide* (Working Paper No. 57). The Hague: Bernard van Leer Foundation.

Lichene, C. (2019). Promoting science education in early childhood: A research in a nursery school. *European Early Childhood Education Research Journal*, 27 (3): 397–408.

Mannello, M., Connolly, M., Dumitrescu, S., Ellis, C., Haughton, C., Sarwar, S. and Tyrie, J. (2019). Opening the school gates: Facilitating after-school play in school grounds. In S. Alcock and N. Stobbs (Eds.), *Rethinking Play as Pedagogy*. London: Routledge. pp. 121–38.

Merewether, J. (2017). Making the outdoors visible in pedagogical documentation. In A. Fleet, C. Patterson and J. Robertson (Eds.), *Pedagogical Documentation in Early Years Practice: Seeing through Multiple Perspectives*. London: Sage. pp. 131–45.

Merewether, J. (2018). Listening to young children outdoors with pedagogical documentation. *International Journal of Early Years Education*, 26 (3): 259–77.

Merewether, J. and Fleet, A. (2014). Seeking children's perspectives: A respectful layered research approach. *Early Child Development and Care*, 184 (6): 897–914.

Muela, A., Larrea, I., Miranda, N. and Barandiaran, A. (2019). Improving the quality of preschool outdoor environments: Getting children involved. *European Early Childhood Education Research Journal*, 27 (3): 385–96.

O'Keefe, A., Lehrer, J. and Harwood, D. (2016). Introduction: Play in the 21st century. *Canadian Journal of Education / Revue Canadienne De L'éducation*, 39 (3): 1–5.

Pacini-Ketchabaw, V., Nxumalo, F., Kocher, L., Elliot, E. and Sanchez, A. (2015). *Journeys: Reconceptualizing Early Childhood Practices through Pedagogical Narration*. Toronto: University of Toronto Press.

Pascal, C. and Bertram, T. (2009). Listening to young citizens: The struggle to make real a participatory paradigm in research with young children. *European Early Childhood Education Research Journal*, 17 (2): 249–62.

Rinaldi, C. (2006). *In Dialogue with Reggio Emilia: Listening, Researching and Learning*. London: Routledge.

Robertson, J. (2019). Playing with digital drawing. In S. Alcock and N. Stobbs (Eds.), *Rethinking Play as Pedagogy*. London: Routledge. pp. 3–16.

UN Commission on Human Rights (1990). *Convention on the Rights of the Child* (E/CN.4/RES/1990/74), 7 March. Available at: www.refworld.org/docid/3b00f03d30.html (accessed 5 September 2020).

Vecchi, V. (2001). The curiosity to understand. In C. Giudici, C. Rinaldi and M. Krechevsky (Eds.), *Making Learning Visible: Children as Individual and Group Learners*. Reggio Emilia: Reggio Children. pp. 158–213.

Vygotsky, L. S. (1978). *Mind in Society*. Cambridge, MA: Harvard University Press.

Wood, E. (2014). The play–pedagogy interface in contemporary debates. In E. Brooker, M. Blaise and S. Edwards (Eds.), *The Sage Handbook of Play and Learning in Early Childhood*. Thousand Oaks, CA: Sage. pp. 145–56.

6

ANALYSING AND INTERPRETING DATA FROM RESEARCH WITH YOUNG CHILDREN: FAITHFULNESS, INTEGRITY AND TRUSTWORTHINESS IN ELICITING MEANING

CATHY NUTBROWN

Thus far in this book, we have introduced some key theorisings, methodologies and conceptual frames to support research through play. We now move forward to consider a key focus in research planning which is often less explored and can be taken for granted, but is vitally important, particularly with research approaches that rely on subjective data. In this chapter, we begin to think about the complexity and deep levels of criticality that are required when interpreting research data that involves play. Without this thinking, consideration and rigour, the approaches you choose run the risk of becoming tokenistic and lacking in authenticity. Understanding how you plan to interpret the data you collect when devising your methods must be considered before any data collection begins. This chapter offers a starting point for reflection on key considerations during the initial research planning stage.

(Continued)

In the context of ethical research conducted with young children or focusing on issues that affect them, this chapter will ask three questions:

- What do we mean by analysis and interpretation?
- Why do we analyse and interpret data?
- How can we rely on our analyses and interpretations?

INTRODUCTION: TRANSPARENCY IN RESEARCH

When it comes to understanding the data gleaned from researching with children, the processes which researchers engage in are not always clear. Something goes on in researchers' heads at the stage between collecting data and presenting findings; and in credible research this process must be made transparent. Such transparency is crucial to research integrity; it is a key ethical element in any research process. *Transparency* refers to making sure that all decisions and practices within the research process are made clear. Clarity around how findings are arrived at, and the process between data collection and reporting of findings, is an important marker of research integrity. Surprisingly, this stage – or at least the report and discussion of it – is often skimped in dissertations, and sometimes in research reports, journal articles and books. A baker needs a recipe; not simply a list of ingredients in various quantities, but also the detail of how to combine them, for how long, at what temperature and so on, so that the end result is a coherent creation which brings together all the separate elements. The recipe allows others to try to create the same cake, to the same standard. And so it is with the analysis and interpretation of data – transparency allows others to know how it was done, to think about, or use, the processes for themselves, and importantly to judge for themselves the integrity and credibility of the project as reported (we will come to these later in the chapter).

Being clear about the steps taken to develop meaning from the data enables other members of the research community to use your approach, and opens up your work to a more rigorous critical appraisal. Researchers have the responsibility to present data – as they have them – and to *faithfully* represent them. This means that researchers must do their utmost accurately to present data and findings, and tell their research stories in ways which bear close relation to their participants' meanings. They also have the right to their own honest (and transparent) interpretation of the data; that is, to present their own impression of what they think the data say. This is not only important for the integrity of the researcher, but also as a matter of respect to the participants who have made the research possible.

This chapter focuses on the thinking that researchers need to engage in when they analyse and interpret data from research with young children. It is not about the specific detail of analytical steps (it is not about coding, or counting, or themes or clusters), but rather it offers some framing to those practical, process decisions. The chapter opened with the need for transparency in data analysis and interpretation. It next highlights the need for ongoing and overarching consideration of ethics and integrity issues in research with young children. Drawing on the wider field of qualitative data interpretation, the chapter then asks three questions: What do we mean by analysis and interpretation? Why do we analyse and interpret data? And finally, with a particular focus on the consideration of faithfulness, integrity and trustworthiness, it asks: How can we rely on our analyses and interpretations? The chapter concludes with a reminder of the responsibilities of researchers when telling their research story.

ETHICS AND INTEGRITY IN RESEARCH WITH YOUNG CHILDREN

Before we can begin any discussion of analysis and interpretation, we must pause to focus attention on the ethical issues which are shot through the whole process of research with young children. Foregrounding ethics at the beginning of this chapter highlights the importance of moral and ethical research conduct at the point of analysis and in interpretative processes.

Having informed consent, from the start, to collect the data is one thing (see Chapter 3 for more on this). Following through to the point of a research report which is faithful to those data requires a diligence and mindset which is ever vigilant to the issues.

Woven through every step and thought of research with young participants are issues of ethics and integrity. Throughout the challenging process of making meaning from the experiences of children, we have moral and ethical responsibilities to do justice to their original intent. In that process, we must endeavour to convey the depth and intricacies of the meanings we find. In her book of autoethnographic stories of early childhood education and care, Henderson (2018) considers the ethical responsibilities she felt to tell her own truths and to protect those young children from whom the stories derive. What she calls 'narrating the heart of practice' is full of pain and tension as well as integrity, honesty and deep thought.

Ethical issues and tensions go well beyond the need for informed consent – they run deep in the veins of the data and through every twist and turn of the research process, from beginning ideas to the final report (see, for example, Mukherji and Albon, 2018; Thompson, 2008). And that final report – whatever form it takes – has its existence apart from the researcher; it stands alone 'out there' on bookshelves or online, for others to scrutinise, available for participants (amongst others) to read, and so the ethical dilemmas continue even after a report is written, a book is published or a degree is awarded. Writing about the experiences of young children, their families and their educators is a crucially important ethical responsibility.

WHAT DO WE MEAN BY ANALYSIS AND INTERPRETATION?

There is no single approach to data analysis and interpretation, and many agree that qualitative data are often 'messy':

> We are in a new age where messy, uncertain multivoiced texts, cultural criticism, and new experimental works will become more common, as will more reflexive forms of fieldwork, analysis, and intertextual representation. (Denzin and Lincoln, 2011: 15)

And this messiness also means that data must be analysed and interpreted in many different ways. One person may develop a set of codes or clusters of meaning, while another, working with the same data, may take a quite different approach and produce a play or a fictional story in response to the data (Clough and Nutbrown, 2019; Henderson, 2019). This is why explaining the process of *how* data are analysed and interpreted is extremely important.

The challenge of analysing qualitative data is not a new problem:

> Qualitative data are attractive for many reasons: they are rich, full, earthy, holistic, 'real'; their face validity seems unimpeachable: they preserve chronological flow where that is important, and suffer minimally from retrospective distortion ... they lend themselves to the production of serendipitous findings and the adumbration of unforeseen theoretical leaps ... (Miles, 1979: 590)

Thus begins Miles's advocacy of qualitative data from over four decades ago. However, he continues with a warning:

> the analyst faced with a bank of qualitative data has very few guidelines for protection against self-delusion, let alone the presentation of 'unreliable' or 'invalid' conclusions to scientific or policy-making audiences. How can we be sure that an 'earthy', 'undeniable', 'serendipitous' finding is not, in fact, *wrong*? (Miles, 1979: 590)

This challenge remains today. Clear and justified processes of analysis are essential to ensure the credibility, through transparency, of qualitative research studies and their findings. Grbich (2013) approaches this problem in terms of 'three Ps': person, process and presentation. She argues that the *person*, the positionality of the researcher and their views and choices impact on the research decisions they make (see Chapter 4 for discussions of reflexivity). Further, she highlights the importance of research design and methods – the research *process*, and finally she suggests that *presentation* of findings and how they were analysed is a key part of the research process.

Analysis and interpretation are processes by which we find meaning in data, and use data to fashion and create meanings. How you choose to analyse data and interpret findings depends on the question that the project began with. Answers to most method and methodology questions are usually to be found somewhere in the original research question. The point at which a study begins provides a guide to how it might conclude. There will be twists and turns along the way – even changes of direction – but generally speaking, clear starting points lay important foundations to the processes involved throughout the study. How data are analysed and interpreted all depends on your research question; analysis and interpretation necessitate interrogation of the data – it is a process of asking questions of the data. In a sense, this is like shining a light, using a different lens. Imagine you are holding a glass bowl – made of different colours and with different angles and facets; to see the full effect of the bowl, you must hold it up – to the light – turning it this way and that, to see the full detail and understand more of its properties and composition. Think of your data as this glass bowl – your analytical approaches are a sort of metaphorical 'holding to the light'. And as you view the data – this way and that – you will begin to find responses to your research question in those data.

Quite how to analyse, or more appropriately to interpret, the kinds of qualitative data generated by using methods which are meaningful to and understood by young children is a slippery and messy business (see, for example, Chapter 5 on pedagogical documentation). The means by which such ephemeral data are brought together in a set of meanings derived by the researcher is often elusive. Such data are less tangible than counting, or ordering, or ranking. They require an immersion in the data, a willingness to be absorbed in and challenged by the meanings they hold. It is for this reason that the previous chapters have focused on reflexivity and the notion of practitioner enquiry as key methodologies and frameworks often employed in this type of research – approaches that embrace the immersion and subjectification of data, rather than trying to bind the meaning into neat and quantifiable packages. As we saw in Chapter 1, play is not neat and quantifiable, and therefore our interpretation of play is likely to be similarly complex.

The boundary-pushing scholars of qualitative research Denzin and Lincoln (2011) expressed this difficulty when they wrote:

> there is **no clear window** into the inner life of an individual. Any gaze is always **filtered** through the lenses of language, gender, social class, race, and ethnicity. There are no objective observations, only observations **socially situated** in the worlds of – and between – the observer and the observed. Subjects, or individuals, are seldom able to give full explanations of their actions or intentions; all they can offer are **accounts or stories** about **what they did and why**. No single method can grasp the subtle variations in ongoing human experience. Consequently, qualitative researchers deploy a wide range of **interconnected interpretive methods**, always **seeking better ways to make more understandable the worlds of experience that have been studied**. (Denzin and Lincoln, 2011: 12)

In this extract from their writing, I have highlighted some terms which I consider to be key to getting under the surface of the interpretation of qualitative data which provide insights into young children's worlds of play, creativity and imagination. Interpretation is exactly that – an interpretation – it is not an exact replication of experience but a version of how this is seen – *through* the data – and through the filter of the researcher's positionality and interests. Researching with children is often not a tidy process, as Eldén notes:

> Through inviting and allowing the messy, children become the social actors that new childhood research strived to represent – simultaneously competent, agentic, vulnerable and dependent. And as such, children's voices can challenge what is known. (Eldén, 2012: 78)

As Chesworth (2016) demonstrates in her work on children's funds of knowledge (see Chapter 1), the accounts which originate in children's worlds must be located in those worlds, and checked out with them for faithfulness of meaning, as their voices become not 'just' heard, but more fully understood.

WHY DO WE ANALYSE AND INTERPRET DATA?

So, having considered the messiness of qualitative data analysis, we need to think about the rationale for analysis and interpretation of those data.

Good qualitative data analysis begins with good quality data – if the data are poor, so will be their analysis, for each step in the research process is dependent upon the last. As will be shown in other chapters in this book (see Part 3, Chapters 7–12), detailed observations, focused film clips, annotated illustrations and attentive listening during interviews and research conversations are essential ingredients which make for analysis which has depth and meaning.

When it comes to research with young children, we also need to consider what place there might be in research for the imagination of the researcher. Clough and Nutbrown (2019) have argued that:

> No test, no observational schedule, no checklist, will adequately uncover the richness of children's minds and hearts, but, we suggest, arts-based responses to critical research questions about childhood and children's learning can take us nearer to a more meaningful portrayal of what it is to be a child and a young learner. (p. 4)

So, having generated rich and focused data, what happens next? How do researchers make decisions about the move from a box of data to a set of findings derived from those data? Some research accounts claim that 'themes' 'emerged' from the data. This, in a sense, denies the active role of the researcher. Did they simply 'emerge' as if by some mystical and invisible process – or were they 'drawn out' by the work done by the researcher? And what is this work? What do researchers *do* with their data in order to draw out their themes? Analysis involves an *active engagement* with the data to draw out, identify and hunt down the salient and meaningful elements of children's experiences. Themes and categories do not 'emerge' – they are identified through a process of systematic (and sometimes serendipitous) working, indeed at times *living* with the data. Themes, codes and categories do not simply 'emerge'. It is not a case of 'data in – findings out'; qualitative data are not merely processed, they are grappled with, pondered over, worried about, and they require our attention in terms of systematic attention and also our emotional engagement – sweat and tears! The researcher *does something* – so what is it that s/he does with their data – often messy and untidy data – to bring *out of it* some sense of order and to bring *to it* their understanding?

Innovative research with young children is increasingly sceptical of the familiar tools of traditional social science qualitative research which often employs observation, questionnaires and interviews as the main means of data collection. As discussed in other chapters of this book (see Part 3, Chapters 7–12), research methods for studies involving young children as participants are increasingly using methods most familiar to those children: drawing, photography, film, objects, and so on. These methods have direct links to those now well established in arts-based educational research, which has developed from an increasing need to render accounts of human experience, not in terms of quantification or generalisation, but rather from a commitment to faithful portrayal, interpretation and understanding of human experience (see, for example, Cahnmann-Taylor, 2018).

This making explicit and visible aspects of living and learning which often remain invisible, *making the familiar strange* (Stronach and MacClure, 1997: 53), brings the often taken-for-granted parts of life into sharp focus and gives them attention. As Clough and Nutbrown (2019) suggest:

> arts-based early childhood research is an area where growth is necessary in order to provide more of the intimate accounts of what is important to young children. For, in the case of young children understanding the 'ordinary' as well as the 'extraordinary' in their living and learning is crucial to understanding *them* as citizens and as learners. (p. 4)

The data that children create can require new ways of looking, new modes of making meaning – from their drawings, objects and play. Deguara (2019: 158) suggests that:

> Drawing, therefore, is a complex process, in which thought, body and emotions are in constant interplay with each other. This notion takes drawing beyond the domain of art to the levels of thinking and meaning-making, which in turn informs the way in which we look at, interpret and understand children's drawings and art education in general.

Deguara argues that 'Children's drawings are impregnated with layers of meaning' (p. 158) and so deserve tailored modes of interpretation. And such is the case when using the things children make as data; it is in the process of understanding both made and treasured artefacts that meaning can be generated:

> Artefacts become data through the questions posed about them and the meanings assigned to them by the researcher. There is no one right way to analyse artefacts ... In the process of analysis, we are asking the data to tell us something. (Norum, 2008: 24)

Analysis and interpretation move a set of data – from a collection of photographs, film, collages, models, poems, discussions and so on – to a research story. Without analysis, there is no research – merely paraphernalia of experience. We engage in analysis and interpretation because it is our responsibility as researchers to work with the data to create meaning. Some do this as part of a co-production process with their research participants, where decisions about processes of meaning-making are negotiated; in other cases, it remains the researcher's sole responsibility.

HOW CAN WE RELY ON OUR ANALYSES AND INTERPRETATIONS? FAITHFULNESS, INTEGRITY AND TRUSTWORTHINESS

Many qualitative researchers have long since rejected the more positivist notions of validity and reliability in favour of more apposite concepts by which research worth is judged. I suggest that three concepts to be considered are faithfulness, integrity and trustworthiness – *FIT*. *FIT* offers a framework for thinking about the processes and responsibilities inherent in interpreting child-focused qualitative research data. This section puts forward some key questions for researchers to ask of their own processes around faithfulness, integrity and trustworthiness in research analysis and interpretation.

FOCUSING ON *FIT* WHEN INTERPRETING CHILD-FOCUSED QUALITATIVE RESEARCH DATA

F ... FAITHFULNESS

the good piece of arts-based research must be able to coax the reader into rethinking the conventionally 'real' world around him or her ... Profound interrogation of that real world by its audience is indeed viewed by many arts-based researchers as the sign of a successful work of their brand of social research. (Barone, 2008: 31–2)

In thinking about the words of Barone above, there are three questions to consider:

- How can interpretation of data encourage a 'rethinking' of – or a different viewing of – children's worlds?
- What kinds of 'interrogation' of your data do you need to carry out to elicit the deep meanings to be found in them?
- What would your participants make of your interpretations? Will you share the meanings you have found with them?

I ... INTEGRITY

critical, reflexive researchers need to reflect on the processes which produce children's voices in research, the power imbalances that shape them and the ideological contexts which inform their production and reception, or in other words issues of representation. (Spyrou, 2011: 151)

Bearing in mind Spyrou's words, three questions bear consideration to ensure *integrity* in analysis and interpretation:

- How can you ensure that your approach to analysis and interpretation of your data is critical and reflexive?
- How can you ensure that children's voices are heard at all stages of the research process, and in the meanings that are elicited?
- How can you ensure that your representations of children's lived experiences are honest and ethically robust?

T ... TRUSTWORTHINESS

trustworthiness provides qualitative researchers with a set of tools by which they can illustrate the worth of their project outside the confines of the often ill-fitting quantitative parameters. (Given and Saumure, 2008: 896)

Unpacking Given and Saumure's four elements of trustworthiness, we can ask questions on four themes:

- **Transferability**: Does the scope of the study mean that users can decide if and how it might be useful to their own settings and contexts?
- **Credibility**: Does the study use the data to describe clearly, accurately and richly what is represented in the data?
- **Confirmability**: How do researchers ensure that their interpretations are rooted in and true to their data?

(Continued)

- **Dependability**: Does the report of the study make clear the processes of analysis so that researchers with similar contexts and data generated in similar ways can use similar processes?

A unique study which applies only to a single context is still worthwhile, and where researchers provide an account of their processes in the interpretation of their data, users of that research can decide how transferable ideas and interpretations are to other contexts and how credible, confirmable and dependable the study is for them.

Involving children in the research process is one way of assuring the quality of the interpretation. It is not necessarily fixed, because children's ideas often change and their interpretation of, say, what was happening in a film of them playing may change from what their ideas were on the occasion the film was shot. Involving children in interpretation of data is not easy, but it is illuminating and, importantly, respects children as rightful participants. As Blaisdell et al. (2019) have reflected:

> As we entered into the 'unruly methods' with young children, it became clear that our research was not, in the first instance, creating concrete, easily categorised data about children's views on voice. We became concerned about the lack of children's own 'voices about voice' – we were not sure how the data being created would fit into the wider Look Who's Talking project. (p. 22)

There are research decisions to be made about when to stick with the original research questions and design, and when it is appropriate to change tack. In the case above, hearing children's voices became important at a point during the research process so new decisions had to be made about its relation to the original aims of the project. It is also a point at which we need to remind ourselves of the need to consider what we can ask children to give their time to. The research that might interest us may not interest or benefit them or their peers, and we have an ethical responsibility not to waste their time. This is an example of research integrity which shows due respect to the young research participants.

These elements come together in a research project not to provide a discrete model or taxonomy to follow rigidly, but to present a list of checkpoints to aid your reflection when analysing and interpreting data related to play. It is not helpful to suggest that there is one key process to interpretation which, if followed, will result in rigorous outcomes. Instead, this chapter offers an overview of key considerations to guide your own unique planning of data analysis and interpretation. Figure 6.1 illustrates how these concepts are brought together to show the process, before we move on in the next Part of the book, which provides examples of real-life research projects which have employed these approaches.

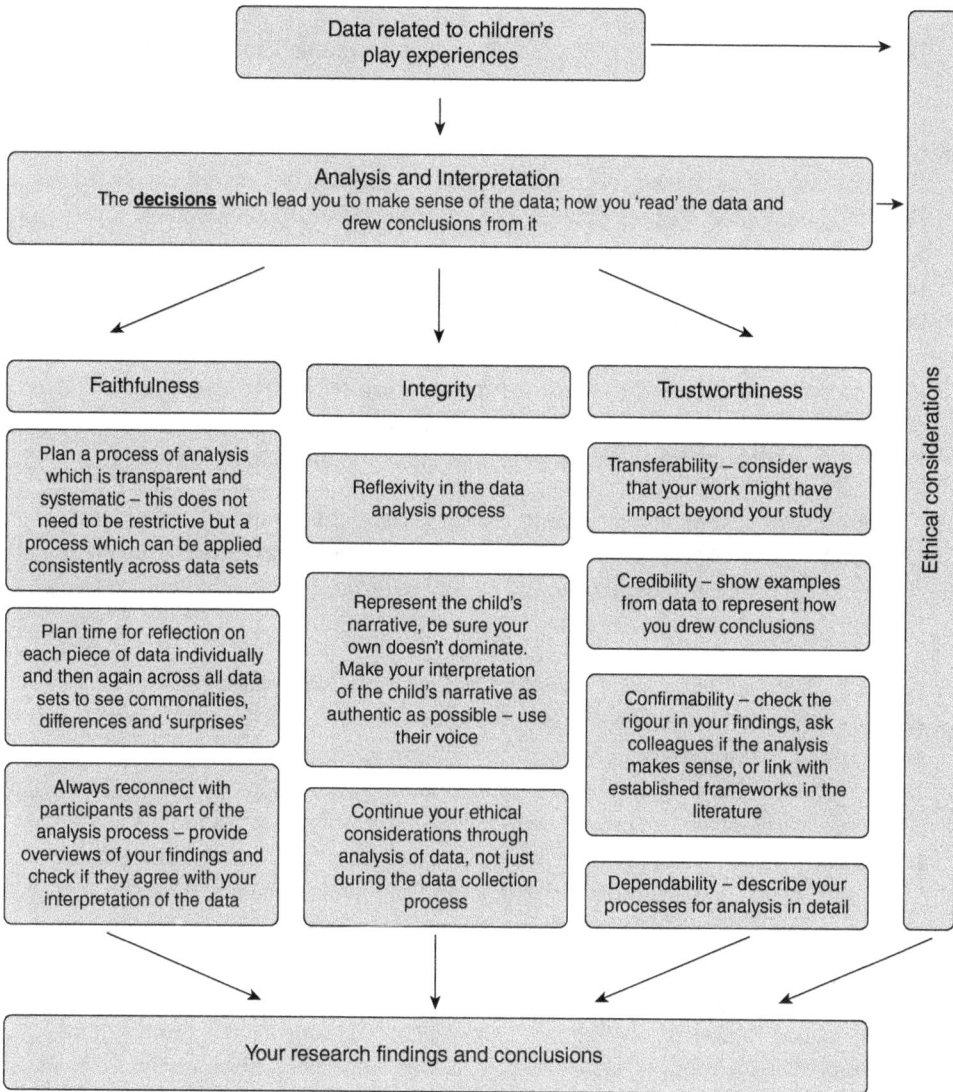

Figure 6.1 Process of analysis and interpretation

CONCLUSION

The interpretation of data is, in the end, about telling a story which has come out of the reality of the research context and represents the lived experiences of participants. In the novel *Life of Pi*, the character Pi asks, 'Which story do you prefer?'

(Continued)

> So tell me, since it makes no factual difference to you and you can't prove the question either way, which story do you prefer? Which is the better story...? (Martel, 2001: 317)

It is not quite the case when reporting research – researchers do not simply tell the story they think their readers might *prefer*; indeed, researchers have a responsibility to render accounts of their work which are faithful to the aims and data, have been conducted with ethical, moral and methodological integrity, and whose accounts can be trusted. Thus, research accounts are not always what others might want to hear and so it is *not* a case of 'which story do you prefer'. The responsibility of researchers is to conduct and publish research reports which tell stories rooted in data, and grounded in the truths of children's lives, play, creativity and imagination, to which those data provide some clues. As Denzin noted some three decades ago:

> Our primary obligation is always to the people we study, not to our project or to a larger discipline. The lives and stories that we hear and study are given to us under a promise, that promise being that we protect those who have shared them with us. (Denzin, 1989: 83)

And this is never more so than when researching with young children. Where participants are considered vulnerable (by virtue of their ages and also other life circumstances), even greater care must be taken to protect them and their identities, and ensure that they understand the processes they are involved in. Blaisdell et al. (2019) have articulated this process and the dilemmas they faced at various stages of their study. This remains important during the process of analysis and interpretation.

Remember to always keep in mind that your research is unique. It must ask *your* questions and investigate them in ways that *you* devise. You can draw on the frameworks that others create, but in the end your study and your research decisions are yours to own. Try always to pay due respect to the data children give you and do rich justice to their ideas through faithful interpretation which is always handled and reported with integrity. Importantly, your decisions need to be trustworthy and clearly justified in ways that enable others to see your processes and thinking, as well as the meanings you make.

REFERENCES

Barone, T. (2008). Arts-based research. In L. M. Given (Ed.), *The SAGE Encyclopaedia of Qualitative Research Methods* (Vols. 1 and 2). Thousand Oaks, CA: Sage. pp. 28–32.

Blaisdell, C., Arnott, L., Wall, K. and Robinson, C. (2019). Look Who's Talking: Using creative, playful arts-based methods in research with young children. *Journal of Early Childhood Research*, 17 (1): 14–31.

Cahnmann-Taylor, M. (2018). Four guiding principles for arts-based research practice. In M. Cahnmann-Taylor and R. Siegesmund (Eds.), *Arts-Based Research in Education: Foundations for Practice*. New York and London: Routledge.

Chesworth, E. A. (2016). A funds of knowledge approach to examining play interests: Listening to children's and parents' perspectives. *International Journal of Early Years Education*, 24 (3): 294–308.

Clough, P. and Nutbrown, C. (2019). Exploring the place of arts-based approaches in early childhood education research. *Journal of Early Childhood Research*, 17 (1): 3–13.

Deguara, J. (2019). Young children's drawings: A methodological tool for data analysis. *Journal of Early Childhood Research*, 17 (2): 157–74.

Denzin, N. K. (1989). *Interpretive Biography*. London: Sage.

Denzin, N. K. and Lincoln, Y. S. (2011). Introduction: The discipline and practice of qualitative research. In N. K. Denzin and Y. S. Lincoln (Eds.), *The Sage Handbook of Qualitative Research* (4th edn). London: Sage. pp. 1–25.

Eldén, S. (2012). Inviting the messy: Drawing methods and 'children's voices'. *Childhood*, 20 (1): 66–81.

Given, L. and Saumure, K. (2008). Trustworthiness. In L. M. Given (Ed.), *The SAGE Encyclopaedia of Qualitative Research Methods* (Vols. 1 and 2). Thousand Oaks, CA: Sage.

Grbich, C. (2013). *Qualitative Data Analysis: An Introduction* (2nd edn). London: Sage.

Henderson, E. (2018). *Autoethnography in Early Childhood and Care: Narrating the Heart of Practice*. Abingdon: Routledge.

Henderson, E. (2019). Researching practitioner experiences through autoethnography: Embodying social policy, exploring emotional landscapes. *Journal of Early Childhood Research*, 17 (1): 32–43.

Martel, Y. (2001). *Life of Pi*. Toronto: Knopf Canada.

Miles, M. B. (1979). Qualitative data as an attractive nuisance: The problem of analysis. *Science Quarterly Qualitative Methodology*, 24 (4): 590–601.

Mukherji, P. and Albon, D. (2018). *Research Methods in Early Childhood: An Introductory Guide* (3rd edn). London: Sage.

Norum, K. E. (2008). Artifact analysis. In L. M. Given (Ed.), *The SAGE Encyclopaedia of Qualitative Research Methods* (Vols. 1 and 2). Thousand Oaks, CA: Sage. p. 24.

Spyrou, S. (2011). The limits of children's voices: From authenticity to critical, reflexive representation. *Childhood*, 18 (2): 151–65.

Stronach, I. and MacClure, M. (1997). *Educational Research Undone: The Postmodern Embrace*. Maidenhead: Open University Press.

Thompson, P. (Ed.) (2008). Children and young people: Voices in visual research. In P. Thompson (Ed.), *Doing Visual Research with Children and Young People*. London and New York: Routledge.

PART 3

ADAPTING PLAY-BASED PEDAGOGIES AS A RESEARCH METHOD

7

APPROACHES TO INFORMED CONSENT WITH YOUNG CHILDREN

LORNA ARNOTT, LOREAIN MARTINEZ-LEJARRETA, KATE WALL, CARALYN BLAISDELL AND SHANNON LUDGATE

This chapter represents our desire to find approaches to research, including informed consent procedures, with early childhood participants that offer a high quality of ethical rigour. They represent the very nature of this book, in that research methods can be devised in line with pedagogy which supports children's understanding. We consider Mayne et al.'s (2017: 301) view of a child having the right to be informed to their level of competence and to be able 'to express a view that is not necessarily fully mature... [This] does not preclude young children from being able to form a carefully considered, rational or informed view'. Thus, the chapter:

- Explores some examples of the ways that you might use play-based and pedagogically appropriate methods to help young children be informed about a research project and be involved in more active consent-giving;
- Finds approaches to informed consent that allow us to move beyond and supplement the generally utilised methods of assent coupled with parental proxy consent.

It is increasingly commonplace to involve children directly as research participants (Christensen and James, 2017; Murray, 2016, 2017). Yet despite literature debating the complexities of ethics and voluntary informed consent (Farrell, 2016; Mayne et al., 2017), children's involvement in negotiating informed consent in research still occupies an ambiguous space. For example, ethical guidance often frames children as a vulnerable or high-risk group, while offering little advice about how to support children to provide consent (Parsons et al., 2015).

This tension may be exacerbated in the case of very young children (under 6 years old). As Farrell (2016) argues, concerns about young children's immaturity could lead to children's restricted possibilities in research. The assumption has been that young children cannot comprehend researchers' explanations of the project, and therefore are never 'truly informed' (Gray and Winter, 2011; Hughes and Helling, 1991: 228). Consequently, it is questioned whether children realise that they have the right to withdraw at any time without consequences.

Finding a path towards supporting children's informed consent is particularly difficult because, with the exception of Mayne et al.'s (2017) discussion of visual manipulatives such as non-fiction narratives, there are still few examples of how to support children to understand research and negotiate consent (Parsons et al., 2015). This chapter therefore makes a significant contribution to the field by examining three practical approaches to negotiating informed consent with young children. Situated within a children's rights perspective, this chapter challenges residual notions that young children's ideas and opinions should be sought *only* via the proxy of a gatekeeper or parent. However, we also challenge simplistic ideas of the child as 'competent' social actor. Instead, we draw on relational understandings of ethics, highlighting the expectations, realities, negotiations and challenges of supporting young children's understanding of, and consent to, participation in research.

APPROACHES FOR INFORMED CONSENT

In this section, we introduce the three approaches we have used for consent with young children, each of which has key benefits, but which are also imperfect and present their own challenges. This is because there are no perfect play-based informed consent processes. They will always be context- and situation-specific, and their usefulness is very much dependent on the participants in the study. This is important to highlight, because we do not suggest that these approaches will suit every occasion. Rather, they offer examples of how you might transform play experiences and activities into meaningful approaches to inform children about research. We invite you to reflect on your own pedagogy and devise your own approaches to informed consent within your practice.

THE ANIMATED VIDEO

Used across two research projects (Arnott et al., 2019; Blaisdell et al., 2018), we created two animated videos using the online space Biteable (https://biteable.com); one to introduce the overall project and one to inform children about their proposed participation in consultation activities. Designed to be engaging, a first point of information for children, and in a format that children were familiar with, the animations were short videos lasting 1.13 minutes and 1.31 minutes, respectively. This was important because the research was taking place in a busy playroom context where children move freely around the room and where the environment is noisy and dynamic. It is our experience, in these particular contexts (see Arnott and Duncan, 2019), that children's engagement with a task can be fleeting due to the broad range of stimuli available, and therefore lengthy video animations would not be pedagogically appropriate for the context. For other settings, boasting a quieter environment or a different demographic of children, longer videos may have been appropriate.

The videos focused on: who we were as researchers; why we were there; what the project entailed; children's roles; dissemination of the data; data security; and children's rights to play with the resources even if they did not want data to be collected about them.

Subsequently, children engaged in a process of discussion about what the research project entailed and developed a joint ethical agreement (see Figure 7.1) with researchers and children directing how we should operate during the project. This agreement

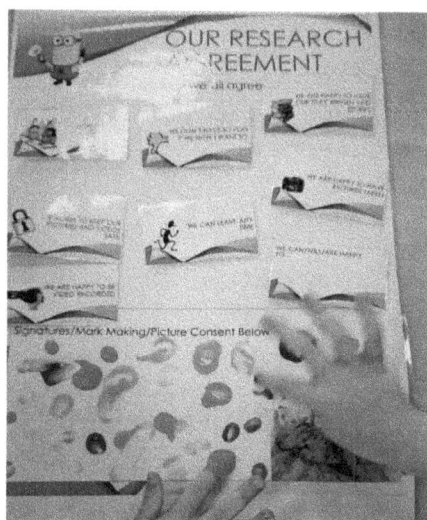

Figure 7.1   Joint agreement

Source: Arnott, L., Martinez-Lejarreta, L., Wall, K., Blaisdell, C. and Palaiologou, I. (2020). Reflecting on three creative approaches to informed consent with children under six. © *British Educational Research Journal*, 46 (4): John Wiley & Sons. Reproduced with permission from the publisher.

was facilitated by a series of removable badges which could be appended to the blank agreement if children agreed (or not) to each element. Badges included statements like 'I can ask questions'; 'I can leave at any time'; 'We are happy to be video recorded'. Blank badges were also available, starting with 'We can/will/are happy to', in order to allow children to add their own statements.

Using the video approach in a large play-based setting, the initial plan was to present it on a large screen, such as a smartboard, to the whole playroom as an introductory ice breaker. However, given the expansive nature of the nursery (accommodating up to 120+ children at one time), it was challenging to screen the film to all children, or even the majority, at one time. Consequently, we ended up only showing the consent video to the first wave of children.

While we agreed that consent is not an isolated act, but is one part of an 'ethical continuum' (Du Toit, 1980: 284), something to be negotiated continually throughout the research (Gallagher, 2009), we had hoped that the initial video process would have provided a springboard or a benchmark to set up the project. Instead, we ended up engaging in a period of ongoing consent with children, some who had seen the video and engaged with the agreement, some who had not. Table 7.1, using extracts of reflective field notes, demonstrates our expectation of how we imagined the ethical process taking place, in comparison to what happened in reality.

Table 7.1 Understanding expectations versus reality in children's informed consent processes

Expectation: Inclusive information sharing	Reality: Fragmented information sharing
All children watch the video on the smartboard, ask questions, then collectively decide on the badges for the consent agreement (Planning from arts-based project)	On reflection, we would have preferred to carry out the ethical agreement with the whole group rather than a select few because other children began approaching the table to find out what we were doing. We allowed them to play with the resources because it seemed unethical to deny children, but it was a continual struggle to explain our purpose in the study when they had already engaged in play. While we asked them if it was okay to take pictures before we did so, they did not want to stop playing to hear about why we were taking pictures and having not heard the ethical agreement discussion previously we were concerned about including the data from these children. (Researcher reflection, day one, 3- to 5-year-old playroom)

In light of these challenges, the approach was subsequently trialled in three different ways, at each stage learning from the last in an informed trial-and-error process. Each iteration offered different insights into children's understanding or engagement with the consent process, as shown in Figure 7.2:

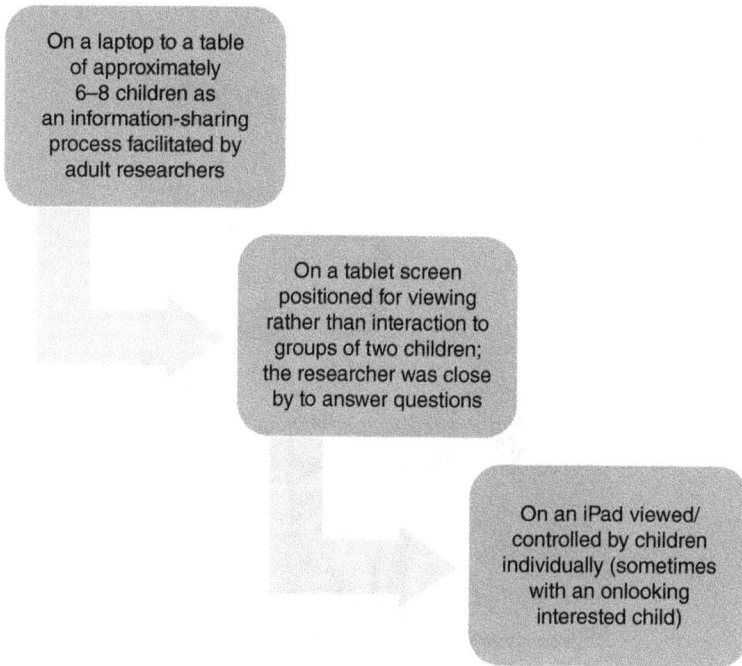

Figure 7.2   Way of presenting the animated video to children

Source: Arnott, L., Martinez-Lejarreta, L., Wall, K., Blaisdell, C. and Palaiologou, I. (2020). Reflecting on three creative approaches to informed consent with children under six. © *British Educational Research Journal*, 46 (4): John Wiley & Sons. Reproduced with permission from the publisher.

Each way of presenting the video led to different outcomes, each bringing their own dilemmas and successes. The first had the advantage of reaching a wider audience, reducing researcher costs in terms of time and investment, but was only moderately successful in reassuring the researcher of the children's understanding. The second demonstrated more static engagement with the children, but surprisingly reduced the level of questioning compared with the first. Children seemed to view the process as a precursor to the 'fun' and therefore were motivated to get the process out of the way as quickly, and as unthoughtfully, as possible. Perhaps a larger group, as evidenced in the first example compared to the second, created a sense of security with more children all familiar with each other, bolstering confidence to ask questions. The final option was more labour-intensive in terms of researcher time but offered more in-depth knowledge of the project on the part of the children because it was coupled with the relational dialogue between researcher and child that created a context where children could extend their knowledge of the project and make more informed decisions.

When the video was presented via the iPad (shown in the third scenario), children maintained ownership of the device and were able to touch and interact physically with the artefact, allowing children to engage more readily in the focus of the research.

Figure 7.3   Children interactively viewing the animated video on an iPad

Source: Arnott, L., Martinez-Lejarreta, L., Wall, K., Blaisdell, C. and Palaiologou, I. (2020). Reflecting on three creative approaches to informed consent with children under six. © *British Educational Research Journal*, 46 (4): John Wiley & Sons. Reproduced with permission from the publisher.

Figure 7.3 shows Mark[1] watching the animated video on an iPad independently (with an onlooker child close by). Mark autonomously took it upon himself to stop the video by touching the iPad screen intuitively, before turning to the researcher to clarify points or questions. For example, when watching the second, follow-up animated video after several months on the project, he turned to the researcher to highlight the toys which he recognised from the previous stage in the research process. Similarly, as he was watching the video in a busy playroom, he used his finger to move the timeline to the left to rewind and re-watch sections that were hard to hear.

NARRATIVE ILLUSTRATED PICTURE BOOK

In Martinez's (2018) project, a picture book was created by the researcher, inspired by children's literature and combining illustrations and narrative. The book was presented via interactive storytelling. This technique was selected as it is a common form of communication, widely used across time in early years pedagogy in the settings involved in this study.

---

[1]Pseudonyms are used throughout.

The picture book contained a linear story represented by cartoon characters of children and the researcher. The storyline was of the researcher exploring how children think when investigating mysteries in the context of super-detective role play. The intent with this form of communication was to 'tell' new and abstract information, through the use of visuals, in the form of an accessible narrative with a clear intent, plot and ending. The picture book storyline covered the purpose of the research visit, research activities, participants' role, data-recording devices, dissemination and voluntary participation, among other things.

Information-sharing via the storytelling session and initial consent happened within a group context. Throughout the remainder of the research, children articulated views individually within and throughout the collective experience and exercised their right to participate, or not, at different times. This included indicating a willingness to take part verbally or asking to leave. Overall, children demonstrated consent via various modes of communication. These were not taken as an indication of firm consent but instead provided an additional non-verbal opportunity for expressing consent, which must be observed in a relational manner. In other cases, some children took ownership and responsibility for the research, reaffirming their consent by reminding the researcher whether the camera had been turned on or moving the focus of the camera to point at the research scenario when perhaps the play had moved to another physical location but the camera had not yet been repositioned.

Children generally demonstrated interest in the picture book. They got physically close to it, pointed, commented and verbally linked content to their experiences, and while referencing the picture book tool they formed and responded to questions. Visuals captured and maintained children's attention and intellectual interest, stimulating interpretation of the visuals and research content. Often, the conversation was more linked to what they saw in the images than what was narrated (for example, see Tim's discussion in Table 7.2 below).

Table 7.2 Reflections from using a narrative picture book for consent

Expectation meets reality (partially): Using manipulatives to make information concrete
When looking at the photograph of the researcher, the children recognised the researcher, and Tim (aged 5) commented:
Yeahhh. I think I know what your work was, I think so. Cause we are doing a full book to learn something. You are talking (*referring to the speech bubble on the photograph*) What does that say? (*Pointing to the speech bubble*). (Tim)
Tim's comments in the beginning of the session showed some understanding about the content as well as the purpose of the informative session by saying 'we are doing a full book to learn something'. He reflected on the process and started to make meaning of the session. Tim interacted with the book by looking and pointing at it. He decoded the meaning of the bubbles but asked for further clarification of the short writing as he was not able to read. I read the bubble and he repeated after me. (Extract from an Observation in a Primary 1 context)

Source: Arnott et al. (2020). Reproduced with permission from the publisher.

The visual nature of the book influenced and catalysed conversation about the research. This was interesting as the researcher had the opportunity to learn about Tim's vision of the research, providing scope for follow-up conversations. Even though the tool was intended to elicit some talk and the researcher was ready to be flexible with the coverage of the story, it was not expected that children would extend their talk so much that at some moments it was difficult to move on from one page to the next. This was particularly the case with the first few pages when the children found most connections to share. Inevitably, some children talked more than others and others had less time to engage with discussions with the researcher. As time went on, the researcher perceived children's attention spans decreasing and excitement started increasing, and as such the session was finished on pedagogical grounds. It became clear that expecting to share full coverage of all ethical issues in one storytelling session with an interested and actively involved small group was not realistic. Having the picture book accessible during the research data collection process and free for children to browse was therefore sensible in the context. This offered another approach to facilitate ongoing negotiated consent.

The book was supplemented by additional resources which helped us understand children's desire to take part. For example, as part of the research activity children could wear themed clothing. The children showed power and ownership regarding their participant role by leaving and coming back to the activities at different times, signalling their participation by putting on and taking off detective clothing. The use of detective clothing created a visual representation for the researcher to interpret during the activity, without the need for the children to verbally express their desire to participate. The children were 'playing' with the idea of being in or out of the research, which for young children is an essential part of developing their understanding. The fact that these symbols were clear to both researcher and children was essential.

CONSENT LANYARDS

In response to the importance of gaining consent and ongoing assent with young children, highlighted by Fraser et al. (2004) and Flewitt (2005), consent lanyards for preschool children can be used as an in-the-moment consent symbol. They allow the children to continually review their desire to consent throughout the duration of the activity.

Ludgate used these lanyards to observe children playing with touchscreen technologies and during focus-group interviews about their touchscreen preferences. The lanyards were designed in order to record consent in an unobtrusive way, with a happy face on one side and a sad face on the other, as shown in Figure 7.4:

Figure 7.4 Both sides of the lanyard design (Ludgate, 2018)

The lanyards were considered to be an age-appropriate way to enable children to signify their informed decision to participate in the study, as the faces removed any communication barriers for young children. The smiley face system is universal and all children were able to recognise emotions such as 'happy' and 'sad' and apply them to being willing (or not) to participate.

The following extracts outline the range of ways that children interacted with the lanyards. These are selected from a range of observations taken in two different early years settings as the children explored the lanyards and tested their 'powers' in terms of what they could control with them. The children demonstrated clear autonomy with the lanyards, choosing to provide or decline permission for other children to watch them playing, and to permit practitioners in having an input in their touchscreen play.

LANYARDS AS A TANGIBLE SIGNAL OF CONSENT

The first extract provides a snapshot of two children playing with their lanyards to give permission to the researcher, but denying permission to others who wanted to watch them play:

(Continued)

> Jack picks up his lanyard, turns the face around from the happy to sad face. He shows the sad face to Billy, saying 'don't look at me'. Jack turns to me, the researcher, showing the happy face, and says 'look at me'.
>
> Billy picks up his own lanyard, commenting 'look at that badge; that is happy, that is sad', as he turns the lanyard around to view both sides. Jack picks up his lanyard and tells Ella 'don't look at me', showing the sad face.
>
> *Source:* Ludgate (2018)

The two boys in this extract clearly demonstrated engagement with the intentions of the lanyards, being decisive when choosing who had permission to watch their own touch-screen play. The boys were confident in their actions, and on other occasions, Jack was keen to watch the researcher after he occasionally denied permission to be observed, just to make sure they did not record any notes. He found this funny, often laughing, and gave back permission to be observed. This demonstrates the awareness of 4-year-old children in making decisions about their lives, as well as their understanding of the lanyards and the associated power they provided. The noticeable actions of Jack to determine who had permission, and who did not, gave him a form of social status amongst his peers, as he established a position for himself in terms of being the rule-maker, and this influenced his play as he gave and removed permission during his time using the touchscreen (Saracho and Spodek, 2007). The actions of Jack were also in line with what Walsh et al. (2010: 14) call 'dominance hierarchies', where he opted to 'include or exclude children' during play.

USING LANYARDS TO EXERCISE POWER

The final extract shows a different way of children using consent lanyards, unlike the playful interactions between Jack and his peers:

A practitioner speaks to Gemma about the consent lanyards, explaining that the happy face means that I can observe her, but if Gemma does not want to be watched and to have notes written about her playing, she should show the sad face, and that means being unhappy to be watched. Gemma nods and wears a consent lanyard, showing the happy face. I sit nearby, as does the practitioner (who plays alongside, giving support where needed), and Gemma begins to play. I start taking notes after a minute of watching, and Gemma notices, with a puzzled look on her face, and turns the lanyard to the sad face. She says 'no thank you' to me, and I put my pen down. Gemma continues playing, every now and then looking up from her iPad to make sure I am not taking notes and my pen is left on the notepad.

Source: Ludgate (2018)

Gemma takes a different approach after understanding the lanyard and initially giving her consent. It was clear that when the researcher started recording observation of her, she was uncomfortable with this. Her clear reaction, to turn the lanyard round and say 'no thank you', demonstrates the importance of empowering children to feel confident to voice their opinion and to be responded to, as was the case by putting the pen down and by not observing her play.

Overall, the two extracts demonstrate that children as young as 4 can clearly demonstrate an understanding of their own role in research, and were able to practise their position of power to have their voices heard and responded to, positioning the consent lanyards as an appropriate tool to use to give children a voice in research.

CONCLUSION

While under the guidance of the UNCRC, society is increasingly acknowledging children's rights. Yet, there is still a challenge to be met regarding children and their involvement in and with research. This is particularly so with young children. Therefore, it is necessary to foreground that while children's understanding of the research will be different to adults', there are ways to negotiate their consent, rather than relying solely on a legal guardian's proxy consent. Indeed, our examples show that when this is done appropriately, even young children can express a fine-grained understanding of what participation, or non-participation, means to them.

It was intended that concrete tools such as those described in this chapter would provide a 'valued space' (Cook-Sather, 2002: 4) for children to engage in questioning and to challenge researchers about research projects. We were under no illusions that any approach would alleviate all issues associated with obtaining consent from young children, but we did want to create *brave spaces* (Cook-Sather, 2016) where children felt they had a voice, could speak up and ask questions about the research. The animated video and the picture book facilitated such reflexive questioning about the purpose of our visits and the research process. These visual manipulatives did

(Continued)

not alleviate the potential power dynamics of adult–child discourse, but rather scaffolded different opportunities for children to engage in dialogue. This resulted in a negotiated consent process more aligned with children's right to voluntarily consent, not just about whether to take part but also in relation to the fine-grained details of what participation involved. In line with Einarsdóttir (2007), the use of visual manipulatives was important in facilitating children's active engagement with the discussions, rather than being a passive recipient of information. For older children, the physical tool allowed the process to be concrete (Harcourt and Conroy, 2005) and facilitated an interactive process.

Having established that ascertaining informed consent from young children is important, this is challenging as a one-time event. Rather, we agree with Abebe and Bessell (2014) that one-off predetermined consent procedures do not adequately take account of power hierarchies, local practices or involve children themselves in determining what is ethical. From our evidence, we would emphasise that of particular concern is the fact that relationships between researcher and child are lacking, yet should be central in an informed consent protocol. This means that iterative ongoing consent needs to be negotiated, similar to Flewitt's (2005) consideration of 'provisional consent'. In practicality, negotiating this consent process is exigent, not least because it is time-intensive to develop the required relationships with participants. As a result, our findings demonstrate that like dominant play-based and child-centred early years pedagogy, informed consent processes with young children are messy and fraught with challenge. Yet they simultaneously offer a rewarding route for children's self-expression, particularly when coupled with tactile concrete consent resources, as described above.

To facilitate this negotiation, attempting to marry the research method with pedagogically appropriate practice is essential. Therefore, creative approaches to consent need to evolve as a project progresses and as the researchers get to know the children and setting. Consideration is needed of the child's experience up to, within and beyond the setting for the research, to ascertain appropriate ways of communicating with and listening to their perspectives. The practicalities of negotiating informed consent with young children should be seen as part of a spectrum of practices sensitive to individual children, the setting in which the research is taking place and the parameters of the researcher and the research project. Consent is not just about asking young children to 'sign their name' in alternative ways or replicating 'stereotypical representations' of consent from young children (Harcourt and Conroy, 2005: 574); rather, it is a holistic consideration that needs to be embedded in the research project. A simplistic approach to consent with young children fails to capture the dynamic and complex nature of how informed consent needs to be conceived with this youngest age range (Kustatscher, 2014).

The use of manipulatives can be conceived as creating spaces for communication, questioning and relational dialogue. They become tools that are catalytic

(Baumfield et al., 2009) of the type of ongoing dialogue between researcher and child needed for a negotiated ongoing approach to informed consent. A well-designed, pedagogically appropriate manipulative or tool will provide an impetus for dialogue around key concepts and processes inherent in the proposed research as well as provide a scaffold or aide memoir that can be returned to by researcher or child as the research progresses. Additionally, it can mediate some of the power dynamics inherent in adult–child interactions, which is important when the relational aspect is foregrounded. With non-verbal and pre-verbal children, then, this concept of a space can be seen as being characterised by familiarity and safety, with active listening behaviours by the adult attuned to the child's perspectives, and particularly their desire to participate, or not.

ACKNOWLEDGEMENT

An extended version of this chapter can be found at https://doi.org/10.1002/berj.3619: Arnott, L., Martinez-Lejarreta, L., Wall, K., Blaisdell, C. and Palaiologou, I. (2020). Reflecting on three creative approaches to informed consent with children under six. *British Educational Research Journal*. Permission for content reused from this article is granted by the publisher, John Wiley & Sons.

REFERENCES

Abebe, T. and Bessell, S. (2014). Advancing ethical research with children: Critical reflections on ethical guidelines. *Children's Geographies*, 12 (1): 126–33.

Arnott, L. and Duncan, P. (2019). Exploring the pedagogic culture of creative play in early childhood education. *Journal of Early Childhood Research*, 17 (4): 309–28.

Arnott, L., Palaiologou, I. and Gray, C. (2019). An ecological exploration of the internet of toys in early childhood everyday life. In G. Mascheroni and D. Holloway (Eds.), *The Internet of Toys: Practices, Affordances and the Political Economy of Children's Play*. New York: Palgrave.

Arnott, L., Martinez-Lejarreta, L., Wall, K., Blaisdell, C. and Palaiologou, I. (2020). Reflecting on three creative approaches to informed consent with children under six. *British Educational Research Journal*, 46 (4, Special Issue): 786–810.

Baumfield, V. M., Hall, E., Higgins, S. and Wall, K. (2009). Catalytic tools: Understanding the interaction of enquiry and feedback in teachers' learning. *European Journal of Teacher Education*, 32 (4): 423–35.

Blaisdell, C., Arnott, L., Wall, K. and Robinson, C. (2018). Look Who's Talking: Using creative, playful arts-based methods in research with young children. *Journal of Early Childhood Research*, 17 (1): 14–31.

Christensen, P. and James, A. (2017). *Research with Children: Perspectives and Practices*. London: Routledge.

Cook-Sather, A. (2002). Authorizing students' perspectives: Toward trust, dialogue, and change in education. *Educational Researcher*, 31 (4): 3–14.

Cook-Sather, A. (2016). Creating brave spaces within and through student–faculty pedagogical partnerships. *Teaching and Learning Together in Higher Education*, 1 (18): 1–5.

Du Toit, B. M. (1980). Ethics, informed consent, and fieldwork. *Journal of Anthropological Research*, 36 (3): 274–86.

Einarsdóttir, J. (2007). Research with children: Methodological and ethical challenges. *European Early Childhood Education Research Journal*, 15 (2): 197–211.

Farrell, A. (2016). Ethics in early childhood research. In A. Farrell, S. L. Kagan and E. K. M. Tisdall (Eds.), *The Sage Handbook of Early Childhood Research*. Thousand Oaks, CA: Sage.

Flewitt, R. (2005). Conducting research with young children: Some ethical considerations. *Early Childhood Development and Care*, 175 (6): 553–65.

Fraser, S., Lewis, V., Ding, S., Kellett, M. and Robinson, C. (Eds.) (2004) *Doing Ethical Research with Children*. London: Sage/Open University.

Gallagher, M. (2009). 'Ethics'. In E. K. M. Tisdall, J. M. Davis and M. Gallagher (Eds.), *Researching with Children and Young People: Research Design, Methods and Analysis*. London: Sage. pp. 11–28.

Gray, C. and Winter, E. (2011). Hearing voices: Participatory research with preschool children with and without disabilities. *European Early Childhood Education Research Journal*, 19 (3): 309–20.

Harcourt, D. and Conroy, H. (2005). Informed assent: Ethics and processes when researching with young children. *Early Child Development and Care*, 175 (6): 567–77.

Hughes, T. and Helling, M. K. (1991). A case for obtaining informed consent from young children. *Early Childhood Research Quarterly*, 6 (2): 225–32.

Kustatscher, M. (2014). Informed consent in school-based ethnography: Using visual magnets to explore participation, power and research relationships. *International Journal of Child, Youth and Family Studies*, 5 (4.1): 686–701.

Ludgate, S. (2018). Exploring the Affordances of Touchscreen Technologies in Early Years Settings in the West Midlands. Doctoral thesis, Birmingham City University, UK.

Martinez, L. (2018). Adapting researchers' approaches towards seeking a more ethically appropriate informed assent/dissent in early years. Paper presented at EECERA, Budapest, Hungary, 28–31 August.

Mayne, F., Howitt, C. and Rennie, L. J. (2017). Using interactive nonfiction narrative to enhance competence in the informed consent process with 3-year-old children. *International Journal of Inclusive Education*, 21 (3): 299–315.

Murray, J. (2016). Young children as researchers: Children aged four to eight years engage in important research behaviour when they base decisions on evidence. *European Early Childhood Education Research Journal*, 24 (5): 705–20.

Murray, J. (2017). Welcome in! How the academy can warrant recognition of young children as researchers. *European Early Childhood Education Research Journal*, 25 (2): 224–42.

Parsons, S., Abbott, C., McKnight, L. and Davies, C. (2015). High risk yet invisible: Conflicting narratives on social research involving children and young people, and the role of research ethics committees. *British Educational Research Journal*, 41 (4): 709–29.

Saracho, O. N. and Spodek, B. (2007). Early childhood teachers' preparation and the quality of program outcomes. *Early Child Development and Care*, 177 (1): 71–91.

Walsh, G., Sproule, L., McGuinness, C., Trew, K. and Ingram, G. (2010). Developmentally appropriate practice and play-based pedagogy in early years education. Available at: www.nicurriculum.org.uk/docs/foundation_stage/eye_curric_project/evaluation/Literature_Review.pdf (accessed 18 December 2016).

8

USING DRAWING AS A PLAYFUL RESEARCH ENCOUNTER WITH YOUNG CHILDREN

PAULINE DUNCAN

Having already presented the theoretical basis for this book and some examples of innovative approaches to informed consent with children in the previous chapters, this chapter now offers the first glimpse into what research methods through play may look like. In this case, the focus is on drawings. There are multiple ways to engage in research involving play. This chapter, and the ones that follow in this Part, are not meant to offer a rigid approach or framework to adopt, but rather the methods presented provide a starting point for you to imagine how you might adapt children's natural ability to play to arrive at meaningful research data which offer an insight into the child's world. The aims of this chapter are to:

- Illustrate some of the benefits of using drawing in research with young children;
- Explore how our conceptualisation of drawing can shape the ways in which we illicit and interpret young children's drawings;
- Consider how a multimodal social-semiotic framework can help us privilege young children's perspectives and natural practices of communication;
- Provide insights into some key methodological factors to consider which can influence the communicative potential of drawing, including the adult role and social and contextual framing.

CHILDREN'S DRAWINGS IN RESEARCH

The continuing developments in social and cultural perceptions of childhood and views towards children as participants (Christensen, 2004; James and Prout, 1997) has resulted in an important shift in research where children's perspectives have been brought to the fore as valued contributors and influencers of their own lives (see Chapter 2 for more on this). Research is now being driven by a more holistic and contextualised approach to childhood, with a focus on accessing children's subjective experiences. Achieving this requires using methods and methodologies which draw on children's natural and everyday practices of communication and ways of being.

Despite the positive changes in research approaches, it is important for us to re-examine the methods commonly used with young children as 'there may be an assumption that the tools themselves somehow automatically enable participation' (Waller and Bitou, 2011: 5). This is particularly true of those often defined as 'child-friendly'. Based on its routine use, drawing may be one of these.

Children's drawings have been studied, analysed and catalogued for centuries, and the method remains consistently popular with professionals engaging in research with children (e.g. Einarsdóttir et al., 2009; Fargas-Malet et al., 2010; Kellogg, 1970; Ricci, 1887). Drawing is embedded in most children's everyday practices (Cox, 2005). Young children use drawings in playful ways to engage in humour, exchange stories and share meanings with others (Anning and Ring, 2004) and to make sense of the world and their experiences (Matthews, 2003). Drawing is known to facilitate meaningful communication, encourage deeper reflection, help build rapport and create a space where we can interact with children through their dynamic self-expression and multimodal narration (Cox, 2005; Kinnunen and Einarsdóttir, 2013). Moyles (1989) refers to drawing as a form of 'intellectual play' involving creativity, innovation, fantasy and problem-solving. A complex interrelationship exists between play and drawing – developing synchronously as the child masters the use of symbol systems, and thought and imagination become visible.

Despite the many advantages of using drawing as a research tool, as with any method, various methodological and social and contextual factors can influence the data produced and the participant's engagement with the tools. Accordingly, the ways in which particular research methods can enable or constrain children's participation deserves careful consideration (Mitchell, 2006: 60) so as not to silence or misrepresent children's voices and lived experiences. For example, historically, researchers have tended to focus on understanding children's drawings from an adult perspective, based on conjecture, rather than using the child's own descriptions and interpretations (Fargas-Malet et al., 2010). The outcomes as such may not reflect the child's perspective but instead result in a strong adult voice. Another caveat is that children may produce drawings simply to satisfy an adult's request or complete a set task (Coates, 2002). This can depend on whether drawing is framed as a play-based activity, and whether the adult is able to engage in the activity in a playful way (see Chapters 5 and 6 for more about authentic representations and interpretations of children's play and experiences).

The research described in this chapter explored the use of drawing as a tool to access children's perspectives on play. For the purposes of this chapter, I focus on two central aspects of this research which are used to show how we can enable, and possibly restrict, the communicative potential of drawing. The first is the theoretical framing. I explore how our understanding of drawing can influence the ways in which we illicit and document children's drawings. A multimodal social-semiotic approach resonates with children's communicative practices and calls for researchers to document the entire drawing process. The second focus is the methodological approach. I examine how playful and child-led drawing enables children to communicate in their own languages, and challenges known ethical issues in research with children.

THE RESEARCH

The study on which this chapter is based examined the use of drawing as a research method for gathering young children's perspectives on play within a social semiotic framework. The research was guided by the following three research questions:

1. How can children's drawings be analysed using a principled approach which privileges children's interpretations?
2. What are the key factors to be considered when using drawing as a research tool?
3. What can drawings reveal about children's perspectives on play?

Adopting a qualitative approach allowed for a flexible research process where the researcher can adapt and accommodate the child's specific interests, needs and level of engagement. Qualitative research also seeks to gain knowledge from the child's perspective by giving voice to individuals and encouraging reflection rather than performance (Lapan et al., 2012).

The research involved visits to the homes of eight children, aged 4, from across central and north-eastern Scotland. The sample included four girls and four boys. Two visits were scheduled with each family, each approximately 90–120 minutes in duration. The primary methodological objective was to create an organic and child-led drawing encounter framed within the children's natural play repertoire in the home context. Visits were therefore unstructured, allowing the child autonomy regarding our level of interaction and the types of activities with which they wished to engage. Often, our interactions were initiated by the children's curiosity as they inquired about the drawing materials I had brought or asked if I wanted to play. If the child expressed a desire to draw immediately then we would create a space for our activities. The flexible approach meant that, for example, one child spent an hour drawing whereas another child drew for 10 minutes then wanted us to play for the remainder of my visit. The resulting engagements were open-ended play episodes which included outdoor play, role play, drawing, pretend play, construction, conversations and child-led tours of their home and play things.

I brought a range of drawing materials to each visit, allowing the child freedom to choose what was most appropriate for their personal drawing needs and styles. Materials included a variety of paper, coloured pencils, felt-tip pens and crayons. Children also used their own drawing materials. I brought a digital still camera, a digital video camera and tripod to document play contexts, play episodes and the children's drawing process. All drawings were photographed. A total of 98 drawings were collected over the two home visits.

Informed by social semiotics (Kress and van Leeuwen, 1996), I developed a four-step approach to the semiotic analysis of children's drawings (4-SASA) which provided a principled technique for interpreting drawings and privileged the children's meanings. Semiotics is a field of study that is concerned with signs, symbols and signification in the production and communication of meaning. Social semiotics is a branch of semiotics which focuses on studying signs and meaning-making within specific social and cultural contexts – exploring how they are created, used and interpreted within these different social processes and social relations (Hodge and Kress, 1988; Kress and van Leeuwen, 1996). The theory of communication here is based on the idea that all language is a form of meaning-making or semiosis involving expressing what one wants to communicate in a particular, or multiple, modes, then representing it in a culturally accepted manner to be interpreted by another (Hodge and Kress, 1988). Sign production generates 'motivated signs' shaped by the individual's interest in a given social situation, context and audience. This theory is used to frame how children's drawings are viewed in the study: as a semiotic vehicle where messages are created through representation and signification, and are always embedded in the social. The adopted framework therefore facilitates an exploration of the child's perspectives as expressed through their choice of representations which are unique to the child, their drawings and their play.

The 4-SASA acknowledged the multimodal process of drawing and privileged children's signification and attribution of meaning as each drawing was analysed in conjunction with transcripts of children's recorded conversations and other modes of expression generated by the drawing process. The 4-SASA involved: (i) identifying and isolating signs within the drawings through manual annotation; (ii) documenting the child's understanding of signs and the significance attributed to them; (iii) organising the signs using specific categories of social semiotic analysis (mode, size, colour, salience) and identifying the child's motivation and interest for specific sign production;

Table 8.1 Summary of the 4-SASA

Step 1	Step 2	Step 3	Step 4
  McKenzie's representation of a person playing: A drawing of herself, her sister and friend, playing football with the 'Fairy Team'			
Begin with a printed copy of the child's original drawing. Identify and isolate signs within the drawing through manual annotation informed by transcriptions of the child's conversation and descriptions of the representations. This technique privileges the child's meanings.	Document the child's understanding of the isolated signs from Step 1 and the significance attributed to them. In social semiotic terms, this is embedding the sign in the social.	Organise the signs using specific categories of social semiotic analysis such as mode, size, colour and salience, and identify the child's motivation and interest for specific sign production.	Synthesis of the child's perspectives from Steps 1–3 with focus on play and choices underlying the criterial aspects (what to include or exclude to illustrate play) producing a summary of the child's perspectives on play.

and (iv) synthesising the child's perspectives from steps 1–3. The four steps, summarised in Table 8.1, were performed on all of the child's drawings. The outcomes from step 4 (summary of the child's perspectives on and conceptualisations of play) were collated from every drawing, from the same child, to produce a rich account of the child's perspectives on play.

The research was undertaken in accordance with the British Educational Research Association's Ethical Guidelines for Educational Research (BERA, 2011). Consent was sought from parents and children. Initial consent from children was viewed as conditional, based on their ongoing willingness to participate (Flewitt, 2005). Pseudonyms are used throughout this chapter to maintain anonymity.

Research outcomes included rich accounts of children's personal experiences and unique perspectives on play, as revealed through their drawings (see Duncan, 2015). Children drew objects to illustrate their favourite toys or play things, produced complex representations of play scenes and drew more abstract concepts. Drawing provided opportunities to explore what children liked to play, and at the same time, discover how a child may conceptualise play.

'INDIANA JONES PUNCHING THE BAD GUYS': THE MULTIMODALITY OF YOUNG CHILDREN'S DRAWINGS

The research on which this chapter is based is informed by Kress and van Leeuwen's (1996) theoretical framework of social semiotics, and multimodality (Kress, 2010). Multimodality considers communication as always using more than one semiotic mode to convey meaning – each chosen for their distinct affordance and the social situation. Modes are resources which we use to represent and convey meaning such as speech, colour, image, text or gaze. These tend to be socially constructed, thus becoming cultural resources. Meaning is typically 'spread' across multiple modes (Kress, 2010). This is particularly true of young children. Children are very experienced at 'making' in a number of media and adeptly create meaning through an array of semiotic modes in their efforts to successfully communicate their message. This is reminiscent of Malaguzzi's discussion of children's 100 languages – the fact that children use different modes of expression.

If we think about young children's drawing practice from our own experiences, whether it be in the home or in education settings, we can begin to understand why defining drawing as a visual method is too narrow. Young children's drawings are typically infused with life through sound, song, gesture, movement, colour, dialogue and dramatisation (Anning and Ring, 2004) (e.g. Figure 8.1 and the narrative below). In their final form, young children's drawings should be more authentically understood as a still moment of capture of the embodied practice of storytelling.

DRAWING AS A MULTIMODAL COMMUNICATIVE PRACTICE

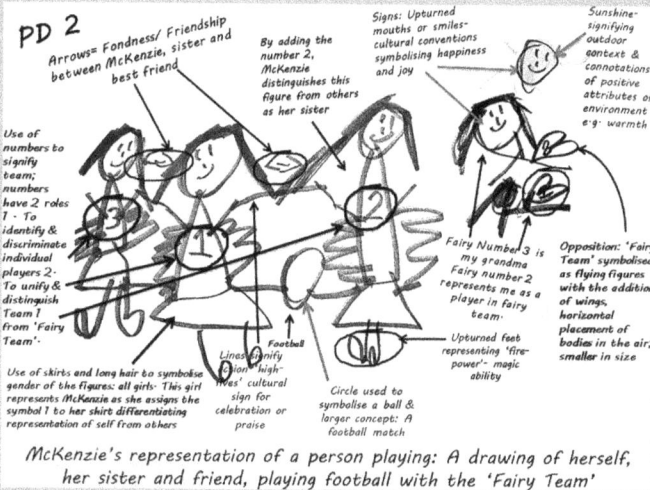

Figure 8.1 McKenzie's drawing of a football match against the fairy team (top), annotated version (bottom)

McKenzie: They had fire powers!

Duncan: Wow!

McKenzie: Like me. That's me. That's my friend [*pointing at one girl in the picture*] and she's got fire power as well. But they don't know that we have fire power, so we get the fire power and wiggled our feet… [*She flings her feet in the air, wiggling them vigorously*] and then… [*Now making stabbing motions with her feet pointed towards me*] Weee!… Weee…! We fire them with our feet!

Conversation and drawing with McKenzie (Transcription, 25 Nov. 2010)

Source: Duncan (2013)

Viewing drawing in this way has two important implications for practice. Firstly, a multi-modal social-semiotic approach recognises that young children's communication is cast across modes in dynamic ways, interwoven with their surroundings. If we are to facilitate young children's communication and expression in research, then we must create situations where they are free to exploit various modes and preferred methods for expressing their views (Kinnunen and Einarsdóttir, 2013). Each mode will have a different affordance and be more apt at representing certain concepts, ideas and experiences, as well as being more effective in different social interactions.

We also have to be aware that children's drawings can be produced in an effort to please the practitioner or researcher rather than follow their own agendas. This is particularly applicable to formal learning contexts. A practitioner, for example, can invite a child to draw whatever they wish – however the reality is that the child will make choices within this invitation based on their own understanding of what they think is expected of them within that particular social encounter (Christensen, 2004) and what they deem appropriate or safe to explore in an education setting or in the presence of a practitioner. If we revisit the theoretical framing of social semiotics, we can interpret the drawing content as potentially reflecting children's awareness of the communicational environment (Kress, 2010) – meaning that the context of drawing, and its framing by the adult, will inevitably shape what children draw. An image will therefore be guided by the child's personal interest, the audience and the most apt or available semiotic resources. Researchers and practitioners who use only prompted drawings or assign parameters to drawing activities such as drawing in silence or restricting drawing materials, run the risk of limiting the communicative potential of drawing for young children.

The second important implication for practice is that by viewing drawing as multi-modal communication, we emphasise the need to document the drawing process in its entirety. As described in the data collection process, the drawing activities were recorded using a digital camera set up on a tripod. The camera was positioned with the child and immediate context of drawing in frame to ensure I captured the children's stories in and around the drawing. On many occasions, children expressed meaning in ways which left no trace on the page. For example, McKenzie's fondness for her sister, who was featured in many of her drawings, was often expressed in her dialogue and interactions with the images. During the creation of McKenzie's drawing in Figure 8.1, she touched the image of her sister and said she was 'tickling' her sister's hair, then followed with the interesting inclusion of arrows between figures to denote their feelings towards each other. These descriptions are an essential part of the annotation process when analysing children's drawings as they allow us to privilege children's signification and perspectives as revealed through their multimodal drawing practice. Here we see links with Merewether and Fleet's discussion of pedagogical documentation (Chapter 5) being more than simply a collection of outputs or a scrapbook, but rather a narrative or story.

CHILDREN'S SIGNIFICATION

[*Pointing at one of the figures*] That's my friend helping me. My sister ... my best friend ... her black hair ... [*scribbling in the hair*] is in my team ... She likes my black hair [*drawing an arrow between the two figures*], and she liked it [*drawing an arrow between another two figures*]. And I liked it as well! [*Drawing more arrows*] ... and my sister liked it as well!

Drawing with McKenzie (Transcription, 25 Nov. 2010)

Source: Duncan (2013)

Alternative interpretations are not uncommon in the reading of children's drawings, especially in the absence of children's descriptions. Young children can produce detailed and realistic images as well as very minimal or abstract representations. We may recognise a figure in a drawing as a person, but who is this person to the child and how do they relate to their lives? For example, Figure 8.2 shows Fynn's drawing; a seemingly simple drawing of a figure with some surrounding objects. If we include his accompanying narrative, we begin to see how children's descriptions breathe life into these static images and help us understand their signification and, in this research, how it relates to children's everyday play. In this example, we learn about Fynn's deep interest in his Lego Indiana Jones video game.

FINDING THE NARRATIVE

Figure 8.2 Fynn's drawing of Indiana Jones punching the bad guys

(Continued)

Fynn:	[*Begins drawing*] This is going to be ... this is the tent of the level we have to get. So ... em ... [*goes quiet*]
Duncan:	So is that the first level?
Fynn:	Yeah, the first level against Indiana Jones.
Duncan:	Ah, OK.
Fynn:	Brown Indiana Jones [*picks up a brown pen and draws quietly until finished*]. There!
Duncan:	Oh, wow. That's really good.
Fynn:	That's Indiana Jones.
Duncan:	Ah, that's Indiana Jones. And what's he doing?
Fynn:	He is ... he's got ... he's punching the bad guys [*begins to draw another figure*]. This is the hair for the next guy ... for Lego man. And the hands ... and the mouth ... and the nose [*verbally labelling each part as he draws them*]. And this is a big giant fish [*drawing a fish*]. So what Indiana Jones' friend is gonna do is ... throw it to a fish, then throw it to a mouse [*pointing to each participant with his pen*]. The mouse is going to throw it to the mice, after it's at the mice, it's dead.
Duncan:	Is it the end of the level once you get past all those mice?
Fynn:	Yeah. The mice is the bad guys.

Conversation and drawing with Fynn (Transcription, 30 Nov. 2010)

Source: Duncan (2013)

These observations emphasise the importance of facilitating and documenting children's unfolding and tangential multimodal narratives. In this way, we can access a more comprehensive and rich account of children's views, understandings and experiences.

'DO YOU LIKE HANNAH MONTANA?' A PLAYFUL APPROACH TO DRAWING WITH YOUNG CHILDREN

If we want to learn about children through drawing, then we must allow for authentic drawing experiences. The activity must sit within its natural social framing for the child, which, particularly in the home context, is within children's play. But how do we ensure that drawing preserves its playful nature for the child in our presence?

Children will typically characterise play experiences as those which are enjoyable, interest-driven, intrinsically motivated and, importantly, experiences which are not shaped or structured by an adult (see Chapter 1 for more detail). Framing interactions in this way, the child is more likely to be engaged, motivated and feel comfortable. Equally important is the adult's ability to engage playfully. Playfulness is understood in this research as a state of mind (Youell, 2008) and a way of being. The important difference between play and the notion of playfulness is that an individual, in this case a researcher or a practitioner, may participate in a play activity without necessarily being playful or having a playful state of mind. This manner of adult interaction has the risk of altering the experience for a child from playing to participating in something that is non-play.

The visits and our interactions in the described research always revolved around play. Children play naturally and instinctively which meant they were keen to play on my arrival. I entered these interactions, whether drawing or engaging in any other form of play, viewing the child as the expert 'player', and I, the less knowledgeable and inexperienced 'player'. Adopting the child's natural repertoire and drawing practice was made simple by allowing children to guide and shape our interactions. I followed and observed the children and learned about their interests, their play things and their natural contexts for drawing. Children assigned me roles and described storylines to follow during role play or gave me a verbal blueprint of what we should build together using Lego or wooden blocks. The context of play deconstructed the formality of the social situation between the unfamiliar adult and the child and provided a dialogic space for meaningful interactions and exchanges. Notably, I engaged playfully and never led activities at the risk of altering their status to 'task'. In these play episodes, I was not perceived as a figure of authority, as indicated in the following data quote.

> You're not a lady; you're just a big girl!
> Conversation with Mia (Field notes, 17 Feb. 2011)
>
> *Source:* Duncan (2013)

Of course, this approach of open drawing, led by the child, has challenges in terms of balancing the needs of the research alongside the interests of the child (Blaisdell et al., 2019). Nevertheless, research based on interpretation always requires continual reflection on the authenticity of the data married with the focus of the study (see Chapter 6's focus on the best FIT when analysing and interpreting data).

Initially, I saw no great methodological innovation when sitting down on the floor with children and drawing. Yet the more studies I examined, the more I realised that researchers did not typically do this. Drawing with the child (if suggested or agreed to by the child) offered valuable benefits pertaining to common ethical issues surrounding research with young children. Children often view the world as adult-centric (Punch, 2002), emphasising the need to constantly strive for new approaches which challenge and disrupt traditional adult–child roles and rework the power dynamic between the researcher and the researched. In doing so, we create opportunities for children to strengthen their position in research and achieve more meaningful experiences. For example, I found that sitting on the floor at the same physical level as the child removed focus from the child as an object of inquiry – observed by a researcher as they 'produce data' – and disrupted power arising from physical difference. Drawing with children also strengthened the rapport between the adult and the child on account of both parties engaging in a shared activity as a form of parallel, social or collaborative play.

The relationship between the researcher and the researched shifted from a one-way process to a responsive and dialogic process where each learns from, engages with and responds to the others' making and creating. Approached in this way, the activity is contextualised within children's social practices and we are able to enter into children's 'cultures of communication' (Christensen, 2004). Together we would sing, laugh, look at each other's drawings, collaborate on drawings, eat snacks and learn about each other. The following example (Figure 8.3) shows how I and the child learned from each other as Eva pondered what to draw next.

DRAWING WITH CHILDREN

Eva: [*thinks for a moment*] maybe ... playing horses!!

Duncan: OK.

Eva: [*begins drawing*] and I'll draw ME!!

Duncan: Good idea.

Eva: [*begins drawing again*] ... and my horse.

[*Continues drawing*]

Eva: Do you like Hannah Montana? I love her!

Duncan: Yeah, she's got some good songs doesn't she?

Eva: Yeah. I've got her CD.

Duncan: Oh really.

Eva: [*starts singing a Hanna Montana song. Then returns to drawing*]

Duncan: That's really good.

Eva: That's my unicorn ... what colour will I do her? [*thinks while putting the pencil to her mouth*] Yellow ... that's my favourite colour [*reaching for the pen*] ... and orange ... [*touching the orange pen*] ... and pink ... [*touching the pink pen*]

Duncan: Oh, they're nice colours.

Eva: What's your favourite colour?

Figure 8.3   Eva's drawing of her horse

The nature of drawing as the practice of 'doing' also creates a space with unique and flexible social rules. Framing it within the context of play (typically viewed by children as a social and cultural space fixed within their domain) allows children to control and manipulate the situation more freely and to be open and confident in expressing their preferences, as illustrated by Tyler and Mia's comments below. There is a level of autonomy in that the familiarity of the activity means that even the youngest of children can initiate, lead and participate in drawing without adult guidance or assistance.

CHILDREN'S AUTONOMY IN DRAWING

Tyler doesn't say anything but takes some paper from my bag of drawing materials and goes back to his small table on the opposite side of the living room placing the paper on the table ... I ask if he wants me to draw with him or just sit on the sofa. He looks at me, smiles, and replies, 'Draw'. He clears a space on the table where he lays a blank piece of paper ready for me to draw next to him.

Interaction with Tyler (Field notes, 17 Jan. 2011)

Mia states that she has had enough of drawing. She places her crayon back in the packet. Instead, she suggests that 'We can go upstairs and play with baby Annabelle'.

Interaction with Mia (Field notes, 17 Feb. 2011)

Source: Duncan (2013)

CONCLUSION

When considering drawing in your own research, the following are key:

- Photograph drawings, as children may want to keep the original.
- Be flexible with time and conditions for drawing. Children will draw for different lengths of time and may see drawing as an ongoing activity, therefore may leave then return to the same drawing.
- Document the entire drawing process through detailed note-taking or video recording to gather the richness that is young children's multimodal communicative practices.
- Be aware that prompting a child to draw may alter the function of drawing for the child – shifting from something that is about playfulness, creativity and self-expression to an adult-initiated task where a correct response is perceived. This can result in sanitised accounts of children's experiences.
- Abstract concepts may be challenging to represent so be mindful of the topics being explored through drawings.

By highlighting some of the key factors to consider when using drawings to access young children's perspectives, I hope to have increased awareness of how our involvement and the framing of the methods we use can alter how a child views and responds to them, and whether the child is given the opportunity to use the method to its full communicative potential.

Drawing can provide a meaningful context for both the child and the adult. It has the potential to provide a rich and authentic space to learn about how children experience the world, using their preferred ways of sharing this. This can be achieved by, firstly, adopting playful, open-ended approaches to drawing where children do not feel bound by mode or material resource, hence are able to use their own languages (Qvortrup, 2005), and, secondly, by developing approaches which enable us as researchers and practitioners to observe, record and interpret the multiplicity of ways children convey meaning.

REFERENCES

Anning, A. and Ring, K. (2004). *Making Sense of Children's Drawings*. Maidenhead: Open University Press.

BERA (2011). *British Educational Research Association: Ethical Guidelines for Educational Research*. Nottingham: BERA.

Blaisdell, C., Arnott, L., Wall, K. and Robinson, C. (2019). Look who's talking: Using creative, playful arts-based methods in research with young children. *Journal of Early Childhood Research*, 17 (1): 14–31.

Christensen, P. H. (2004). Children's participation in ethnographic research: Issues of power and representation. *Children and Society*, 18: 165–76.

Coates, E. (2002). 'I forgot the sky!' Children's stories contained within their drawings. *International Journal of Early Years Education*, 10 (1): 21–35.

Cox, M. (2005). *The Pictorial World of the Child*. Cambridge: Cambridge University Press.

Duncan, P. (2013). Drawing as a Method for Accessing Young Children's Perspectives in Research. PhD thesis, University of Stirling, UK.

Duncan, P. (2015). Pigs, planes, and play-doh: Children's perspectives on play as revealed through their drawings. *American Journal of Play*, 8 (1): 50–73.

Einarsdóttir, J., Dockett, S. and Perry, B. (2009). Making meaning: Children's perspectives expressed through drawings. *Early Child Development and Care*, 179 (2): 217–32.

Fargas-Malet, M., McSherry, D., Larkin, E. and Robinson, C. (2010). Research with children: Methodological issues and innovative techniques. *Journal of Early Childhood Research*, 8 (2): 175–92.

Flewitt, R. (2005). Conducting research with young children: Some ethical issues. *Early Child Development and Care*, 175 (6): 553–65.

Hodge, R. and Kress, G. (1988). *Social Semiotics*. Cambridge: Polity Press.

James, A. and Prout, A. (eds.) (1997). *Constructing and Reconstructing Childhood: Contemporary Issues in the Sociological Study of Childhood*. London: Falmer Press.

Kellogg, R. (1970). *Analyzing Children's Art*. Palo Alto, CA: Mayfield Publishing Company.

Kinnunen, S. and Einarsdóttir, J. (2013). Feeling, wondering, sharing and constructing life: Aesthetic experience and life changes in young children's drawing stories. *International Journal of Early Childhood*, 45 (3): 359–85.

Kress, G. (2010). *Multimodality: A Social Semiotic Approach to Contemporary Communication*. Abingdon: Routledge.

Kress, G. and van Leeuwen, T. (1996). *Reading Images: The Grammar of Visual Design*. London: Routledge.

Lapan, S., Quartaroli, M. and Riemer, F. (2012). *Qualitative Research: An Introduction to Methods and Designs*. San Francisco, CA: Jossey-Bass.

Matthews, J. (2003). *Drawing and Painting: Children and Visual Representation*. London: Paul Chapman.

Mitchell, L. M. (2006). Child-centered? Thinking critically about children's drawings as a visual research method. *Visual Anthropology Review*, 22: 60–73.

Moyles, J. R. (1989). *Just Playing? The Role and Status of Play in Early Childhood Education*. Maidenhead: Open University Press.

Punch, S. (2002). Research with children: The same or different from research with adults? *Childhood*, 9 (3): 321–41.

Qvortrup, J. (2005). Varieties of childhood. In J. Qvortrup (Ed.), *Studies in Modern Childhood: Society, Agency, Culture*. New York: Palgrave Macmillan. pp. 1–21.

Ricci, C. (1887). *L'arte dei Bambini [The Art of Children]*. Bologna: Biblio Bazaar.

Waller, T. and Bitou, A. (2011). Research with children: Three challenges for participatory research in early childhood. *European Early Childhood Education Research Journal*, 19 (1): 5–20.

Youell, B. (2008). The importance of play and playfulness. *European Journal of Psychotherapy and Counselling*, 10 (2): 121–9.

9

OBSERVING AND INTERPRETING EMBODIED INTERACTIONS: INTERPRETING VOICE FROM BIRTH TO 3 YEARS

LORNA ARNOTT, TIMOTHY J. MCGOWAN AND JONATHAN DELAFIELD-BUTT

The majority of the examples in this book support research through play with children from 3 years and older. Of course, the chapters in Parts 1 and 2 that are foundational, theoretical and conceptual are relevant to children under 3 years old but in this Part the under-3s have yet to be explored. That is not because under-3s are less important or incapable; it simply reflects the novelty in this work. It is important to recognise that children under 3 still have valuable stories to share, and therefore this chapter offers a unique contribution to how we might draw on play and key scientific approaches to the analysis of observational data to support our understanding of children's experiences from birth to 3.

- We consider the place of consulting with, and understanding the perspectives of, children from birth to 3 years old, in a broad sense.
- The chapter is positioned within the perspective that 'voice' should not necessarily privilege verbal voice, articulating that all children also communicate in

(Continued)

embodied ways that are non-verbal. This is especially important in pre-verbal children and those who do not develop language.

• Linking with research in neuropsychology, we articulate how the embodied voice, especially evident in young children and babies' pre-verbal behaviour, communicates intentional and affective interests.

• From the above theoretical perspective, we demonstrate example ways to tune into children's intentional actions to interpret their meaning in research.

In this chapter, we take a unique approach in framing consultation with babies and very young children. We offer an interdisciplinary dialogue, as we marry perspectives on pedagogies of listening in education (Bath, 2013), as part of the overall discussion of play in this book, with the neuropsychology of infant minds (Delafield-Butt and Trevarthen, 2013; Trevarthen and Delafield-Butt, 2013). We draw on educational knowledge and high-quality early childhood pedagogies about how best to listen to children by following their actions and interests, their 'non-verbal voice' that allows access to their minds (Reddy, 2008). This technique, we will show, is routine in knowledge from neuropsychology and paediatrics (Brazelton, 2006) where we understand that even before birth, children's movements and behaviours offer an insight into the very young child's intentions and desires (Delafield-Butt and Gangopadhyay, 2013; Quintero and De Jaegher, 2020).

In Chapter 2, Murray details the rights of children to be listened to – all children, regardless of age-related competences. Yet much of the work that is taking place is still happening with older children, and the knowledge of how to consult with very young children and babies is still considered challenging. This is largely because methods for consultation with children, even play-based methods, can privilege verbal voices or means of communication which ultimately showcase children's perspectives on adults' agendas. For example, in the case described in Chapter 12 of this book, Mertala engages children in designing and building objectives related to digital play. A discrete output was sought. While this was appropriate for the more mature age group, for babies and younger children, such explicit contributions are unrealistic.

With babies and young children, it is much more challenging to start with an adult agenda and then to extract children's ideas and perspectives on matters that affect them (UN Commission on Human Rights, 1990). A shift in perspective of what we mean by listening is required to better understand babies' participation in research and design. Listening must include much more than linguistic, verbal utterances and instead take into account the infant's or non-verbal child's perspectives, understood by following their lead and reading their feelings, intentions and desires. Children communicate with one hundred languages (Malaguzzi, 1996), and in this chapter, we explore the bodily language of movement and expressive gesture. We will demonstrate through world-leading neuropsychological research that every movement made by children holds a degree of intentionality that demonstrates their motivations and feelings in expressions of body and (non-verbal) voice (Delafield-Butt and Trevarthen, 2020; Malloch et al., 2019).

Understanding that babies' movements are not arbitrary opens up possibilities to engage in fine-grained observations of babies' play to understand their perspectives, which offers a meaningful route to involving even small babies in the collection of research data about their interests and feelings of participation. This requires a particular skill in how we observe babies' movements – a process of watching and re-watching is often required. Learning this technique from how psychologists conduct observations of babies offers a route to data collection that is systematic, allowing for the collection of rigorous and articulated evidence. Findings can then be interpreted with the help of educational frameworks to successfully interpret babies' voices in early childhood practice. Furthermore, we can learn similar lessons from clinical perspectives that attend to the mental health and well-being of infants and young children (Douglas, 2007; Zeanah, 2009). Yet before we can understand these observational techniques, we must first understand the theory behind babies' intentional actions.

WHAT WE CAN LEARN FROM NEUROPSYCHOLOGY

Infant psychology now recognises the expressive movements and gestures of young babies as being intentional from birth (Delafield-Butt and Gangopadhyay, 2013; Delafield-Butt and Trevarthen, 2020; Delafield-Butt et al., 2018). They express the feelings, interests and desires of the infant through their form and direction, soliciting attention and interest in a reciprocal dialogue with others (Stern, 2000). These patterns of interaction start to form small stories that begin, develop, and very often reach a point of maximal tension in a climax, before receding to a quiet state again and concluding (Delafield-Butt and Trevarthen, 2015). Altogether, these projects are experienced as a story, or narrative event, and their experience is held in memory.

Infant narratives are made through experience and shared experience with others. They are pre-verbal and embodied, rather than being linguistic and structured by ideas and concepts, as they are in adult storytelling (Delafield-Butt, 2018). Rather, infant stories are directly experienced in body action and interaction. But despite the fact these are not told in the language that adult stories are, they hold the same temporal pattern and four-part structure of (i) introduction, (ii) development, (iii) climax, and (iv) resolution (Figure 9.1). This is a structure of human narrative meaning-making invariant across the lifespan, and it is used to share the drama of life events from birth, right though to the technical sharing of ideas in adult industry (Bruner, 1987, 1990). Narratives structure the way we experience the world and remember it in shared stories with others, or as we reflect and make plans for the future. And its lived, shared experiences can form a bedrock of meaning-making in school (Delafield-Butt and Adie, 2016).

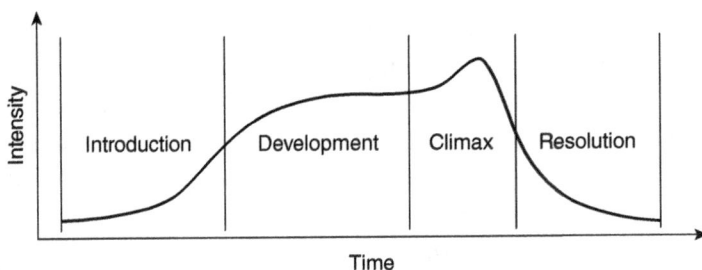

Figure 9.1   The intensity contour of a narrative over its four phases

Source: Trevarthen, C. and Delafield-Butt, J. T. (2013) Biology of shared meaning and language development: Regulating the life of narratives. In M. Legerstee, D. Haley and M. Bornstein (Eds.), *The Infant Mind: Origins of the Social Brain.* New York: Guilford Press. pp. 167–99. Reproduced with permission of the publisher.

(i) 'interest' in the narrative begins at a low intensity in the *introduction*, which 'invites' participation in purposefulness; (ii) the coordination of the actions and interests of real and imagined agents intensifies over the *development*, as the 'plan' or 'project' is developed; (iii) a peak of excitation with achievement of a goal in mutual intention is reached at the *climax*; after which (iv) the intensity reduces as the purposes of the participants share a *resolution*, and those who were closely engaged separate (Trevarthen and Delafield-Butt, 2013).

Even the pre-verbal speech of newborn infants made in proto-conversation – vocal and movement-based interactions – communicates the emotions, intentions and interests of the infant, and is important for professional understanding (Trevarthen and Delafield-Butt, 2015). A musicality of shared tempo, reciprocal to-and-fro of timbre, pitch and intensity of vocalisation altogether communicate and share reciprocal feelings and interest, and the mutual pleasure in sensitive care and support (Malloch, 2000; Malloch and Trevarthen, 2009). Interestingly, these vocal interactions follow the rules of jazz music: partners can withhold their contribution and wait for a split second, increasing dramatic tension in the expectant partner with uncertainty. Or a partner can interrupt early, disrupting the flow and creating new patterns of interaction (Gratier and Apter-Danon, 2009).

What is clear from these studies is that infants and their adult partners follow the same formal patterns of engagement, sharing feelings and interest, and structuring their discourse in shared time with each other as we do as adults. And this sharing of time and experience is deeply rooted in our common neurobiological rhythms and expectations (Trevarthen, 2009; Trevarthen et al., 2014).

This 'communicative musicality' that exists between individuals allows humans (including infants) to share time meaningfully, and collaborate not only in interaction but also in the completion of tasks (Malloch and Trevarthen, 2009). It is important to note that the definition of 'musicality' here differs somewhat from what would be generally understood by the term – it refers to the basic and foundational human ability for the production and appreciation of music (Blacking, 1969/1995), alongside other temporal endeavours such as dance or theatre. Malloch and Trevarthen (2009) link musicality with the attraction to cultural learning exhibited by humans, and the affinity and appreciation we have for moving in coordination with others (particularly within the narrative structures found in the temporal arts of music, poetry, dance and drama). Narrative structuring forms a key component of communicative musicality, bringing structure to interpersonal interactions that serve to frame knowledge and enhance the feeling within social relationships and individual experience.

The earliest form of proto-conversations, or the 'first dialogue', is evident in the imitative interactions of the neonate (newborn baby) with an adult partner (Nagy and Molnar, 2004). Neonates are sensitivite to the actions and intentions of another human being, and may imitate them from as early as the first hours after birth (e.g. Kugiumutzakis, 1998; Meltzoff & Moore, 1983, 1989). Imitation is one of multiple ways neonates can express themselves to join a shared, social behavioural repertoire (Trevarthen, 1979). The importance of these imitative interactions in building attachment and developing cultural intelligence has been supported through recent findings in neuroscience (Ammaniti and Gallese, 2014). Adults can use imitation as an effective method of engagement with infants and children yet to develop language skills. Its function runs deeper than being purely reactionary, as it enables engagement in meaningful and purposeful interaction without language for infants and children of all ages, and it can be especially important in reaching hard-to-reach children averse to social engagement, such as those with autism spectrum disorder (Delafield-Butt et al., 2020; Nadel, 2014). Neonatal imitation appears to be a foundation stone for primary intersubjectivity (a shared understanding), which goes on to develop into the full-blown proto-conversations of later infancy. It is a useful tool for professionals.

Children learn and explore the world in narrative cycles of interaction all of the time, whether in solitary play in engagement with objects or in social, intersubjective interaction with others. These narrative 'projects' underpin learning and structure communication with others. Recognising these moments of learning and communication allow researchers and practitioners to make sense of the experiences of the infant, recognising their body actions of interest or disinterest, aroused excitement or under-aroused weariness, and expressive of inner feelings of confidence or uncertainty, or pride and shame in shared performance with others (Trevarthen and Delafield-Butt, 2017). Tuning in to these embodied feelings expressed in short narratives allows the researcher or practitioner to recognise those movements as purposeful engagements that give access to the child's perspective, and that are displays – in body actions and vocalisations – of the infant's voice.

METHODS OF OBSERVATION: TRANSLATING BABIES' COMMUNICATIONS

Once tuned into the child's attempts at embodied communication, the practitioner researcher can find ways to observe and follow the child's interests and feelings to learn the story the child is creating as he or she moves step-by-step, movement-by-movement into his or her self-generated future. In this way, the infant creates his or her own world, constructing its experience and structuring it in body action that expresses his or her feelings of interest and care. The practitioner researcher must watch and observe sensitively to put one's own 'eye' in the perspective of the child. What is the infant or child attending to and experiencing now? What feelings accompany these interests and actions? Is the infant or child seeking engagement with an object, or a person of interest? Or is he or she seeking to disengage and withdraw? Why and how is he or she doing this? Through simple observation, the observer can place his or her mind into the mind of the infant or child. And the interests and feelings of the infant or child will resonate with the observer, because we have evolved as a social species to intuit the feelings and intentions of another without needing to think reflectively (mentalise) about them (Ammaniti and Gallese, 2014). By doing so, one can gain insight into the lived experiences of the young child to understand those experiences, understand where they are enjoyed and successful in their engagement with the world, and where they require support and assistance to help the infant realise his or her intentions.

In this section, we demonstrate examples of what these observations may look like when conducted in a systematic way. We present an example of a baby's attempts to communicate and how this observation is framed. After each example, we re-draw your attention to an educational perspective by analysing the case studies using key educational analytical tools.

EXAMPLE 1: ACCOMPLISHING A TASK, AND SHARING THE JOY OF SUCCESS

This example is one narrative episode taken from a chain of narratively structured projects in which a toddler walks with the support of a toy push-truck, as her father watches, films and encourages. The narrative we are interested in here follows immediately from the conclusion of another. The toddler's attention and gaze are firmly focused on her supporting partner (her father), who has been making positive vocalisations in joint celebration with her previous accomplishment. She holds her hands together in a moment of apparent contemplation lasting 1.5 seconds, closing the previous narrative with a resolution phase. Her gaze and attention remain focused on her father. Immediately following this brief pause, the toddler's attention returns to her toy truck. Her gaze shifts from her father to the handle bars of the truck and she moves her hands so as to grasp them – therefore beginning a new narrative and bringing us into its introduction phase. As soon as her hands have grasped the handle bars, the toddler's left leg makes a step forward, her gaze and focus entirely on her hands and the truck. She moves forward, placing one foot in front of the other, her gaze remaining fixed on her hands and the truck as she travels forward. Continuing to travel forward, her gaze shifts to her father and we enter the development phase of the project. Her hands remain firmly placed on the toy but her stance and weight distribution shift awkwardly as she navigates the multiple layers of this action chain. Her gaze shifts to the direction of travel as she continues to move towards her goal, her velocity increasing as the narrative progresses. Briefly, the toddler's gaze shifts to her table (containing other colourful items of interest) but she continues to travel forward. At this point, approximately 4 seconds since the beginning of the narrative, peak velocity is reached and the toddler begins to slow. The development stage of this narrative project is ending and the climatic segment is beginning. The toddler comes to a standstill, and returns her focus and gaze to her father. She releases the truck, first with her left hand, and then (after a short delay) with her right hand. As she does so, she redistributes her weight in order to maintain balance and then vocalises triumphantly, her gaze all the while remaining fixed on her supporting partner. She has successfully completed her goal, and the climax of the project and narrative has been reached. The toddler applauds herself for her accomplishment whilst maintaining eye contact with her father, encouraging him to join her in celebrating the achievement (this he does as he vocalises positively, congratulating his daughter). As the narrative begins to enter the resolution stage, the toddler stops applauding but continues to take pleasure in the completion of her goal and pride in sharing these with her caring parent. In the final acts of the project, the toddler disengages from her father, shifting her gaze back to her toy and her hands. She vocalises again to herself, gesturing and whirling with her hands as she does so. With this the narrative is concluded and the toddler starts the process of beginning a new project.

(Continued)

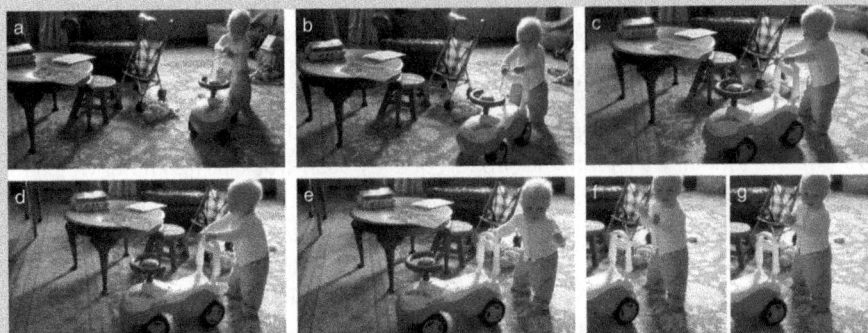

Figure 9.2   A toddler performing a short narrative project, walking with the help of a push-truck

Source: Delafield-Butt, J. (2018). The emotional and embodied nature of human understanding: Sharing narratives of meaning. In C. Trevarthen, J. Delafield-Butt and A.-W. Dunlop (Eds.), *The Child's Curriculum: Working with the Natural Voices of Young Children* © Oxford University Press, 2018. Reproduced with permission of the Licensor through PLSclear.

Note: The project (a) initiates with attention to the task and (b–d) develops over repeated steps, one in front of the other, maintaining difficult shifts in balance with support from the truck until (e–g) final conclusion, accomplishment shared with delight and applause with her father filming.

STRUCTURING OBSERVATIONS AND ANALYSIS

What we have described above, from a neuropsychology perspective, is an observation of a young child's play and learning (about how to move her body, and value moments of accomplishment with others) shared in companionship. The narrative perspective adds structure to that observation and helps unpick the meaning associated with fine-grained movements and expressions. What is really interesting when applying this perspective – that babies' movements have meaning and intentions – in an educational setting is that these fine-grained observations of children's play highlight what skilled practitioners do as part of their daily professional work with children. Detailed observation can give explicit framing of the actions and interactions in everyday settings, and taking the time to observe young children's movements and infer meaning from them adds insight and value to that work (Palaiologou, 2019). These observations form the basis for key pedagogical documentation (Fleet et al., 2017) and records of children's achievements through approaches like Learning Stories (Carr and Lee, 2019).

What we are suggesting here is that everyday observation of play and babies' and toddlers' experiences can be refined to produce data for research projects or to inform practice and to offer a unique insight into babies' perspectives. In order to do so in a way that builds on the neuropsychological knowledge of babies' intentional movements (Delafield-Butt and Trevarthen, 2020), you impose some structure on the analysis process, whether that be the focus on moment-by-moment interpretations of the contour of a narrative (see Figure 9.1) or something broader like Broadhead's Social Play Continuum, where children's reciprocal actions and behaviours are mapped out over multiple episodes of time to interpret the social nature of the play (Broadhead, 2006). Or indeed, it could be any other framework which helps structure how you interpret meaning from data, such as Laevers' well-being scale, as is discussed later in this chapter. This does not necessarily mean the observation changes. If using video to support the analysis process, for example, the play episode remains the focus, but the interpretation of that observation changes depending upon the structure imposed. The example above in Figure 9.2 could be analysed with a different frame and the insight would be different.

This process of imposing some structure on the observation analysis offers a supporting tool or guide to help you draw conclusions. For example, in the following snippet of analysis (see Figure 9.3), a 7-week-old baby interacts with her mother, practising her first smile. Her mother playfully interacts with her, making different sounds to maintain the baby's engagement and focus and to encourage a smile in response. The play interaction does not need to change to generate research data; instead, the episode only becomes data in the way that the observation is analysed and interpreted, and this is facilitated by video footage to allow the baby's experience to remain as naturalistic as possible.

In the example above the process is supported by identifying 'critical moments' in the child's playful experience; moments that represent a turning point in the play or are of some significance to the narrative. In relation to a teacher context, Coultas (2015: 32) describes these as 'the moments [that] helped them [teacher] to learn something'. The process builds on traditional approaches from disciplines like Industrial Psychology where the Critical Incident Technique was employed (Corbally, 1956) and was later re-imagined for research in educational contexts. As it became embedded in education, the identification of these critical moments offered a starting point for deep self-reflection and was often the precursor to a process of change (Labercane et al., 1998).

In Figure 9.3 below, we draw on this notion of moments of significance and turning points in the play to instigate that enhanced self-reflection. At each point that Rosie appears to shift in her expression and movement, we are afforded the opportunity to interpret the narrative of her story and infer meaning. In this case, the reflection is guided by the previous knowledge of children's narratives of communication, set out in the previous section, and is contextualised by 'storying' the video screenshots to provide necessary richness to the example.

Throughout this process, the structure imposed to help analyse the playful experience is facilitated by three components:

1. The recognition of critical moments in the play where specific elements of the baby's expression and embodied movements have significance and tell another snippet of the child's story.
2. A focus on narrative descriptions of the play experience, to contextualise the data.
3. The neuropsychological model of babies' communication processes, laid out in the previous section, helps understand the babies' attempts at communication.

Drawing conclusions from this simple and very short exploration of data (the video footage for this analysis lasted 1.08 minutes) allows us to unpick Rosie's perspective. You can see:

- The cycles of interaction emerging and the period of time that Rosie can remain focused and engaged. Her desire to interact, or not, becomes clear. We can also see how that process of re-introducing an interaction again after a period of distraction can extend the play.
- Instances of developmental milestones like first smiles or responding to her name.
- Moments of discomfort and frustration from Rosie's perspective.
- Moments of joy and her ability to express that joy.

In this example, we take what first appears to be rather complex interpretations of babies' communication, set out in neuropsychology and described in the previous sections, and apply the systematic process of observation to a simple and short extract about a playful encounter.

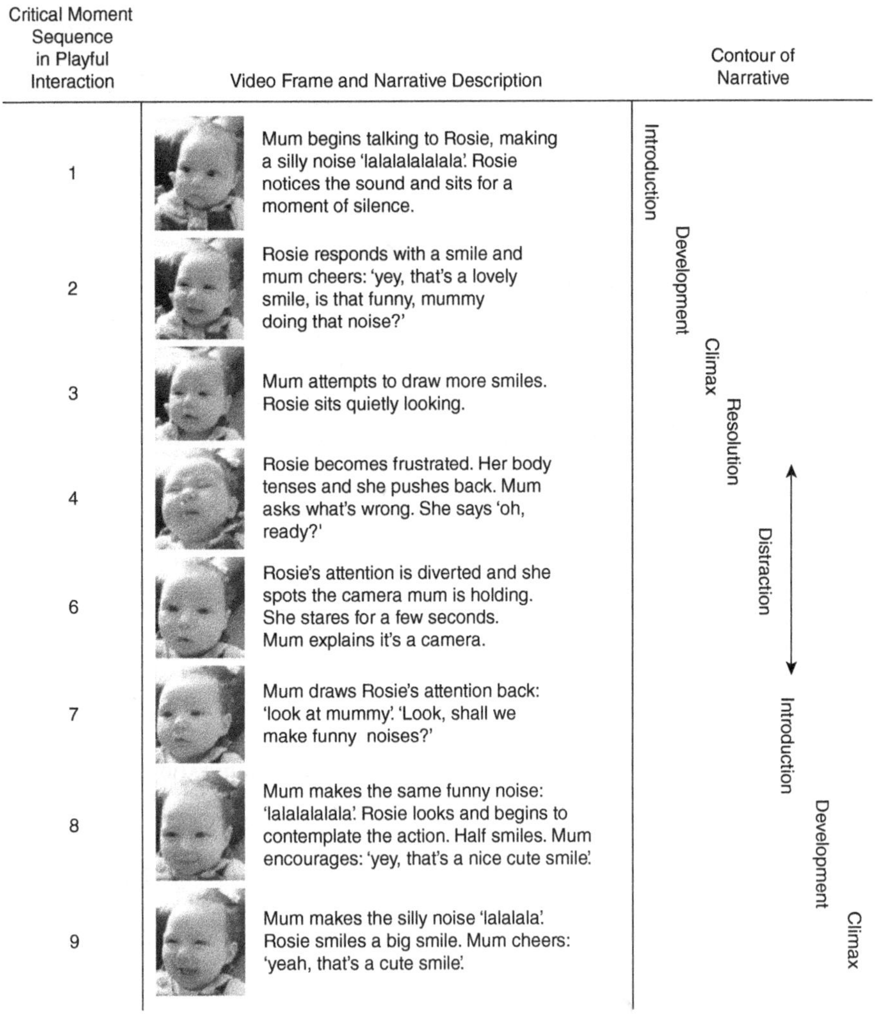

Critical Moment Sequence in Playful Interaction	Video Frame and Narrative Description	Contour of Narrative
1	Mum begins talking to Rosie, making a silly noise 'lalalalalalala'. Rosie notices the sound and sits for a moment of silence.	Introduction
2	Rosie responds with a smile and mum cheers: 'yey, that's a lovely smile, is that funny, mummy doing that noise?'	Development
3	Mum attempts to draw more smiles. Rosie sits quietly looking.	Climax / Resolution
4	Rosie becomes frustrated. Her body tenses and she pushes back. Mum asks what's wrong. She says 'oh, ready?'	Distraction
6	Rosie's attention is diverted and she spots the camera mum is holding. She stares for a few seconds. Mum explains it's a camera.	
7	Mum draws Rosie's attention back: 'look at mummy'. 'Look, shall we make funny noises?'	Introduction
8	Mum makes the same funny noise: 'lalalalalala'. Rosie looks and begins to contemplate the action. Half smiles. Mum encourages: 'yey, that's a nice cute smile'.	Development
9	Mum makes the silly noise 'lalalala'. Rosie smiles a big smile. Mum cheers: 'yeah, that's a cute smile'.	Climax

Figure 9.3   Rosie's smile and contour of narrative

Although the theory about babies' communication may seem complex, when applied with an educational lens, we show that the process is important, relevant and applicable in early childhood settings for practitioner research. We then begin to understand that neuropsychology gives us a grounding to govern our analysis in rigorous ways and with the confidence that we are understanding the child's story.

Such analysis could be extended with alternative frameworks to help support how you interrogate the data and draw meaning. For example, you could re-analyse the data from the perspective of key pedagogical tools, such as Ferre Laevers' emotional well-being scale (2017). Laevers' process may be better suited to longitudinal interpretations of a particular child, but nevertheless the various points on the scale can still help structure interpretations of a snapshot in time. In doing so, you gain a new interpretation of the data. You can even combine two approaches to analyse across frameworks to see similarities or differences (Figure 9.4).

Critical Moment Sequence in Playful Interaction	Video Frame and Narrative Description	Contour of Narrative	Laevers' Emotional Well-Being Scale
1	 Mum begins talking to Rosie, making a silly noise 'lalalalalalala'. Rosie notices the sound and sits for a moment of silence.	Introduction	Moderate
2	 Rosie responds with a smile and mum cheers 'yey, that's a lovely smile, is that funny, mummy doing that noise?'	Development	High
3	 Mum attempts to draw more smiles. Rosie sits quietly looking.	Climax	Moderate
4	 Rosie becomes frustrated. Her body tenses and she pushes back. Mum asks what's wrong. She says 'oh, ready?'	Resolution	Extremely low
6	 Rosie's attention is diverted and she spots the camera mum is holding. She stares for a few seconds. Mum explains it's a camera.	Distraction	Moderate
7	 Mum draws Rosie's attention back 'look at mummy'. 'Look, shall we make funny noises?'	Introduction	
8	 Mum makes the same funny noise 'lalalalalala'. Rosie looks and begins to contemplate the action. Half smiles. Mum encourages 'yey, that's a nice cute smile'.	Development	High
9	 Mum makes the silly noise 'lalalala'. Rosie smiles a big smile. Mum cheers, 'yeah that's a cute smile'.	Climax	Extremely High

Figure 9.4 Extended analysis

What was key in this episode, when comparing the neuropsychological framework to Laevers' well-being scale (2017), was that it became clear that the two frameworks somewhat align. The contours of the narrative of communication tied in with varying levels of emotional well-being. As you see the conversation reaching a climax, so too is the child's emotional well-being, according to Laevers' scale. This drops as the communication narrative is interrupted by a period of distraction, and then increases again as the communication narrative is re-introduced.

By adopting this approach, you make reasoned judgements and choices about what to analyse and from what perspective. The episode can be interpreted differently depending upon your conceptual or theoretical stance. This process of adopting a particular stance was described in Part 2 and is also reaffirmed in Chapter 11 where Marilyn Fleer demonstrates the influence of a Vygotskian perspective in shaping her findings. As Nutbrown points out in Chapter 6, high-quality research makes this process of analysis explicit. Thus, we are not suggesting here that this is the only way to understand babies' voices in practice, but rather that, for us, drawing on the neuropsychological knowledge of children's intentional movements provides us with a framework to guide our interpretation and offers us a degree of confidence in the findings.

ETHICAL CONSIDERATIONS

One practical consideration which must be deliberated in this chapter is the complexity of ensuring assent or consent with babies to participate in research. As the UNCRC (UN Commission on Human Rights, 1990) continues to guide the children's rights movement, and countries likes Scotland begin to enshrine the convention in Scots Law, now more than ever we must make an attempt to be respectful of children's rights to participate (or not) in research (see Chapters 2, 3 and 7 for more on this). While more challenging when working with babies, it should not be disregarded as impossible. Palaiologou, for example, has developed an Ethical Helix as a set of reflective questions which researchers and practitioners may ask themselves when conducting research with babies to better evaluate the child's desire to assent to or dissent from participation (Arnott et al., 2020; Palaiologou, 2015). Consent or assent should not privilege verbal voice because we know when considering children's participation that 'training in "listening" skills should take appropriate account of the range of non-verbal "cues" which children deploy when expressing themselves' (Lundy, 2007: 937). What we have described in this chapter is that one form of 'listening' to children requires attuning to their experiences and listening to their interests and feelings by attending to their embodied forms of non-verbal communication, and the structure of those actions through time in narratives of solitary play or shared engagement. Thus, the same principle of interpretation and inference of non-verbal expression for understanding communication can be extended to issues of consent with children under 3 years old and those with language delays.

While we do not have space here to debate this process in full, we advocate the need to make ethical choices, engage in iterative critical reflection and attempt to interpret babies' expressions in considerate ways when involving them in research.

CONCLUSION

This chapter combines knowledge from neuropsychology about children's communication capabilities with knowledge of pedagogies when working with babies/toddlers to arrive at some practical examples of how children's communication techniques can be utilised in research data to help understand the child's perspective. The chapter extends new knowledge that babies' actions are intentional from birth, and so research data at this stage doesn't need to be overly complex but instead should find ways to document and observe children's patterns of communication to understand meaning.

Importantly, this chapter demonstrates techniques which relate to pedagogy:

- For practitioners – you already listen to children, but this chapter articulates how this information can be translated to serve research or develop practice.
- For researchers – it documents the need to look at pedagogy and children's ways of communicating to pinpoint what to focus on in your data collection.

By amalgamating interdisciplinary perspectives from neuropsychology with pedagogies relating to children's play and listening in early childhood education, this chapter offers a useful approach to help solidify what observations of embodied actions, engagements and interactions may look like in practice and in research in order to articulate infant, young children's and non-verbal children's perspectives.

REFERENCES

Ammaniti, M. and Gallese, V. (2014). *The Birth of Intersubjectivity: Psychodynamics, Neurobiology, and the Self.* New York: Norton.

Arnott, L., Martinez-Lejarreta, L., Wall, K., Blaisdell, C. and Palaiologou, I. (2020). Reflecting on three creative approaches to informed consent with children under six. *British Educational Research Journal,* 46 (4): 786–810.

Bath, C. (2013). Conceptualising listening to young children as an ethic of care in early childhood education and care. *Children & Society,* 27 (5): 361–71.

Blacking, J. (1969/1995). The value of music in human experience. *The 1969 Yearbook of the International Folk Music Council*. Chicago, IL: University of Chicago Press. (Republished as Chapter 1: Expressing human experience through music. In P. Bohlman and B. Nettl (Eds.) (1995). *Music, Culture and Experience: Selected Papers of John Blacking*. Chicago, IL: University of Chicago Press.)

Brazelton, T. B. (2006). *Touchpoints: Birth to Three*. Cambridge, MA: Da Capo Press.

Broadhead, P. (2006). Developing an understanding of young children's learning through play: The place of observation, interaction and reflection. *British Journal of Educational Research*, 32 (2): 191–207.

Bruner, J. S. (1987). *Actual Minds, Possible Worlds*. Cambridge, MA: Harvard University Press.

Bruner, J. S. (1990). *Acts of Meaning*. Cambridge, MA: Harvard University Press.

Carr, M. and Lee, W. (2019). *Learning Stories in Practice*. London: Sage.

Corbally Jr, J. E. (1956). The critical incident technique and educational research. *Educational Research Bulletin*, 35 (3): 57–62.

Coultas, V. (2015). Case studies of teachers' understandings of the pedagogy of classroom talk: Some critical moments explored. *Literacy*, 50: 32–39. DOI: 10.1111/lit.12065.

Delafield-Butt, J. (2018). The emotional and embodied nature of human understanding: Sharing narratives of meaning. In C. Trevarthen, J. Delafield-Butt and A.-W. Dunlop (Eds.), *The Child's Curriculum: Working with the Natural Voices of Young Children*. Oxford: Oxford University Press.

Delafield-Butt, J. and Adie, J. (2016). The embodied narrative nature of learning: Nurture in school. *Mind, Brain, & Education*, 10 (2): 117–31.

Delafield-Butt, J. T. and Gangopadhyay, N. (2013). Sensorimotor intentionality: The origins of intentionality in prospective agent action. *Developmental Review*, 33 (4): 399–425.

Delafield-Butt, J. T. and Trevarthen, C. (2013). Theories of the development of human communication. *Theories and Models of Communication*. DOI: https://doi.org/10.1515/9783110240450.199.

Delafield-Butt, J. T. and Trevarthen, C. (2015). The ontogenesis of narrative: From moving to meaning. *Frontiers in Psychology*. DOI: https://doi.org/10.3389/fpsyg.2015.01157.

Delafield-Butt, J. and Trevarthen, C. (2020). Infant Intentions: The role of agency in learning with affectionate companions. In M. Peter (Ed.), *Encyclopedia of Teacher Education*. Singapore: Springer Nature.

Delafield-Butt, J. T., Freer, Y., Perkins, J., Skulina, D., Schögler, B. and Lee, D. N. (2018). Prospective organization of neonatal arm movements: A motor foundation of embodied agency, disrupted in premature birth. *Developmental Science*, 21 (6): e12693.

Delafield-Butt, J. T., Zeedyk, M. S., Harder, S., Vaever, M. S. and Caldwell, P. (2020). Making meaning together: Embodied narratives in a case of severe autism. *Psychopathology*, 53 (2): 60–73.

Douglas, H. (2007). *Containment and Reciprocity: Integrating Psychoanalytic Theory and Child Development Research for Work with Children*. London and New York: Routledge.

Fleet, A., Patterson, C., Robertson, J. and Robertson, J. (2017). *Pedagogical Documentation in Early Years Practice: Seeing through Multiple Perspectives*. London: Sage.

Gratier, M. and Apter-Danon, G. (2009). The musicality of belonging: Repetition and variation in mother–infant vocal interaction. In S. Malloch and C. Trevarthen (Eds.), *Communicative Musicality*. Oxford: Oxford University Press.

Kugiumutzakis, G. (1998). Neonatal imitation in the intersubjective companion space. In S. Braten (Ed.), *Intersubjective Communication and Emotion in Early Ontogeny* (pp. 63–88). Cambridge: Cambridge University Press.

Labercane, G., Last, S., Nichols, S. and Johnson, W. (1998). Critical moments and the art of teaching. *Teacher Development*, 2 (2): 191–205. DOI: 10.1080/13664539800200050.

Laevers, F. (2017). How are children doing in ECEC? Monitoring quality within a process-oriented approach. In German Youth Institute (Ed.), *Monitoring Quality in Early Childhood Education and Care*. pp. 178–200. Available at: www.dji.de/fileadmin/user_upload/bibs2017/Monitoring_Sammelband_E_final.pdf (accessed 15 November 2020).

Lundy, L. (2007). 'Voice' is not enough: Conceptualising Article 12 of the United Nations Convention on the Rights of the Child. *British Educational Research Journal*, 33 (6): 927–42.

Malaguzzi, L. (1996). *The Hundred Languages of Children: The Reggio Emilia Approach to Early Childhood Education*. Norwood, NJ: Ablex Publishing Corporation.

Malloch, S. (2000). Mothers and infants and communicative musicality. *Musicae Scientiae*, Special Issue on Rhythms, Musical Narrative, and the Origins of Human Communication, 3: 29–57.

Malloch, S. and Trevarthen, C. (2009). Musicality: Communicating the vitality and interests of life. In S. Malloch and C. Trevarthen (Eds.), *Communicative Musicality: Exploring the Basis of Human Companionship* (pp. 1–12). Oxford: Oxford University Press.

Malloch, S., Delafield-Butt, J. and Trevarthen, C. (2019). Embodied musicality of infant intersubjectivity in learning and teaching. In M. A. Peters (Ed.), *Encyclopedia of Teacher Education*. Singapore: Springer Singapore. pp. 1–5.

Meltzoff, A. N. and Moore, M. K. (1983). Newborn infants imitate adult facial gestures. *Child Development*, 54 (3): 702–9.

Meltzoff, A. N. and Moore, M. K. (1989). Imitation in newborn infants: Exploring the range of gestures imitated and the underlying mechanisms. *Developmental Psychology*, 25 (6): 954–62.

Nadel, J. (2014). *How Imitation Boosts Development in Infancy and Autism Spectrum Disorder*. Oxford: Oxford University Press.

Nagy, E. and Molnar, P. (2004). Homo imitants or homo provocans? Human imprinting model of neonatal imitations. *Infant Behavior and Development*, 27 (1): 54–63.

Palaiologou, I. (2015). Ethical issues associated with educational research. In I. Palaiologou, M. Needham and T. Male (Eds.), *Doing Research in Education: Theory and Practice*. London: Sage.

Palaiologou, I. (2019). *Child-Observation: A Guide for Students of Early Childhood*. London: Sage.

Quintero, A. M. and De Jaegher, H. (2020). Pregnant agencies: Movement and participation in maternal–fetal interactions. *Frontiers in Psychology*. DOI: https://doi.org/10.3389/fpsyg.2020.01977.

Reddy, V. (2008). *How Infants Know Minds*. Cambridge, MA: Harvard University Press.

Stern, D. N. (2000). *The Interpersonal World of the Infant: A View from Psychoanalysis and Development Psychology* (2nd edn). New York: Basic Books.

Trevarthen, C. (1979). Communication and cooperation in early infancy: A description of primary intersubjectivity. In M. Bullowa (Ed.), *Before Speech: The Beginning of Human Communication*. London: Cambridge University Press. pp. 321–47.

Trevarthen, C. (2009). Human biochronology: On the source and functions of 'musicality'. In R. Haas and V. Brandes (Eds.), *Music that Works*. Vienna: Springer. pp. 221–65.

Trevarthen, C. and Delafield-Butt, J. T. (2013). Biology of shared meaning and language development: Regulating the life of narratives. In M. Legerstee, D. Haley and M. Bornstein (Eds.), *The Infant Mind: Origins of the Social Brain*. New York: Guilford Press. pp. 167–99.

Trevarthen, C. and Delafield-Butt, J. T. (2015). The infant's creative vitality, in projects of self-discovery and shared meaning: How they anticipate school, and make it fruitful. In S. Robson and S. F. Quinn (Eds.), *International Handbook of Young Children's Thinking and Understanding*. Abingdon and New York: Routledge. pp. 3–18.

Trevarthen, C. and Delafield-Butt, J. T. (2017). Intersubjectivity in the imagination and feelings of the infant: Implications for education in the early years. In E. J. White and C. Dalli (Eds.), *Under-Three Year Olds in Policy and Practice*. New York: Springer. pp. 17–39.

Trevarthen, C., Gratier, M. and Osborne, N. (2014). The human nature of culture and education. *Wiley Interdisciplinary Reviews: Cognitive Science*, 5 (2): 173–92.

UN Commission on Human Rights (1990). *Convention on the Rights of the Child* (E/CN.4/RES/1990/74), 7 March. Available at: www.refworld.org/docid/3b00f03d30.html (accessed 5 September 2020).

Zeanah, C. H. (2009). *Handbook of Infant Mental Health* (3rd edn). New York: The Guilford Press.

10

THE USE OF PEDAGOGICAL DOCUMENTATION AND ARTISTIC LANGUAGES IN RESEARCH WITH YOUNG CHILDREN

ELISABETTA BIFFI, IOANNA PALAIOLOGOU AND FRANCA ZUCCOLI

In Chapter 5, Merewether and Fleet presented an overview of pedagogical documentation, and the complexity associated with the approach, to explore children's experiences and research through play. The current chapter offers practical examples of what pedagogical documentation could entail when used in a research project. The focus is different from Merewether and Fleet in some ways because in this chapter we show how pedagogical documentation can be used as a methodology with arts-informed methods as a play based approach for participatory research with children.

Thus, this chapter aims to explore:

- The nature of pedagogical documentation for capturing the educational experiences of children;
- The nature of pedagogical documentation as a methodology for participatory research;
- The use of arts in research as a method of involving children in their meaning-making that words sometimes cannot achieve.

A s has been discussed elsewhere in this book, the quest for participatory research has led to the examination of child-friendly, play-based methods that are mainly qualitative, such as observations, use of visual media, narrative inquiries and forms of art such as drawings, the most influential approach being the Mosaic Approach introduced by Clark and Moss (2001). Research has also examined ways of documenting children's voices, with an emphasis on pedagogical documentation (see Chapter 5) as a friendly and playful way to make children's voices and experiences heard and visible through recording them in a variety of ways (e.g. Biffi, 2019). Such approaches have led to task-based methods with children, such as drawings, photographs and videos, or a merging of traditional methods with a playful context such as play-based interviews, to make comprehensible meaning of children's lives. However in this chapter, based on a transnational study, we aim to explore how pedagogical documentation can be used as a 'methodological attitude' (Gallacher and Gallagher, 2008: 513) with arts-informed methods as our main tool for data collection.

This book explores research through play in a broad and eclectic sense. In this chapter, we take a complementary approach to researching through play where we explore arts-informed methods and link this to well-established notions of pedagogical documentation, which, as Merewether and Fleet have described in Chapter 5, are well placed to unpick children's natural play experiences. Play-based approaches often enhance children's experiences in taking part in research and offer a shift from adult-oriented control to a child-friendly data collection where consideration is given to children's rights, their languages (oral or embodied) are respected and the context is familiar to and suitable for them. Arts-informed methods and how they are used in our study cannot be characterised as play-based methods. Nevertheless, their inclusion in this book is still helpful because arts-informed methods do have playful attributes where children can express themselves through creativity; however, the actual techniques to be used (e.g drawing, drama) are adult- rather than child-initiated approaches.

The chapter starts with the context of the study, then discusses a means of recording children's experiences to locate our argument for pedagogical documentation as methodology and not simply as a research strategy. Arts-informed methods are explored as a way to collect data to enable children's involvement in their meaning-making process. Finally, we conclude that such an approach enables children to take part in research by 'listening' to their many languages.

THE STUDY

This chapter is based on a transnational project, the purposes of which were twofold. Firstly, it aimed to examine how children understand abstract concepts and express them; secondly, we were interested in exploring methodology and methods that allow children to elicit their voices to make meaning and engage with research that maybe would have not been possible through language only. Building on valuing children's 'Hundred Languages' (Malaguzzi, 1996), children in our research are positioned as being able to reflect on ideas and concepts with high levels of complexity (Bateson, 1972), make meaning of their own experiences and thus engage in research. This engagement was conceptualised as being how children express their ideas and feelings beyond 'the limiting constraints of discursive communication in order to express meanings' (Barone and Eisner, 2012: 1) within 'a semiotic modality, presentational, orientational and [where] organisational semiotic interpretation is both gestalt and iterative' (Lemke, 2002: 305) (see Chapter 8 for more on semiotic multi-modality).

Thus, we employed pedagogical documentation as a methodology, as it allows for the recording of children's voices in a variety of ways. Arts-informed methods were chosen as the main method of data collection to offer data not dependent merely on oral and/or written language, but also on other modes of expression which enable children to represent their own lives. These methods also offered a route that linked with children's natural play experiences, despite not being child-led.

The abstract concepts of inside/outside were also considered for their several dimensions. Examining relevant research, it was found that these concepts can refer to real space, with a connection to a special dimension such as school buildings and classrooms (Clark, 2010), as well as to embodied spaces and their influence in learning experienced by children and adults (Farman, 2015). They also align with social relationships and how one positions oneself within a group. Finally, perceptions of the inside/outside reflect on the sense of self (identity) which mirrors how one expresses meanings and ideas to relate to space and interact with others. So, in our research, data collection was conducted under three main themes: Space, Social Relationships and Self (identity), facilitated by arts-informed techniques (artistic language).

In this chapter, we present examples from the Italian and English data with children aged 3–6 years. This data was collected in a wider project including early childhood education setting, children (aged 12 months–6 years) and educators in Italy, Greece, the UK (England), Norway and Japan. The researcher in each country carried out the data collection with educators and children as part of their pedagogical documentation within practice. The main artistic techniques used were: drawing, collage, cartography, drama, sculpting, video, digital animation and dance.

PEDAGOGICAL DOCUMENTATION FOR UNDERSTANDING EDUCATIONAL EXPERIENCE

To explain how pedagogical documentation was used as a methodology, it is important to see how we conceptualise it. In capturing children's experiences, we draw upon the principles of pedagogical documentation as a tool to claim that it can be used as a methodology in research. As shown elsewhere in this book (see Chapter 5), pedagogical documentation has been recognised as an effective way of capturing not only children's experiences, but also the educational experiences of early childhood education. However, in our study we conceptualise pedagogical documentation in line with Biffi (2019: 71–2), who argues that the traditional cycle of pedagogical documentation of 'observe-think-act-document-reflect' should be enriched with 'explore-collect-assemble-perform' (see Figure 10.1). Such an approach:

> offers an effective strategy for tapping into the multiple dimensions of human experience in its overall complexity ... Thus, the documentation ... is not only defined as pedagogical because of the nature of its object (i.e. the education and development of children) but also, and above all, because of how it is conceived and put into practice: it is itself an educational opportunity for all involved. (Biffi, 2019: 78)

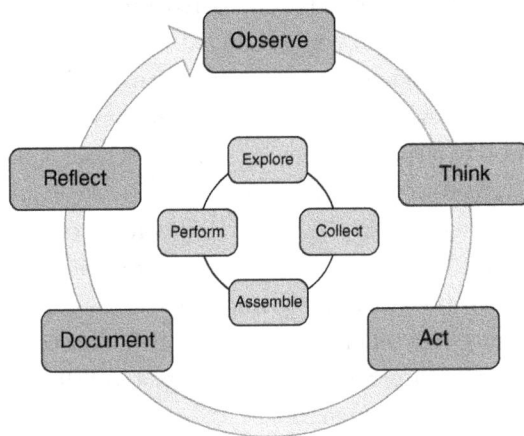

Figure 10.1   Conceptualisation of pedagogical documentation (Biffi, 2019: 71)

Source: Copyright © 2019 From 'Pedagogical documentation as a shared experience of understanding childhood' by Biffi, E. in Understanding Pedagogic Documentation in Early Childhood Education: Revealing and reflecting on high quality learning and teaching J. Formoshino & J. Peeters. Reproduced by permission of Taylor and Francis Group, LLC, a division of Informa plc.

Inspired by the Reggio Emilia philosophy, pedagogical documentation can be viewed as a specific strategy for educators and children (Rinaldi, 2012), which moves from observing children to developing an action and evaluating the action itself, to allow a return to the action with an increased pedagogical awareness. The approach is rooted in the idea that children are rich, competent and capable of acting autonomously in their own creative ways (Malaguzzi, 1996), where:

> a young child exists just if there is an adult next to him that gives him/her voice, that valourizes his/her competences and his/her potentialities. Documenting means taking

the responsibility of giving visibility and value to the children and to the ones that work and live with them ... It means – as Carla Rinaldi says (2009) – making the culture of childhood visible. In this perspective, giving visibility to pedagogical actions through documentation represents a democratic practice ... or participation for all involved subjects, it allows share and exchange, making difference visible, recognisable and valuable. (Malavasi and Zoccatelli, 2012: 37)

Pedagogical documentation mainly relies on observations and evaluation of recordings that blend visuals, artistic artefacts and narratives. The main focus has 'an educational intentionality that attunes children and educators' participation in co-constructing learning journeys' (Oliveira-Formoshino and de Sousa, 2019: 35). At its heart is the notion that educators and children are the 'protagonists' of their experiences (Biffi, 2019) so that these experiences are recorded and shared in a meaningful way to everyone (teachers, children and families). Based on the participatory nature and value of pedagogical documentation and its multi-modal presentation, in our quest for a methodology that encapsulates all modes of children's expressions when meaning-making, it made sense to conceptualise it as a methodology.

PEDAGOGICAL DOCUMENTATION AS 'METHODOLOGICAL ATTITUDE' RESEARCHING EXPERIENCES

Children's participation in research is now a dominant discourse with researchers who have been examining methods that can engage young children as partners (i.e. research with children). Although much research examines methods, few attempts have been made to examine alternative methodologies based on playful contexts beyond qualitative ones. We argue for the importance of examining methodologies rooted in playful elements and attitudes to make research accessible to educators, children and their families, rather than adopting or importing other related disciplines.

Previously it was argued that participatory research with young children cannot be fully achieved just by children taking part and by the use of child-friendly methods (Pascal and Bertram, 2009), but also requires shared methodological understandings (Gallacher and Gallagher, 2008: 513). In this study, we conceptualise methodology as an attitude where all participants (children and adults) are respected for their diversities, can engage in contextualised ways with the research process (e.g. play-based) and can narrate it in an ethical, emotional and cognisant way.

Thus, building on the principles of pedagogical documentation as a participatory and democratic tool in practice, we conceptualise it as a methodological attitude in research. As such, we define it as a bricolage based not only on linguistic and written narratives, but also on visuals such as artistic work. Subsequently, pedagogical documentation as a methodology becomes a platform for research that gives children more than a voice because it allows for the connection of actions, emotions and the patterns that shaped them. All these relate to tell the story of the connected research events that represent multiple realities to make meaning, filtering them through the lenses of participants.

EXAMPLE FROM THE ENGLISH DATA

A teacher with a group of 17 children aged 4 and 5 years old leads the process of explaining to the children the research project. She explains that the research aims to collect their views on what inside/outside means. The aim is for the children to choose materials to create a collage of what inside/outside means to them. With the use of photographs, she initiates the discussion of what inside/outside might mean to the children. The teacher writes down what the children are saying (Figure 10.2).

This is a fairly common play-based approach, whereby preceding many play activities, verbal consultation takes place with children, whose perspectives are scribed onto some sort of visual representation, like a spider diagram. Thus, while adult-led, the approach represents a pedagogically playful tool that children can engage with.

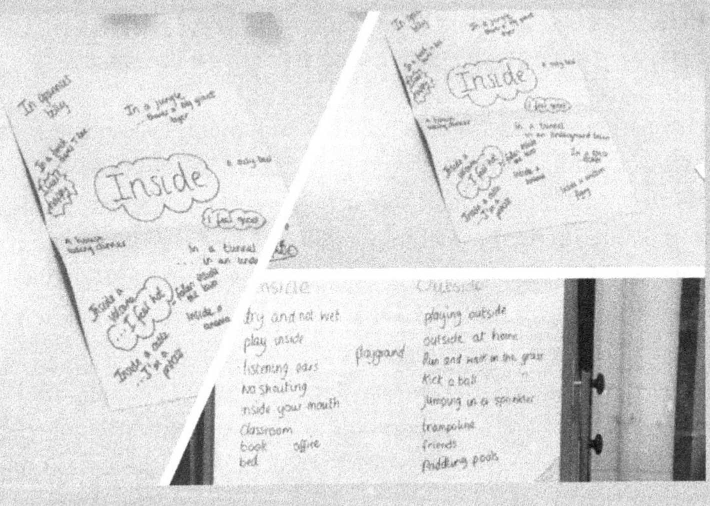

Figure 10.2 Children's ideas of what inside/outside means

After the initial discussion, the teacher encourages the children to choose materials to create their collages of what the terms mean to them. Children start producing two collages, either in pairs or individually, for the inside and the outside, shown in Figure 10.3, with final representations shown below in Figure 10.4.

Figure 10.3   Children choose materials for their collages

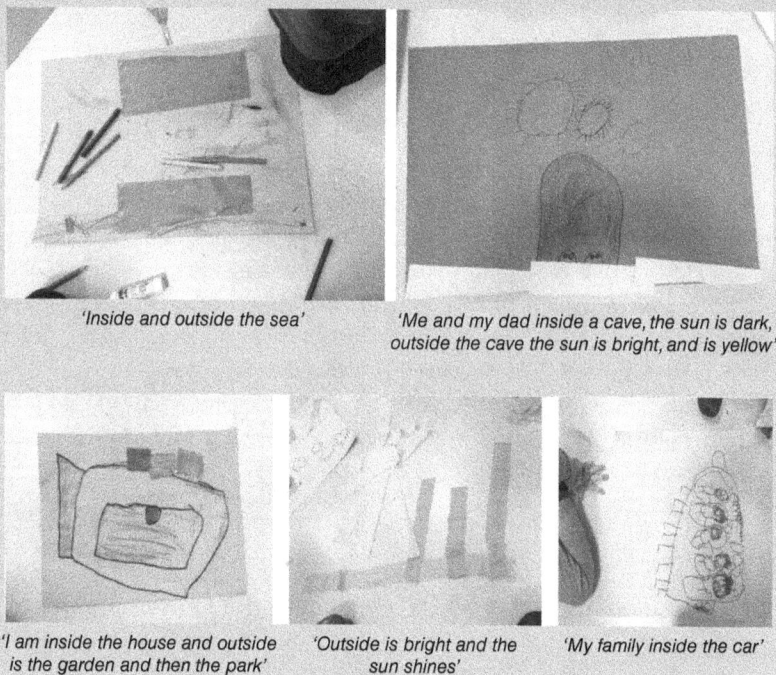

'Inside and outside the sea'   *'Me and my dad inside a cave, the sun is dark, outside the cave the sun is bright, and is yellow'*

'I am inside the house and outside is the garden and then the park'   *'Outside is bright and the sun shines'*   *'My family inside the car'*

Figure 10.4   Examples of children's artistic creations

Two girls leave the area where children were creating their drawings and collages, and move into the deconstructed role-play area. They start by asking each other what inside/

(Continued)

outside means and pretending they keep notes. Then they try to say what inside/outside means to them with materials from the role-play area to create a 'stage' with a 'curtain' where they can be both inside and outside (i.e. although inside, they can see the outside as well). They ask the researcher whether they can audio-record their discussion and take photos of what they are doing.

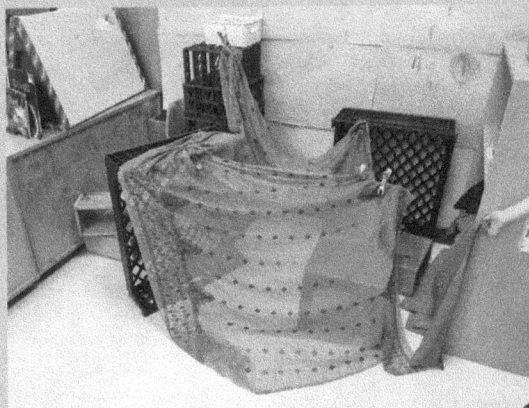

Figure 10.5   'Our stage inside, but we can see what happens outside'

Here we see that the children were stimulated by the research activity and, through their social connectivity, took control of their own documentation. Although the suggested method was to create a collage, they decided to use ephemeral (temporary) materials as they knew the drawing or the collage would not stay there, and asked the researcher to use the digital recorder to capture their 'notes' and to take photographs of their representation of inside/outside. In that sense, they chose their own methodology: photography and recording to document their views and visualise them via their creation (Figure 10.5). Thus, they used their imagination to express their thoughts about the concepts. As such, documentation as a methodological attitude enabled them to explore their views and reshape the methods used.

In line with our positioning in this study, we view young children taking part in research as not only being about oral and/or written words, but also about representing the emotional cognisance of their lives through other modes – such as the above boxed example – and how they relate to themselves in the situations researched. Thus, we propose the conceptualisation of pedagogical documentation as a methodology as it offers an opportunity for young children to express themselves in diverse modes where they feel comfortable, allowing them to make meaning of their experiences *per se* and *per time* rather than based on merely oral and/or written interpretations. It represents an approach more aligned with their natural curiosity to explore in playful ways.

In that sense, children are viewed as omniscient. The term is used as a metaphor to describe a wise child that has his/her own views, not filtered by adults and able to know, see and contribute beyond what is communicated with language only.

Such a conceptualisation allows for a view that in research with young children some things cannot be narrated with words only, thus the use of pedagogical documentation as a methodological bricolage telling of diverse modes (oral, gestural, visual, arts) allows for sharing with others the deeper meanings of those actions. Moreover, it offers opportunities for children to connect with their personal understandings of these actions and express them, which might be difficult with a written text. The bricolage telling of the research process allows for the creation of events, however, 'by means of structures and the "bricoleur" [children in this case] creating structures by means of events' (Levi-Strauss, 1962: 22). Thus, we argue in the next section that the meaning of these events and actions can be captured with arts-informed methods, as:

> when young children create art, they can be expressing astonishing conceptual understandings and imagination, well beyond what they can communicate through language. (McArdle and Wright, 2014: 22)

USING ARTS TO EXPRESS EMOTIONS: AN EXAMPLE FROM THE ENGLISH DATA

Thomas (3 years old – not real name[1]) participated in a circle time when photos were shown on the theme of inside/outside and the teacher asked how the children felt about it and what it meant to them.

Figure 10.6 Children in the carpet area are shown photos of inside and outside

(Continued)

---

[1]Psuedonyms used throughout.

Thomas did not participate during this brief discussion despite the teacher prompting him to speak. At the end, the teacher explained to the researcher that Thomas had some difficulty in expressing his views either in a group or on a one-to-one basis. After the circle time, the teacher encouraged the children to move to the 'creative arts' area to choose any materials they wanted and start creating their own collage of inside/outside.

Thomas worked with two other children of the same age to create a collage. Thomas did not actively take part but just watched the other two as they started creating the inside of a house by putting down beds, chairs, tables and then a fence to protect the house. Thomas then picked up some silver paper, sticks and red strings and went to the corner of the A2 paper that the other two children were using to make a house, and glued them onto the paper. He said that he was making a volcano and the white sticks were the lava, with the red strings the fire. The teacher asked him where the volcano would be and he said 'it is scary, so it will be outside the house and far far away'. The teacher then asked him to say how he felt about the volcano: Thomas said it was scary and that he would run straightaway into the house the other two children created when he saw the lava approaching. He pointed to the bed they had made and said 'I will hide inside the bed'. The teacher asked him why and Thomas replied 'because it is warm and makes me feel safe'.

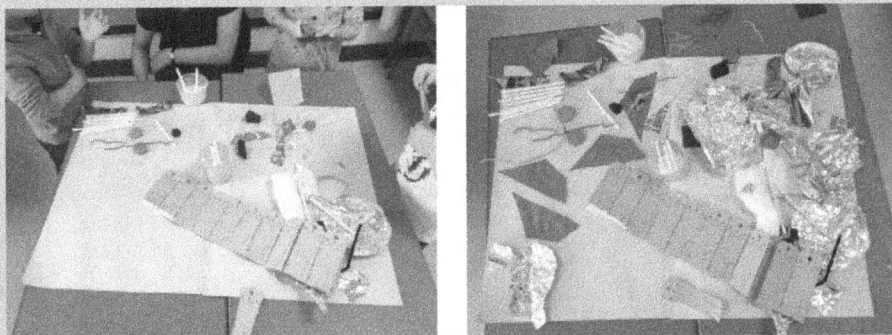

Figure 10.7   'Our house with the volcano far away ... the fence protects us'

In this example, we can see that although Thomas did not articulate his feelings and views when first shown the photos, when he took part in the collage, he was able to start expressing his feelings and thoughts. The process of engaging in activities similar to those play experiences normally apparent in early childhood education, created a space for Thomas to feel comfortable in taking part.

METHODS OF ARTS AS INFORMING PEDAGOGICAL DOCUMENTATION

The choice to use artistic languages (such as drawing, photography, collage and bodily movement) derived from the desire to offer children an opportunity to express their experiences. Asking them to explore the theme proposed through the simple use of words could have excluded some children who are not yet able to manage, in a complete way, the linguistic dimension. This was the case with Thomas. The possibility for children to express themselves in more than one way, possibly through playful activities, and to be able to model their way of thinking with their way of sharing their ideas is not only a needed opportunity, but also an authentic right, as stated in Article 13 of the United Nations Convention on the Rights of the Child (UN Commission on Human Rights, 1990):

> The child has the right to freedom of expression. This right includes the freedom to search, receive and disseminate information and ideas of all kinds, regardless of the frontiers, whether verbally or in writing or in print or in art form or by any other means chosen by the child.

Moreover, Article 12 of the UNCRC claims the right to listen to the children's point of view about their daily experience that deserves to be accepted and taken into consideration by the reference adults. As such, the use of artistic languages can be considered as a different form of listening from the adults to the children.

When used with young children, as mentioned above, while similar in nature to play-based approaches through initiating play activities to express their voices, they also differ as they use pure artistic techniques such as drawing, collage, dance and drama, that are adult-initiated, and children express themselves 'by the act of doing it', but their meaning-making is 'invoked in artistic efforts and encounters' (Sullivan, 2008: 241).

As Barone and Eisner (2012: 8–9) explain:

> Arts-based research is the utilisation of aesthetic judgment and the application of aesthetic criteria in making judgements about what the character of the intended outcome is to be. In arts-based research, the aim is to create an expressive form that will enable an individual to secure an empathic participant in the lives of others and in the situations studied.

Within an arts-informed perspective, however, art becomes a set of languages that allows individuals to express themselves in ways that would not have been possible solely by the use of words. This perspective is underpinned by the suggestion that artistic languages are able to reach different dimensions, not-rational or preverbal, and that art can be considered as a method of inquiry in a wider way (Biffi and Zuccoli, 2019). Artistic perspectives can enable researchers to understand phenomena either through different lenses, or that other methods cannot explicate in the same way (Rolling, 2013).

Arts-based methods offer young children opportunities to make meaning through a number of modes of expression such as visual, aural, movement or gestural (Barone and Eisner, 2012) and provide a tool for children to express themselves where words alone might not (Barton, 2015). They refer not only to specific practices, but also to a theoretical conceptualisation connected to the idea of thinking about art as a rigorous research method (Biffi and Zuccoli, 2019). As such, research becomes a creative, not linear, process of exploration for which the use of different languages is needed. Children thus have multiple ways of expressing themselves through the use of arts and to make meaning in different ways:

> This is critically important in the lives of young children and if there was not the opportunity for young children to express themselves in any form they feel comfortable, then we would be at risk of not knowing the full meaning of their experience. (Barton, 2015: 74)

In this context, artistic techniques can become tools for pedagogical documentation as a methodology. Its core dimension not only refers to a technical strategy for gathering images, but is rather an ideological approach for creating different relationships between the meanings and ideas to be shared. Consequently, we argue that pedagogical documentation as a methodology (with artistic languages as its main method) becomes a bricolage telling of connected meaning and action. It is a concrete space for anchoring the ideas to allow their sharing within the group in a way that words might not have been able to achieve. Children, in these lenses, become bricoleurs – researchers who are able to contribute to data collection and interpretation in forms where they feel comfortable – and make meaning of their experiences which other research methodologies and methods might not allow.

THE USE OF ARTISTIC LANGUAGE: AN EXAMPLE FROM THE ITALIAN DATA WITH CHILDREN AGED 4–6 YEARS

The Italian team delivered three workshops using artistic methods in relation to the inside/outside theme. The team, with the help of the teachers, carried out the workshops in different periods of time. Once each workshop was carried out, the teachers, when the researchers were not in the school, encouraged children to express themselves in relation to each theme. In this way children had a continuation of the theme in between the workshops where data was collected.

WORKSHOP 1: EXPRESSING VIEWS THROUGH DRAWINGS AND COLLAGES

Here the aim was to find what children think the concepts of inside/outside mean in relation to the spaces they occupy. Initially, during circle time, the researchers introduced themselves and the aims of the project and, with the use of prompts such as photos, asked the children what they think about inside and outside.

During the initial conversation, some general ideas were explored by children in an intuitive way, often following what the previous child had said before, in a sort of repetition (something that is evident in the English data as well). So, for example, if a child said that inside 'keeps you dry and not get wet', the data shows that others who followed this child said similar things.

Children offered ideas and numerous references to the world of colours, animals and nature (such as volcanoes, holes) as well as family and personal experiences (for example, moments of celebration, games or sports). These discussions were vivid and always enriched with narratives, that emerged either spontaneously or following questions or bodily movements (such as holding hands in a circle, or creating with one's own hands the dimensions of 'inside/ outside'). Once the discussions had come to a natural end, the children were asked to represent, with felt-tip pens and coloured pencils, their ideas of inside and outside on a sheet of A4 or A3 paper.

During the creation of their drawings, children were trying to visualise their ideas, which gave them the opportunity not only to narrate even further what they thought about the concepts, but also to articulate their feelings that they were not able to express during the initial discussion.

WORKSHOP 2: EXPRESSING VIEWS THROUGH THE USE OF CARTOGRAPHY

The second workshop opened with a video showing the children the multimedia material collected from the previous workshop. This first moment proved to be not only a valuable opportunity to take in the contents of the workshop together, allowing children to identify themselves in the various phases of work, but also an opportunity to give back to children, in a narrative form and with the artistic language, their perspectives of what inside/outside means. Children viewing their journey from the first workshop were able to add more views, feelings or even change the narrative that the researcher offered them as interpretation and offer another one, taking control of their own interpretation of the data.

Building on this discussion, children were encouraged to reflect on the dimension of space inside and outside of their school. The children were invited to guide the researchers on a tour through what they considered to be the most significant spaces within their school, in the various rooms and in the garden, indicating from time to time which were the elements or areas that they considered their favourites for different reasons.

(Continued)

Children were given A4-size sheets and were asked to represent their favourite places in the school without the researchers specifying how, with children to choose places that either existed in the school or were enriched with imaginary elements. Children were able to articulate their favourite spaces, which were mainly related to physical environments (such as their garden and specifically the little house and the grove within).

WORKSHOP 3: EXPRESSING OUR VIEWS AS A GROUP

Building on the narratives and the artistic work of the first two workshops, children were asked to create on their own in the third workshop before the researchers reflected together with the children as a group. Using the artistic technique of collage, researchers invited the children to make a work representing them as a group on a cardboard sheet. Working as a group during the creation of their artefacts, children shared their ideas of what it means to be inside/outside a group by referring to family or friends, but also cities and natural elements such as trees. Creating the collage as a group, children not only shared ideas but also negotiated ideas where there was disagreement. To make the collage children used a lot of glue, but the metaphorical 'gluing effect' of the collage was also evident in children's emotions, such as love, affection, enthusiasm and their physical–spatial closeness, coordination and collaboration.

At the end of each artistic creation, the researchers dedicated a few minutes to each child individually, asking them to describe what the subject of the artistic work was and their feelings throughout the process. Children shared their views and feelings by pointing to their contribution in the collage and explaining it. In some instances, instead of using words, children pointed to an area of the collage to express how they viewed the concepts of inside/outside.

CONCLUSION

In this chapter, we sought to explain how pedagogical documentation, apart from being a valuable tool, can also become a methodology in research with young children. We argued that in the quest for participatory methods, it is important to shift our thinking beyond the methods and seek home-grown methodologies for early childhood education research based on playful contexts. We do not claim that we have the only methodology for early childhood education, but claim that methods themselves – even arts-based, friendly methods where children can participate – are not enough and methodology should be the focus. If we accept the definition of methodology as being the narration of the research process, we propose that pedagogical documentation as a methodology for research is a bricolage that enables all participants to go beyond words and connect actions and events with personal understandings.

We argue that we do need to create our own methodology/ies rooted in playful attitudes. Based on the evaluation of our research, we argue that when drawing from practice we can refine several ideas about how children can participate in research. Research with children might go beyond verbal responses by including new criteria such as practice- and/or play-rooted approaches like pedagogical documentation, and rethinking educational research terms. The recognition that verbal and visual data can go beyond oral or written interpretations leads us to the conclusion that where research cannot be transmitted effectively to young children, a re-examination of research methodologies previously dominant in the field is needed.

We propose that in order to achieve such a move, there are two criteria that need to be satisfied. First, we need to rethink the structural approach to research that involves using data only in oral or written form, and instead think about using different modes (such as artistic forms that might be permanent – e.g. drawings or collages – or ephemeral – e.g. dance performances or role play). In this way, we should not seek to make interpretations of children's context and meaning-making, but acknowledge that this meaning-making makes sense only in a specific context and may not offer concrete findings/answers. Rather, we should be making meaning and raising questions about a certain phenomenon that makes sense in a specific context. Second, we should be prepared as researchers to recognise that we might not be able to reach conclusions or answers to the phenomena we witness. Instead, we should seek to empower young children to express complex ideas which may be different in nature from those of adults. Such an approach would enhance the core values of equality and equity and contribute to the view that children are capable of making meaning, given the appropriate methodology/ies.

ACKNOWLEDGEMENTS

The English team would like to thank Middleton Primary and Nursery School in Nottingham for hosting the research project. We would also like to thank all children, parents, teachers and headteachers for taking part in the project.

REFERENCES

Barone, T. and Eisner, E. (2012). *Arts-Based Research*. Thousand Oaks: Sage.

Barton, G. (2015). Arts-based educational research in the early years. *International Research in Early Childhood Education*, 6 (1): 62–78.

Bateson, G. (1972). *Steps to an Ecology of Mind*. London: Intertext Books, International Textbook Company Ltd & Chandler Publishing Company.

Biffi, E. (2019). Pedagogical documentation as a shared experience of understanding child-hood. In J. Formoshino and J. Peeters (Eds.), *Understanding Pedagogic Documentation in Early Childhood Education: Revealing and Reflecting on High Quality Learning and Teaching.* London: Routledge. pp. 67–80.

Biffi, E. and Zuccoli, F. (2019). Art as a method of research. In Z. Brown and H. Perkins (Eds.), *Using Innovative Methods in Early Years Research: Beyond the Conventional.* London: Routledge. pp. 49–62.

Clark, A. (2010). *Transforming Children's Spaces: Children's and Adults' Involvement in Designing Learning Environments.* London: Routledge.

Clark, A. and Moss, P. (2001). *Listening to Young Children: The Mosaic Approach.* London: Joseph Rowntree Foundation.

Farman, J. (2015). Stories, spaces, and bodies: The production of embodied space through mobile media storytelling. *Communication Research and Practice*, 1 (2): 101–16.

Gallacher, L. A. and Gallagher, M. (2008). Methodological immaturity in childhood research: Thinking through 'participatory methods'. *Childhood*, 15 (4): 499–516.

Lemke, J. (2002). Travels in hypermodality. *Visual Communication*, 1 (3): 299–325.

Levi-Strauss, C. (1962). *La Pensée Sauvage.* Paris: Librairie Plon (published in translation in English 1966 with the title: *The Savage Mind*). Chicago, IL: University of Chicago Press.

Malaguzzi, L. (1996). *The Hundred Languages of Children: The Reggio Emilia Approach to Early Childhood Education.* Norwood, NJ: Ablex Publishing Corporation.

Malavasi, L. and Zoccatelli, B. (2012). *Documentare le Progettualità Nei Servizi e Nelle Scuole Dell'Infanzia.* Bergamo: Junior.

McArdle, F. and Wright, S. (2014). First literacies: Art, creativity, play, constructive mean-ing-making. In G. M. Barton (Ed.), *Literacy in the Arts: Retheorising Learning and Teaching.* Cham: Springer International Publishing. pp. 21–8.

Oliveira-Formoshino, J. and de Sousa, J. (2019). Developing pedagogic documentation. In J. Formoshino and J. Peeters (Eds.), *Understanding Pedagogical Documentation in Early Childhood Education: Revealing and Reflecting High Quality Learning and Teaching.* London: Routledge. pp. 32–51.

Pascal, C. and Bertram, T. (2009). Listening to young citizens: The struggle to make real a participator paradigm in research with young children. *European Early Childhood Education Research Journal*, 17 (2): 249–62.

Rinaldi, C. (2012) Re-imagining childhood: The inspiration of Reggio Emilia education principles in South Australia, Government of South Australia.

Rolling, J. H. (2013). *Arts-Based Research.* New York: Peter Lang.

Sullivan, G. (2008). Painting as research: create and critique. In J. G. Knoles and A. L. Cole (Eds.), *Handbook of the Arts in Qualitative Research: Perspectives, Methodologies, Examples and Issues.* London: Sage. pp. 239–50.

UN Commission on Human Rights (1990). *Convention on the Rights of the Child.* Available at: www.refworld.org/docid/3b00f03d30.html (accessed 24 September 2019).

11

FRAME, EXPLAIN AND THEORISE: USING AN APP AS A TOOL TO INTERPRET IMAGINARY PLAY WITH CHILDREN AND TEACHERS

MARILYN FLEER

This chapter explains how to capture, interpret and theorise imaginary play using an app, purposefully designed to document and interpret data in ways that bring together children and their teachers in a process of meaning-making through play.

The chapter:

- Begins with a discussion about why more needs to be known about how to research imaginary play in early childhood settings;
- Is followed by an example of a free app designed to collect digital data of imagination in play and imagination in learning (www.monash.edu/conceptual-playworld/app);
- Highlights the importance of positioning such analysis within a clear theoretical frame – driven by the researcher but supported by the app.

In this way, an example of interpreting the meaning of children's play through the lens of cultural-historical theory is presented. The example is illustrative of the new

(Continued)

affordances now available to teachers and researchers interested in capturing, analysing and theorising imaginary play so they can better understand children through
the lens of their play. The chapter brings into focus a cultural-historical approach
to interpreting and theorising imaginary play through a research practice model of
'frame, explain and theorise'.

BACKGROUND

Vygotsky (1933/1967) argued that play acts as a mirror into the child's world, revealing
how they give meaning and how they interpret their social and material environment. In studying and interpreting their actions, teachers and researchers gain insights
into children's thinking and meaning-making processes. But to do this with rigour, sensitivity and robustness, we need tools to help make this doable within the dynamics of the
play as it unfolds in practice.

In this chapter, the teacher and the researcher are conceptualised as the same person
who asks, 'How should we conceptualise the object of our study, formulate a methodology, and develop an analytical frame for studying children's play in ways that open up
new understandings of the meaning children show through their play?' This is because
the researcher was a staff member within the setting where the research took place and, in
line with Chapter 4, research related to play is often relevant to those engaging in enquiry
about their own practice. In the remainder of the chapter, we talk about the teacher/
researcher for consistency.

In line with previous cultural-historical research, this chapter puts forward a methodology and a method to help teachers/researchers to study and interpret children's play
within early childhood settings. Using an app to capture imaginary play and a framework
to support *an interpretation* of imaginary play that transcends that moment, gives teacher/
researchers understandings about how children are making meaning of their social and
material world. This chapter discusses this app as an example of one way of consulting with children, explains the framework that supports the interpretation process, and
argues why teacher/researchers together with children can better understand the meaning-
making process when the focus is on play.

RESEARCHING IMAGINARY PLAY

A great deal was learned about imaginary play in the 1970s, and a significant amount is
now known about how to research imaginary play (see Chapter 1 for more discussions
on theorising and researching play). Yet in recent times, the early childhood education

research community has seen a resurgence of interest in studying children's imaginary play. What has changed?

First, we now have new tools for undertaking research, such as digital video cameras, digital still cameras and digital audio tools. We also have a range of different apps designed to support teachers and researchers with data analysis and interpretations of children's play. These tools were not available to teacher/researchers studying children's play in the 1970s. They offer different possibilities and give new directions for teachers and play researchers. *Consequently, we need to know more about how to use these new tools and emerging methods to see what they afford for the study of imaginary play.*

Second, we now have unprecedented numbers of early childhood education research-ers contributing to scholarship by doing postgraduate studies and practitioner enquiry. For the first time in the history of early childhood education, the field has been supported by research from within its profession. Rather than relying almost exclusively on other professions, such as psychology, to inform early childhood teachers on the nature of chil-dren's play, education now has its own emerging researchers (see Chapter 10 for more on the need for methodologies from within education).

Early childhood teacher-led inquiries and researchers with education backgrounds are likely to ask different kinds of research questions to other professions. Rather than a study of a focus child at play, a dyad of children playing together, or laboratory-based conditions to study mother–child interactions during play, early childhood researchers have contributed to play research by examining play pedagogy, collective play, and play in naturalistic settings in preschools. As we have seen throughout this book, teachers and researchers are also drawing on deep understandings of play as a cultural practice, which is used to capture and gain insight into what is meaningful for a child in a broad range of ways. *Consequently, with different kinds of research questions being asked, new kinds of methods and methodologies are needed to support teachers and researchers working from within educa-tional contexts through and about play.*

In summary, there is a contemporary need for play research that can help us bet-ter understand the institutional conditions that support imaginary play, to be better informed about the possibilities of the new digital tools being used to capture imaginary play, and to theorise the new approaches emerging through the practice of researching play. This chapter contributes to this methodological and analytical need by offering one case example to support teachers and researchers with this important work.

ITERATIVE INTERPRETATION WHEN RESEARCHING PLAY

To better understand this process of imaginary play, we propose that an iterative inter-pretation cycle is helpful when following the child's actions within an activity setting, observing their play actions, and making tentative claims about their intentions.

By paying close attention to the demands placed upon the child, and also the play motives of the child (see Hedegaard, 2012), as they enter into the activity setting and by contributing to and shaping play practices, we can determine important relations between events, people and cultural and historical institutional rules, values and practices (Hedegaard, 2008a, b). But this requires a theorisation of a high order, and this is where the researcher draws upon the system of concepts for theorising the findings of the research on imaginary play.

First, the process of validation of studies of imaginary play needs to occur from within the theoretical frame used. In this chapter, validation from a cultural-historical perspective asks the question about imaginary play in relation to the different perspectives of the participants. That is, when asking the research question, 'How can we conceptualise children's participation in imaginary play within preschools as the basis for understanding and guiding practice?' (Hedegaard, 2008b: 43), we need to capture not only the child's play activity from the different perspectives (teachers, children, institutional rules, societal expectations of play or learning from preschools), but also how they are contributing to the conditions for the development of children's imaginary play.

Second, the question of reliability of data in researching imaginary play is also an important consideration (see Chapter 6 for more). Unlike research that uses predetermined categories to frame and explain the data and analysis process, the approach illustrated in this chapter of using an app deals with the question of the reliability of data by conceptualising the role of the teacher/researcher in relation to the data collection process, but also by tagging data in relation to what the teacher/researcher was doing at the time. The selfie feature of the app, described later in the chapter, makes the actions of the teacher/researcher explicit in the data set. Hedegaard (2008b) has argued that we must 'conceptualise the projects of the researcher as different from the persons being researched, and at the same time conceptualise the researcher as a partner in their activities' (p. 44). Meaningful insights can be gained during the research process when children are comfortable having the teacher/researcher with them during imaginary play. Capturing the moments of imagination in play, and in the case of the example of the app, imagination in learning on the app, means the teacher/researcher must build a relationship with the children so that when they ask questions and react, it is relevant to the situation. Hedegaard (2008a) refers to this as a double subjectivity of the researcher. She says, 'Because the researcher's project is the scientific activity and not the project of the activity of those being researched, the concept of double relevance comes into focus' (p. 44).

Finally, a theoretical alignment between how the data collection is framed, how the interpretations are made, and how the insights are drawn is imperative to both the validity and reliability of the study of children's imaginary play. If we use different theories to guide these different research processes, then we may lose confidence in the results, but also the process of interpreting imaginary play becomes difficult. In using the metaphor of a skeletal system, it can be argued that different theoretical traditions have their own internal conceptual skeletal system and integrity. If we mix these in different parts of the research, it is difficult to draw conclusions and to theorise from our findings – especially in imaginary play where we can never be inside the head of a child. We will always need to fill gaps in our own interpretations by drawing upon theory to guide us. If we begin with one conceptual theoretical skeletal system, we can use the basic conceptual structure to guide us in writing about our findings. This is shown in Figure 11.1.

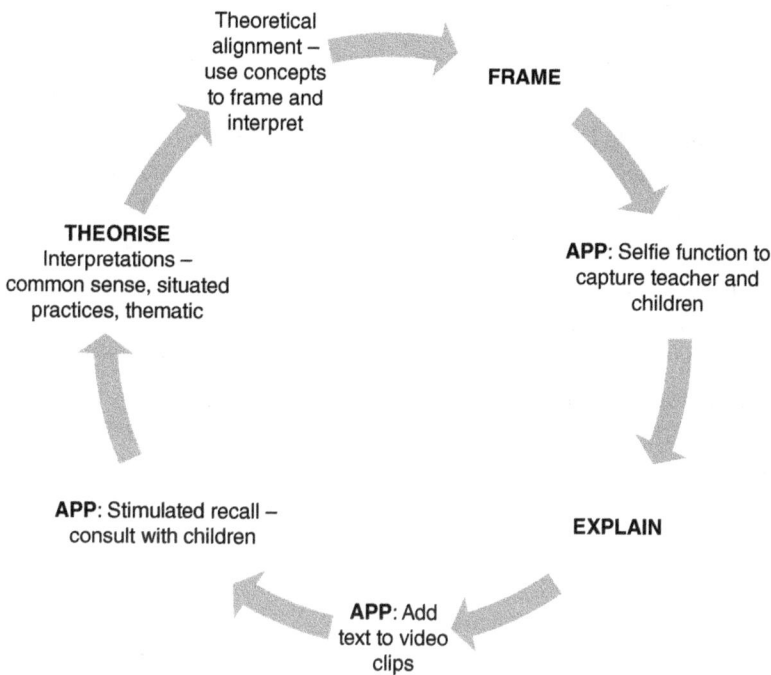

Figure 11.1 Iterative interpretation process when studying complex imaginary play with children

We have developed an app to help us move through these steps in the process, which can be found here: www.monash.edu/conceptual-playworld/app. The free app was designed specifically to capture moments of imagination in play within the naturalistic settings of a preschool, and allows us to work within our chosen theoretical frame. The app is available for mobile devices, such as phones and tablets. It is used in this chapter to illustrate how to frame, explain and theorise imaginary play.

We now turn our attention to an example as being illustrative of how to frame, explain and theorise imaginary play using our app. As you read the case example, we invite you to consider what you need to think about when interpreting children's play in your own context. In this chapter, we frame the work from a cultural-historical perspective to demonstrate what this may look like in practice. If you choose a different framework, different findings may emerge (as described in Chapter 6 by Cathy Nutbrown). In other chapters, different theoretical lenses are discussed and other ways of researching imaginary play are presented, and together they broaden the theoretical toolkit of the teacher and researcher.

FRAME, EXPLAIN AND THEORISE

A cultural-historical view of play is defined as the creation of an imaginary situation where children change the meaning of objects and actions to give them a new sense (Vygotsky, 1933/1967). The stick becomes the hobby horse and the child becomes a rider. In the imaginary situation, the child no longer sees a stick, but sees a horse. A new sense is given to the situation and new actions are performed by the child of horse riding. Researching imaginary play is complex because the actions and the objects are given meaning by the child. As researchers, we are charged with capturing the child's action and their intentions in relation to the objects they are using, and analysing what this might mean. We capture imaginary play in different contexts, over time, and with others (children and/or adults). Therefore, it becomes important to ask: What kinds of tools are needed for the collection, analysis and interpretation of data of imaginary play situations? An example of this problem follows and represents Ruth's experiences within a conceptual PlayWorld. The PlayWorld is shown on the app that is the case example of this chapter.

CAPTURING THE TEACHER AND THE CHILD IN PLAY

Example 1: Ruth (teacher) is sitting in the outdoor area together with the children and her co-teacher Olivia. The children and the teachers have created a new imaginary situation, inspired by reading the story of *Charlotte's Web* by E. B. White (1952). Ruth's teacher inquiry seeks to interpret the children's play and, at the same time, to better understand their thinking about the STEM concepts that they become increasingly interested in exploring so she can expand their experiences. But how can Ruth be both with the children and, at the same time, capturing the PlayWorld that is developing over the morning, over the week and over the month? How can she capture and interpret the children's play? How can Ruth and Olivia better understand the meaning-making process emerging in the dynamics of the play over time, which Vygotsky has said will act as a mirror into children's thinking?

FRAME

We cannot just point a camera at a group of children playing and announce that we are collecting data. We would end up with hours and hours of video recordings. How would we know if this constituted quality data? What do we focus the camera on – the child, the objects, the adults, or all of these? But also, as a teacher/researcher we would be absent from the child's world. Similarly, when do we turn the camera on and when do we turn it off? How do we position ourselves in the context – as a play partner, as a fly on the wall, inside or outside of the imaginary situation? There are many decisions to make before we enter the field, and, equally important, before we begin to analyse the data and draw conclusions about imaginary play.

By declaring what theory of play you subscribe to, you consciously frame the data collection process and frame how you organise your interpretation of imaginary play. You should use a theory that is well understood in the literature, and not simply an intuitive view of what you 'just know is play'. For example, a cultural-historical view of play frames how you point the camera, because you will be looking for moments where a child or an adult creates an imaginary situation, and you will capture these moments by following a child as they set up, engage in and end the imaginary play situations. This is a holistic conception of the play activity and the play context (Hedegaard and Fleer, 2008). That is why Ruth and Olivia used the app, because it allowed them to be with the children and, at the same time, to capture the PlayWorld they were creating together, as shown in Figure 11.2 below.

Figure 11.2   How can the teacher/researcher be with the children and be capturing the children's play?

The dashboard of the app is organised around three specific windows. The first window is a planning tool for educators who are designing and implementing play-based programs. The second window is shown in Figure 11.3, and is the tool that captures the imagination in play moments. The researcher or the teacher can record continuously, but unlike a general filming app, the device frames the recordings as 30-second imaginary play episodes that can be saved and stored as 30-second video clips – perfect for systematic analysis. This is the continuous capture mode of the tool. The researcher can also record a particular imaginary play moment that is shorter or longer, and this will also be stored as a video clip. All the imaginary play moments are then stored on the device along a breadcrumb for easy scrolling between clips (see Figure 11.5).

Figure 11.3   Imaginary play data collection tool – for capturing imagination in play and imagination in STEM moments

The researcher also has an opportunity to tag each video clip with information about what just happened, what took place before and what occurred after the moment of imaginary play was recorded. This feature is shown in Figure 11.4.

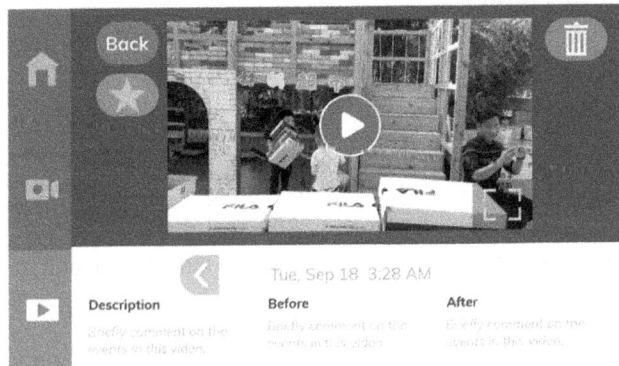

Figure 11.4   Imaginary play data collection tool – inserting text and tagging each video clip

In the example of the app shown in Figures 11.3 and 11.4, the teacher/researcher is supported to frame their research from a cultural-historical perspective because they can capture holistically all the adults and the children together – which is the norm for preschool practice. The mobile device is placed in situ close to children who are playing. The camera in selfie mode, can gather a sequence of clips of imaginary play. The teacher/researcher can also follow the child (or other teachers) in imaginary play situations. The continuous capture of the 30-second segments of imaginary play gives an analytical structure to the interpretation, yet maintains the holistic context of the play. The ability to add text to each clip means the teacher/researcher can begin a pre-interpretation through saving and tagging all the clips relevant to their research question onto the device as material for consulting with children about their play. For example, the teacher/researcher can document in situ what is said by the children, as the example below shows.

TAGGING DATA WITH TEXT

TEXT ON APP

Example 2: After recording a clip, Ruth adds comments on the children's play. She enters into the app a quick description of the context:

Description: *We are playing spider house.*

She then adds text about what happened prior to capturing this particular clip, recalling where possible what the children said.

Before Comment: *We saw lots of spiders outside and wanted to make a house for them.*

Similarly, she captures what the children did or said afterwards by adding text into the app.

After Comment: *Yuwen saw a spider in the spider house we made. Xingji squealed but Yumen said spiders like Charlotte are strong and wise and he shouldn't be frightened.* *

* pseudonyms are used

The teacher/researcher can also invite the children to use the device themselves to capture their play when the adults are not with the children. Adding the children's comments means that the children's perspective on the moments of play can be dynamically captured.

EXPLAIN

The researcher not only frames their data collection of imaginary play following a particular theoretical perspective, but they also use the same theoretical lenses for analysing and explaining the data they have collected. In Figure 11.5, all the video clips of imaginary play are shown in the breadcrumb at the bottom of the screen. The teacher/researcher or children can select and drag an imaginary play video clip to the top of the screen, in the section labelled 'Clips for discussion'. The selection of clips is centered around the research question. For instance, if the teacher/researcher is studying how a child changes the meaning of objects and actions in the imaginary situation, then the researcher would drag from the continuous capture of data in the breadcrumb all the clips that showed evidence of this. This feature is designed to also allow the teacher/researcher to consult with the child or other teacher in relation to particular data by simply selecting and playing the relevant video clip. This gives more meaning to the data – for instance, gaining the other teacher's perspective of the play practice or the child's perspective about the play activity. As a stimulated recall (Lyle, 2003), the video can also be played and the teacher interviewed or child consulted about the imaginary play situation captured on the device.

For example, the teacher/researcher can begin consultations with the children by first sharing with them the video clip (Figure 11.4), and then asking them about what happened before the moment they are viewing on the app of their play (Example 2, Tagging Data with Text). The children's comments about what happened afterwards can also be documented on the app (as 'After' comments). But also, the teacher/researcher can invite the children to describe the meaning of the play for them and document this on the app (as 'Description' comments). This gives the possibility of interpreting through the play that some children identify with the characters in the story of *Charlotte's Web*, where the spider is wise and strong, and others who bring to the play a possible fear of spiders.

An example of a teacher being interviewed is shown in Figure 11.6. Some of the questions that we posed that were related to the research question surrounding the relations between play and learning (Fleer, 2018) were:

1. What concept or big idea did you intend the children to learn in the imaginary situation of the PlayWorld?
2. How did you engage the children in learning the content in a meaningful and interesting way?
3. How did you document and analyse children's learning in the imaginary play?
4. How did you make children's learning visible for the parents?

Responses to these questions can be found in the overview video on the app, and these are all in the context of the PlayWorld that was documented as a curriculum inquiry by the teachers.

The ability to keep the whole data set together is featured in the app. Vygotsky (1934/1987) argued for the importance of examining the whole system of a phenomenon, whilst at the same time examining the process of development of that system

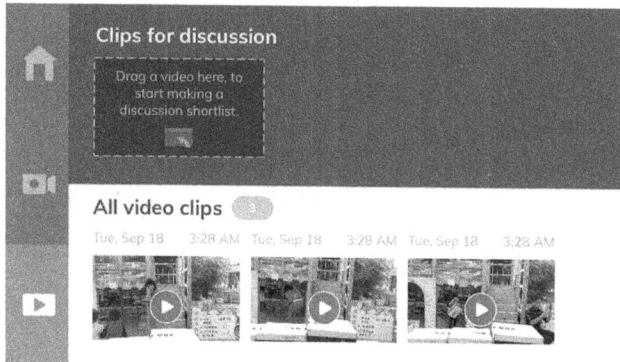

Figure 11.5 Imaginary play data collection tool – selecting data clips of imaginary play for stimulated recall

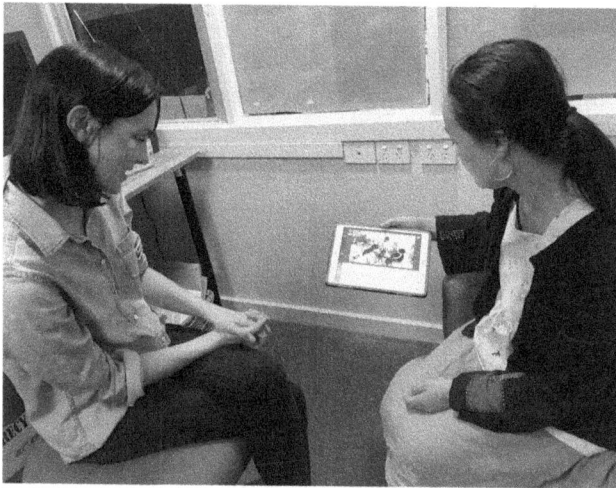

Figure 11.6 Imaginary play data collection tool – stimulated recall

(Vygotsky, 1997). Rather than examining the end product, Vygotsky (1997) used a skipping metaphor to capture and analyse development. In a cultural-historical view of imaginary play, it is argued that the play activity of the child is a mirror of the child's development – their thinking, their intentions and their understandings (Vygotsky, 1933/1967). Play is both the source of development and the product of that development. Skipping captures the nature of how a teacher/researcher would look over the data, again and again, deepening their explanation of the data set with each skip. Vygotsky suggested that in doing this kind of analysis, it becomes possible to determine the unit that is characteristic of the whole.

Vygotsky had a particular theoretical reading of unit of analysis. He suggests that if we simply identify elements, as one does when studying the chemical formulae of water – H2O – we miss the characteristics of the whole. He says this 'causes the researcher to ignore the unified and integral nature of the process being studied … The internal relationships of the unified whole are replaced with external mechanical relationships between … processes' (Vygotsky, 1934/1987: 49). That is, the phrase '2 hydrogen atoms and 1 oxygen atom' tells us very little about the nature of water – its characteristics, how it behaves, its social significance, cultural beliefs surrounding it, and so on.

Unit is the result of the research, Vygotsky argued, when he said, 'the term "unit" designates a product of analysis that possesses *all the basic characteristics of the whole*' (Vygotsky, 1934/1987: 46; original emphasis). For instance, Vygotsky notes, 'the living cell is the real unit of biological analysis because it preserves the basic characteristics of life that are inherent in the living organism' (p. 46). Therefore, a Vygotskian analysis which determines the unit that makes up the whole of the system, is sensitive to unearthing the assumptions that are characteristics of the whole – that is, the outcomes of the research.

As cultural-historical teacher/researchers, it is important to undertake an analysis which preserves the whole of the imaginary play, whilst at the same time being able to systematically examine multiple video clips across time, across children, across contexts and so on as is relevant to the research question.

The key question is, 'How can collections of research protocols documented in the research field be turned into reliable and valid interpretations?' (Hedegaard, 2008a: 47). That is, the teacher/researcher needs to systematically examine the data and make explicit the theoretical model building of imaginary play. Hedegaard (2012) has explained how this can be done through discussing the data analysis process as holistic, and in introducing the analytical interpretation of a common-sense analysis, a situated practice analysis and a thematic analysis.

A common sense analysis: The app encapsulates a common-sense analysis because the process of tagging the relevant recordings of the continuous capture of 30-second video clips is done in situ or shortly after. The researcher organises and draws out of the data set those video clips that show:

- The intentional orientation of the researched persons (e.g. to be looking for spiders in the outdoor area and then to make a spider house).
- The ways interaction occurs between the participants (interaction patterns) (e.g. girls appear to identify with the main character of Charlotte who is strong and wise).
- The conflicts between different persons' intentions and projects in the activity (e.g. spiders are often presented as something to be frightened by, and this is often gendered, but in the story of *Charlotte's Web* the image was dramatically different and this gave different possibilities for the children's play and search for spiders).

- The competence and motives that the researched persons demonstrate during their interactions (see Hedegaard, 2008a: 55) (e.g. expressions of new understandings about spiders).

The identified digital video clips must then be interpreted. At the common-sense level, the interpretations are formulated as pre-concepts because of the distance between being in the field and being at your desk analysing the data. However, these are framed in accordance with the theoretical lens that was advanced before beginning data collection. This means the framing and the explaining will be aligned and, as will be shown in the next section, this gives the foundations for the theorisation needed to move from explanation to a full theoretical interpretation.

In a common sense analysis, the interpreter is using the app to make comments on their understandings of the interactions of the imaginary play, as we saw in Example 2. Hedegaard (2008a) has said:

> The interpretation 'objectifies' the person's interactions in the activity settings where the interpreter is not part of the shared activity settings. This kind of interpretation is useful in validating the observation with the pedagogues or others who have participated in the observed activities. (p. 58)

A situated practice analysis: A situated practice analysis is centered on looking for patterns across activity settings related to the goals of the research. Clustering video clips on the app for discussion is an example of a situated practice interpretation of imaginary play. For example, identification of the range of ways that children enter into imaginary play situations will draw attention to how a child reads the play situation. Looking for 'how a child enters the play' across video clips over time and in different contexts with different imaginary play situations could reveal important patterns of interaction. For instance, expressions about spiders (positive or negative) are brought together as a set of clips to gain an overview of the whole group of children's play, where an interpretation can be made about children's thinking about spiders. A density of video clips can show a pattern, such as spiders help the environment and are an important part of the ecosystem (see teacher/researcher comments on the overview video in the app), and this could point to something important in the analysis process, and gives more confidence to the interpretations that would be made.

A thematic analysis: A thematic analysis is focused on the research questions driving the study of imaginary play. At this third level of analysis, it becomes important to discover the relations between the situated practices that emerged through the analysis of the imaginary play data. Imaginary play is complex, and therefore it is at this time that it becomes important to bring concepts to the interpretations of the data. For instance, in a PlayWorld, emotionally charged play situations can be designed into children's play through the careful selection of books (such as *Charlotte's Web*), where prior thinking about spiders can emerge in the play, but this thinking can be changed through imaginary play of a PlayWorld of Charlotte's Web and Zuckerman's Farm, and girls can identify positively with a character who is wise and strong (Figure 11.7 below). Consequently, it is imperative that the conception of play that framed the study is now used explicitly. That is, by using a cultural-historical conception of play, it is possible to formulate new conceptual relations within a problem area being investigated. This means that several digital video data sets will be analysed to see if the various patterns that emerged can be related to each other in some way (e.g. emotionally charged play about spiders, actions that show children imagining the outdoor area as a farm). That is, the researcher needs to find meaningful patterns in relation to the research questions driving the study of imaginary play.

Figure 11.7   Children and teachers ready to enter Zuckerman's Farm

The three levels of interpretation of imaginary play described here with examples from the app should be considered iteratively (see Figures 11.1–11.6 and Examples 1 and 2), because digital technologies allow the teacher/researcher to revisit the data and look for things not previously conceptualised (Fleer, 2014). With new concepts or new insights as a result of the ongoing interpretation process, captured through the skipping metaphor, it becomes possible to theorise in new ways about imaginary play.

THEORISE

Imaginary play is complex. It is not possible to go inside the mind of a child and to determine with confidence an interpretation of their play actions to build insights related to the research question. Rather, we use theory to bring together what we learn from a systematic study of children's imaginary play (see Chapter 6 for more on this). We also use theory to tie together aspects of evidence, where we make tentative claims. But how do we do this in practice?

Psychologically, there is a tension that exists between the real world (cultural rules and actual roles) and the 'as if' world of ideas and actions within imaginary situations. In a cultural-historical interpretation, we are looking for these dynamic moments in the data, and we theorise these as the Zone of Proximal Development in play situations (see Vygotsky, 1933/1967), acting as a dynamic force for children's development.

CONCLUSION

In this chapter, the example of an app designed to gather moments of imagination in play and imagination in learning was used to discuss how to gather, analyse and theorise when researching imaginary play, where the child is central to the process. The dynamics of this complex process are summarised and mapped out as an interactive process, as shown in Figure 11.1. It is because the play narratives of the children develop over time that we need powerful tools to capture the dynamic as a process of development, and not just an end product. In this cultural-historical conceptualisation of development, the inclusion of the teacher/researcher in the data set (often missing) is as important as consulting with children, if a holistic interpretation is to be achieved. In using the skipping metaphor, it becomes possible to realise that the research model of frame, explain and theorise can guide our thinking on how to interpret imaginary play. The app gives one doable way for the teacher/researcher to be *with the children* in the play setting, whilst at the same time *capturing the play setting* and *consulting with children*.

ACKNOWLEDGEMENTS

Funding from the Australian Research Council (ARC) supported the development of the app which grew out of insights across a series of ARC-funded studies over ten years, culminating in the ARC 2018 Kathleen Fitzpatrick Laureate Fellowship and ARC Programmatic Research Number FL180100161. Special thanks to the teachers Rebecca and Oriana for supporting the development of the video resources featured in the app.

REFERENCES

Fleer, M. (2014). Beyond developmental geology: A cultural-historical theorization of digital technologies for studying young children's development. In M. Fleer and

A. Ridgway (Eds.), *Visual Methodologies for Researching with Children: Transforming Visuality*. Amsterdam: Springer. pp. 3–13.

Fleer, M. (2018). Conceptual playworlds: The role of imagination in play and learning. *Early Years*. DOI: 10.1080/09575146.2018.1549024.

Hedegaard, M. (2008a). Principles for interpreting research protocols. In M. Hedegaard and M. Fleer (Eds.), *Studying Children: A Cultural Historical Perspective*. New York: Open University Press. pp. 46–64.

Hedegaard, M. (2008b). A dialectic approach to researching children's development. In M. Hedegaard and M. Fleer (Eds.), *Studying Children: A Cultural Historical Perspective*. New York: Open University Press. pp. 30–45.

Hedegaard, M. (2012). Analyzing children's learning and development in everyday settings from a cultural-historical wholeness approach. *Mind, Culture and Activity*, 19 (2): 127–38.

Hedegaard, M. and Fleer, M. (Eds.) (2008). *Studying Children: A Cultural Historical Perspective*. New York: Open University Press.

Lyle, J. (2003). Stimulated recall: A report on its use in naturalistic research. *British Educational Research Journal*, 29 (6): 861–78.

Vygotsky, L. S. (1933/1967). Play and its role in the mental development of the child. *Soviet Psychology*, 5 (3): 6–18.

Vygotsky, L. S. (1934/1987). Thinking and speech. In R. W. Rieber and A. S. Carton (Eds.), *The Collected Works of L. S. Vygotsky* (Vol. 1). New York: Plenum Press. pp. 39–285.

Vygotsky, L. S. (1997). *The Collected Works of L. S. Vygotsky: The History of the Development of Higher Mental Functions* (Vol. 4. Trans. M.J. Hall. Editor of English Translation, R.W. Rieber). New York: Kluwer Academic and Plenum Publishers.

12

USING PLAYFUL METHODS TO UNDERSTAND CHILDREN'S DIGITAL LITERACIES

PEKKA MERTALA

This chapter is the final one for Part 3 and in many ways stands as an example of how many of the individual elements presented thus far in the book can come together in a holistic way. This chapter demonstrates how we can adopt play, make it unique to the project and the children, and still arrive at meaningful research data. It describes a research project wherein 3- to 6-year-old Finnish children's digital literacies were studied and supported via playful methods. The key theses this chapter advocates are:

- The use of playful methods in early childhood education (ECE) research is one way to acknowledge and respect the characteristics of the research context;
- The ambiguity of play should be acknowledged when planning, conducting and evaluating playful research projects;
- Studying and supporting children's digital literacies does not always require digital devices.

The chapter is structured as follows. First, a reflective discussion on the ambiguity of play and the use of playful methods as a context-sensitive research approach is presented. Then, an overview of the research project and its objectives are provided. In the end, three concrete examples of how children's digital literacy was studied and supported using playful methods are given.

PLAY OR PLAYFUL(NESS): ENTERING THE GREY AREA

In August 2019, a major Finnish newspaper interviewed me about a game design study we had conducted with a group of preschoolers (Mertala and Meriläinen, 2019). In the interview, I mentioned that the study was perhaps the most fun project I had ever been involved in. Interestingly, one reader commented that because the project was fun, it was not proper research. I have given this comment a great deal of thought, and the more I think about it, the more I am opposed to it. In fact, I would argue that fun is often a requisite for conducting high-quality research with young children in the context of institutional ECE.

What I mean by this is that research is never context-free, and research tasks, such as data collection, should be designed in a manner that acknowledges and respects the characteristics of the context. Children's right to play, to learn by playing and to enjoy what they have learned is emphasised by the United Nations' Convention on the Rights of the Child (UN Commission on Human Rights, 1990), which has influenced various national and international ECE curriculums (Pramling Samuelsson and Johansson, 2006). Indeed, play has been highlighted as the most important pedagogical medium in ECE (Edwards, 2013), and play and learning have even been referred to as 'inseparable dimensions of preschool practice' (Pramling Samuelsson and Johansson, 2006: 47). Play is one of the key characteristics in the National Association for the Education of Young Children's (NAEYC, 2009: 14) influential framework of Developmentally Appropriate Practices. In the Finnish National Curriculum Guidelines, the word 'play' is mentioned 102 times (FNAE, 2018). As such, it would be justified to say that play is one of the leading concepts in contemporary ECE (see Chapter 1 for more on play).

Although references to play are common in curricular texts as well as in the everyday language of ECE, it is at the same time an extremely ambiguous phenomenon (Sutton-Smith, 1997), and, as such, has been theorised and defined in various and even contradicting ways in the extant research literature (Pyle and Danniels, 2017). There are some commonalities, however. One of them is freedom. In their classical and canonised definitions of play, Huizinga (1949) and Caillois (1961) argued that play is free from goals other than those created by the play itself. Accordingly, children tend to consider the freedom from outside demands as one of the fundamental characteristics of play (Wong et al., 2011).

The strong emphasis on the autonomy of play provides an interesting perspective on the theme of this book, research through play. What I mean by this is, if play is being used as a research method, the activity we refer to as play is not free from outside demands, as every research process has its own objectives. Thus, if we are to believe Huizinga and Caillois, what we call play in research would not be play at all. Actually, since education is always an intentional and goal-oriented activity (Siljander, 2002), the very same thing could be said about practically everything done in ECE settings.

Teachers' intentions are present, even in the play forms we typically refer to as free play. An illustrative example would be that teachers allow children free play time so that they can learn how to get along with others and socialise appropriately (Pyle and Danniels, 2017: 279).

That being said, it is evident that a straightforward and binary division between play and non-play is counterproductive, as it leaves practitioners and researchers without interpretative tools to discover and understand the multifaceted nature of play. First, it is important to acknowledge that a theory-driven (deductive) approach to defining and understanding play is just one possible starting point among others. For example, from a phenomenological point of view, it is not the theory (nor the type of activity) but the individual's experience that determines whether s/he is playing or not (Rasmussen, 2001). Indeed, the research on children's views on play is full of contradicting accounts of whether engaging in certain activities – for example, drawing and building with blocks – would be considered playing or not (Ólafsdóttir and Einarsdóttir, 2017; Wu, 2014). These contradictions are partially explained by situational factors, and instead of focusing solely on the type of activity, all activities should instead always be interpreted with an understanding of the broader situation. While children can conceptualise guided drawing as (pre)school work instead of play (Theobald et al., 2015), drawing can also take place within a broader framework of socio-dramatic, dramatic or fantasy play (Kukkonen and Chang-Kredl, 2018), as a child can, for example, draw in an imagined role other than her/his real self. Actually, a child can also draw in an imagined role *during* a guided drawing activity, which further underlines the ambiguity of play.

Talking about imagination, it needs to be borne in mind that even if we opt for a theory-driven approach to understanding play, freedom from outside goals is not the only thing that defines what is counted as play and what is not. The possibility to immerse oneself in imaginative realities and situations is included in Huizinga's (1949) and Caillois' (1961) play definitions as well as in Vygotsky's (1978) theoretical ideas on play. The fundamental question then is should an activity that is imaginative but not free from outside goals be understood as play or as non-play? Once again, a binary view is restrictive and counterproductive, and I find concepts such as play-based learning/pedagogy and playful learning/pedagogy extremely useful for solving this dilemma. To me, play and non-play are the end points of a continuum rather than distinct categories. Playfulness, in turn, refers to the grey area between these two absolutes (see Figure 12.1).

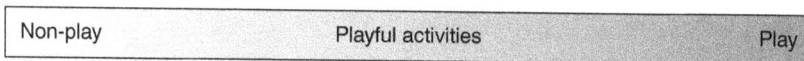

Non-play	Playful activities	Play

Figure 12.1   Playful activities as the grey area between non-play and play

In other words, play-based learning/pedagogy and playful learning/pedagogy convey an idea that despite all requirements and principles of pure play – which may not be met in full in the context of education and research – there are still various aspects that locate the activity closer to the play end of the play–non-play continuum. In the following sections, I will explain what this means in the context of our project: I will start with an overview of the project and then focus on the different ways in which playful activities were included and used in the methods employed.

OVERVIEW OF THE PROJECT OBJECTIVES

In this section, the research objectives and outline of the phases of the research process are discussed. As mentioned at the beginning of the chapter, the overarching theme of the project was digital literacy; specifically, it is about children's understanding of ubiquitous computing (ubicomp) and the Internet of Things (IoT). The term ubicomp refers to the proliferation of computing in the physical world (Abowd and Mynatt, 2000) – in other words, the core idea of ubicomp is that any tangible object can either include or be a computer. The idea behind IoT, in turn, is that any *thing* or object that is appropriately tagged can communicate through an internet-like structure with other objects that are similarly tagged (Espada et al., 2011). Put differently, when appropriately tagged, any tangible object can include internet connectivity.

The first research objective was to explore children's initial perceptions of ubicomp and the IoT. Ubicomp and IoT are a timely topic of study, as these technologies shape children's digital landscapes and lifeworlds, for example in the form of computer and/or internet-enabled tangible toys (Statista, 2019). Nevertheless, empirical research on children's perceptions of these technologies has been practically non-existent, with the exception of Manches et al. (2015), who studied how cognisant 10- to 11-year-old children are of IoT toys. As no studies have been conducted with younger children, there was a clear gap in the literature which our study was designed to fill.

The second research objective was to design and test playful methods to teach children about ubicomp and IoT. The importance of supporting young children's digital literacy has been addressed by various stakeholders, including scholars (Marsh, 2017); global agents, such as the Organisation for Economic Co-operation and Development (Taguma et al., 2013); and national educational administrations, such as the Finnish National Agency for Education (FNAE, 2018). Play and digital technologies are seldomly integrated into curriculum texts (Edwards, 2013), and the pedagogics of early years digital literacies education are still in an emerging stage (Edwards et al., 2018b; Salomaa and Mertala, 2019). Thus, there is an urgent need for research-based methods that acknowledge the pedagogical principles of ECE, including play.

Since this chapter focuses on the guiding principles behind playful study design, it does not go into detail on the results, which were reported in another publication (Mertala, 2020a).

However, to give a brief overview, the children were initially sceptical about the idea that tangible objects, such as plush toys, could be a computer and/or internet-enabled. These perceptions changed when the scientific concept of computers and the internet were provided.

OVERVIEW OF THE PROJECT ACTIVITIES

The research project was conducted in a Finnish early childhood centre in December 2018 by the author and a group of first-year ECE student teachers who were participating in a compulsory course about technology-enhanced teaching and learning. The activities undertaken during the project were designed to acknowledge the pedagogical principles of Finnish ECE outlined in the National Core Curriculum (FNAE, 2018) and to familiarise the student teachers with the transversal model of supporting digital literacies in ECE (Mertala, 2020b). The model consists of three orientations: technology education (i.e. teaching children about how technologies work), media education (i.e. teaching children about critical media literacy) and technology-enhanced learning (i.e. using technology to support learning processes). The structure of the three-day project and its linkages to the three orientations are summarised in Figure 12.2, which is followed by a detailed outline of the activities undertaken on each of the three days.

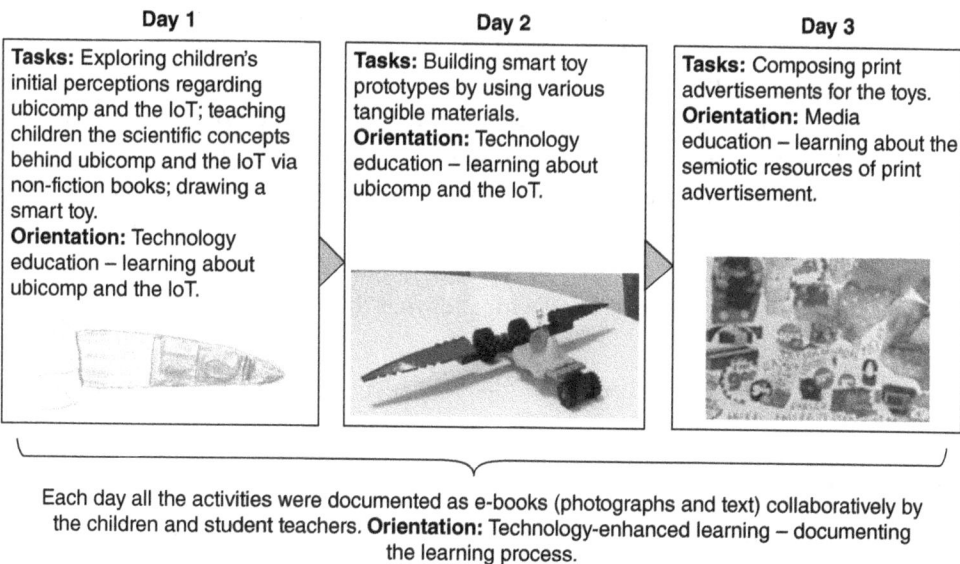

Day 1	Day 2	Day 3
Tasks: Exploring children's initial perceptions regarding ubicomp and the IoT; teaching children the scientific concepts behind ubicomp and the IoT via non-fiction books; drawing a smart toy. **Orientation:** Technology education – learning about ubicomp and the IoT.	**Tasks:** Building smart toy prototypes by using various tangible materials. **Orientation:** Technology education – learning about ubicomp and the IoT.	**Tasks:** Composing print advertisements for the toys. **Orientation:** Media education – learning about the semiotic resources of print advertisement.

Each day all the activities were documented as e-books (photographs and text) collaboratively by the children and student teachers. **Orientation:** Technology-enhanced learning – documenting the learning process.

Figure 12.2   Structure of the project and its linkages to the three orientations of the transversal model of supporting young children's digital literacies

DAY 1

On the first day, the children's initial conceptions were explored by having them freely explain what they knew and understood about computers and the internet. This decision reflected the sociocultural tradition of Finnish ECE that places emphasis on children's initial knowledge and prior experiences (FNAE, 2018: 22). There were, indeed, variations in children's initial perceptions. While many children found it difficult to verbalise what computers and the internet are, they were able to tell what can be done with them, a notion familiar from previous research (Edwards et al., 2018a; Mertala, 2019). However, one child explained that computers are built from different types of parts. His knowledge had strong sociocultural roots, as he related that he knew this because his grandfather had different types of computer parts.

Then, the children were shown pictures of a car, washing machine and teddy bear one by one and asked whether these objects could include a computer or an internet connection. These specific items were chosen because they present a pool of everyday objects that are likely to be familiar to all children. All these objects can also contain computers and connectivity. For example, all modern cars have at least one computer in them and many have integrated on-board computers that can display error signals and/or be used for navigation purposes.

After this, a short scientific explanation of computers and the internet was introduced to the children by reading selected parts of non-fiction children's books: *Miten Tietokone Toimii? Kurkista ja Koodaa* ([*Flip-the-Flap: Computers and Coding*] Dickins and Nielsen, 2015) and *Miten Internet Toimii* ([*How the Internet Works*] Nilsson, 2015). Next, the children were shown the same three pictures again, and they were asked whether the objects could contain a computer or an internet connection. Finally, the children were asked to draw a design of a toy that would have a computer or connectivity in it. The children were oriented towards the task through a fairytale about a Christmas elf who hit her/his head on a tree in a sledging accident and was therefore unable to invent any new toys for the coming Christmas and needed help from the children. During and after the drawing, the children were interviewed about the design by asking, for instance, how the toy could be played with and what the connectivity/computer would do in the toy.

DAYS 2 AND 3

On the second day, the drawings made during the first day were reexamined with the children by reading to them what they had said about their toy and by giving them an opportunity to refine the design. When the children were happy with their design, they began to build prototypes of their toys by using all the materials available in the centre (e.g. toys, cardboard, Play-Doh). The children were given an opportunity to use battery-operated light-emitting diode (LED) lights to signal the presence of digitality and electricity. Digital photos of the prototypes were taken for use on Day 3, which was devoted to composing print advertisements for the toys. When the prototypes were ready, the children were able to play with them. Pedagogy-wise, the idea of building concrete prototypes was catalysed by various sources. Working with physical materials to understand the digital world was inspired by Dufva and Dufva's (2019) ideas of 'digi-grasping' – that is, holistic and embodied sense-making in and of the world where the digital and physical worlds are deeply intertwined. Other sources of inspiration were the tactile tradition of ECE (Parker and Neuharth-Pritchett, 2006) and the general principles of technology education: one goal of technology education is to teach children that technology is always an outcome of human activity, and the creation of their own technological products is named as one method for achieving this objective (FNAE, 2018: 47).

On the third day, the digital photos of the prototypes were printed. Then, the children were invited to compose print advertisements for their toys. A collage technique combining drawing, writing, cutting, and gluing pieces from actual ads was used. The orientation of this activity was media education and to engage children in the investigation of semiotic resources used in print advertisement, such as boldface capital letters, exclamation marks, bright colours, smiling people, and so on. The activity was guided by the Finnish National Core Curriculum that requires an educator to support children's critical media literacy; the playful creation of their own media texts is mentioned as being a pedagogically appropriate method (FNAE, 2018: 45).

PLAYFUL ELEMENTS OF THE PROJECT

Three different kinds of playful activities can be identified in the project: (i) imaginative framing; (ii) playing around with materials; and (iii) 'free' play with self-designed toys. Figure 12.3 illustrates where these activities fit in relation to each other in the continuum of play. The aforementioned themes are elaborated in the following sections.

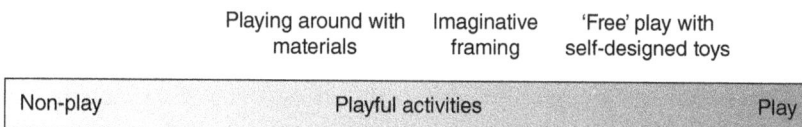

Figure 12.3   Playful activities of the project in the continuum of play

IMAGINATIVE FRAMING

Imaginative situations were present in our research process in several ways and on several levels. Actually, the whole process of designing and building ubicomp and IoT toys was framed via an imaginative situation. As previously mentioned, the activity of toy design was introduced to the children in the form of a short story. The full story went as follows:

> Did you know that all the elves in Santa's village have specific responsibilities? Lekolar Playful, for example, is one of the oldest and most respected elves, and their task is to design new toys. Lekolar is extremely proud that for centuries, she/he has come up with wonderful new inventions for Christmas. However, this year, all that has changed. Despite their age, Lekolar loves sledging. Unfortunately, while racing down a steep slope at a furious pace, Lekolar lost control of the sledge and hit their head on a tree. As a result of the shock, Lekolar has been unable to create any new ideas for toys. Mixture Meiram, the doctor elf, is sure that Lekolar will return to normal, but this will not happen in time for Christmas. Now Santa needs help from skillful and creative children like you. Your task will be to design new types of toys – toys that have a computer inside them and can also be connected to the internet.

The idea behind the use of imaginative framing is that children are not merely asked to draw a design; playful fantasy elements are included in the task. In other words, the children are not drawing the designs and building the prototypes simply because they have been instructed to do so – an activity that would be approached as non-play by many children (Brooker, 2014) and play theorists (Pyle and Danniels, 2017). Instead, they are provided with a narrative to give the task a purpose – helping the poor elf – and to stimulate their creativity. From a pedagogical point of view, methods like these can be interpreted as a playful learning approach in which the learning of targeted skills will occur in a manner that is playful, engaging and enjoyable for the children (Pyle and Danniels, 2017).

PLAYING AROUND WITH MATERIALS

Playing around with materials can be initially located at the non-play end of the continuum. As noted by Brooker (2014), children often view activities with specific outcomes as non-play, and it is certainly true that explicit instructions were included in this project. The children were asked to draw the design of a toy, build a tangible prototype of the toy, and compose an advertisement for the toy. Additionally, some of the materials used (e.g. LED lights and print advertisements) were offered to the children by us instead of giving them total freedom of choice. While the instructions to use these particular materials to design predefined artifacts may appear contradictory in relation to the autonomy of play, they, at the same time, served an important communicative purpose – objects and artifacts can act as mediating tools that allow different parties to understand each other's thinking by creating a transitional space in which their thoughts and ideas can be externalised in a concrete form (Lipponen et al., 2016). It can also be argued that such tools are needed, especially when addressing phenomena as abstract and complex as ubicomp and IoT, as they allow us to approach the digital world through the physical world (see also Dufva and Dufva, 2019). For instance, the children were able to illustrate and concretise the location of the computer in their toys by pointing to the exact area in their drawings and/or prototypes where it was placed, instead of merely stating that there would be a computer somewhere.

Furthermore, while the tasks were not totally free or open, there was a great sense of freedom regarding the kinds of toys the children were able to draw and build. The variation in children's ideas and creations is perhaps best illustrated by looking at the actual prototypes. Figure 12.4 provides some examples of the various ways the children employed different materials in their designs. The toy shown on the far left is a moving dollhouse made from Lego bricks, Play-Doh and LED lights. The upper-right image is a super robot (which shoots laser beams from its legs) made out of Play-Doh, plastic beads and LED lights. The lower-right image is a prototype of a smartphone-operated concrete truck with LED lights tied on (the arrow points to the lights). Since the concrete truck was not remote-controlled nor was the robot actually able to shoot lasers from its legs, imaginative framing was present in the playful use of materials.

Figure 12.4   Smart toy prototypes made from different materials

'FREE' PLAY WITH SELF-DESIGNED TOYS

The third and final form of playful activity was 'free' play with the self-designed toys. The term *free* here indicates that the children's play activities were not guided or instructed at this stage. Quotation marks around the term are thus used to pinpoint that in the context of institutional education, teachers' intentions are present even in child-initiated activities. In our case, the inclusion of the 'free' play period was influenced by the Finnish core curriculum, which states that 'while playing, children have an opportunity to use their imagination and creativity, try out their ideas and explore the world', which supports their thinking and learning skills (FNAE, 2018: 24). We believed that playing with the self-made prototypes would be a novel experience for the children. Thus, it would provide new elements to the children's play, which again would contribute positively to their learning and development. While it is impossible (and needless, I would add) to point out any explicit learning outcomes from the 'free' play period, its inclusion in the project is justified by the observation that the children seemed to enjoy the opportunity to play with the prototypes. In the end, it is the children and their happiness and well-being that matter the most.

CONCLUSION

This chapter has presented a research project in which 3- to 6-year-old Finnish children's digital literacies were studied and supported via playful methods. The first key thesis of the chapter was that research processes should be designed with respect to the characteristics of the research context, and the chapter has demonstrated that research projects conducted in ECE can be playful as well as pedagogical (which here refers to contributing to children's learning). The second key thesis was that the ambiguity of play should be acknowledged when planning, conducting and evaluating playful research projects. In this chapter, I problematised the idea of totally free play in the context of education and/or research, and suggested that the concept of playfulness better captures the multifaceted nature of play. The third and final thesis was that studying and supporting children's digital literacies does not always require digital devices. To support this claim, this chapter provided practical examples of how children's understanding of ubicomp and IoT were studied and supported by using printed books, Play-Doh and traditional toys. That being said, these practices should not be approached as a one-size-fits-all solution, as the pedagogical value and meaningfulness of playful projects are always highly contextual.

REFERENCES

Abowd, G. D. and Mynatt, E. D. (2000). Charting past, present, and future research in ubiquitous computing. *ACM Transactions on Computer–Human Interaction*, 7 (1): 29–58.

Brooker, L. (2014). Children's perspectives on play. In L. Brooker, M. Blaise and S. Edwards (Eds.), *The Sage Handbook of Play and Learning in Early Childhood*. Thousand Oaks, CA: Sage. pp. 319–29.

Caillois, R. (1961). *Man, Play and Games*. New York: Free Press of Glencoe.

Dickins, P. and Nielsen, S. (2015). *Kuinka Tietokone Toimii? Kurkista ja Koodaa*. Helsinki: Tammi.

Dufva, T. and Dufva, M. (2019). Grasping the future of the digital society. *Futures*, 107: 17–28.

Edwards, S. (2013). Digital play in the early years: A contextual response to the problem of integrating technologies and play-based pedagogies in the early childhood curriculum. *European Early Childhood Education Research Journal*, 21 (2): 199–212.

Edwards, S., Mantilla, A., Henderson, M., Nolan, A., Skouteris, H. and Plowman, L. (2018a). Teacher practices for building young children's concepts of the internet through play-based learning. *Educational Practice and Theory*, 40 (1): 29–50.

Edwards, S., Nolan, A., Henderson, M., Mantilla, A., Plowman, L. and Skouteris, H. (2018b). Young children's everyday concepts of the internet: A platform for cyber-safety education in the early years. *British Journal of Educational Technology*, 49 (1): 45–55.

Espada, J. P., Martínez, O. S., Lovelle, J. M. C., G-Bustelo, B. C. P., Álvarez, M. Á. and García, A. G. (2011). Modeling architecture for collaborative virtual objects based on services. *Journal of Network and Computer Applications*, 34 (5): 1634–47.

Finnish National Agency for Education (FNAE) (2018). *National Core Curriculum for Early Childhood Education and Care 2016* (Regulations and Guidelines 3a). Helsinki: Finnish National Agency for Education.

Huizinga, J. (1949). *Homo Ludens: A Study of the Play-Element in Culture*. London: Routledge.

Kukkonen, T. and Chang-Kredl, S. (2018). Drawing as social play: Shared meaning-making in young children's collective drawing activities. *International Journal of Art & Design Education*, 37 (1): 74–87.

Lipponen, L., Rajala, A., Hilppö, J. and Paananen, M. (2016). Exploring the foundations of visual methods used in research with children. *European Early Childhood Research Journal*, 24 (6): 936–46.

Manches, A., Duncan, P., Plowman, L. and Sabeti, S. (2015). Three questions about the Internet of Things and children. *TechTrends*, 59 (1): 76–83.

Marsh, J. (2017). Introduction. In Marsh et al. (Eds.), *Makerspaces in the Early Years: A Literature Review*. pp. 6–11. Available at: http://makeyproject.eu/wp-content/uploads/2017/02/Makey_Literature_Review.pdf (accessed 24 September 2019).

Mertala, P. (2019). Young children's conceptions of computers, code, and the internet. *International Journal of Child–Computer Interaction*, 19: 56–66.

Mertala, P. (2020a). Young children's perceptions of ubiquitous computing and the Internet of Things. *British Journal of Educational Technology*, 51 (1): 84–102.

Mertala, P. (2020b). Laaja-alaisen tieto – ja viestintäteknologisen osaamisen tukeminen varhaiskasvatuksessa ja esiopetuksessa. *Journal of Early Childhood Education Research*, 9 (1): 6–31.

Mertala, P. and Meriläinen, M. (2019). The best game in the world: Exploring young children's digital game-related meaning-making via design activity. *Global Studies of Childhood*, 9 (4): 275–89.

NAEYC (2009) Developmentally Appropriate Practice in Early Childhood Programs Serving Children from Birth through Age 8, Position statement. Available from: www.naeyc.org/sites/default/files/globally-shared/downloads/PDFs/resources/position-statements/PSDAP.pdf

Nilsson, H. (2015). *Miten Internet Toimii*. Helsinki: Kansallinen Audiovisuaalinen Instituutti.

Ólafsdóttir, S. M. and Einarsdóttir, J. (2017). 'Drawing and playing are not the same': Children's views on their activities in Icelandic preschools. *Early Years*, 39 (1): 51–63.

Parker, A. and Neuharth-Pritchett, S. (2006). Developmentally appropriate practice in kindergarten: Factors shaping teacher beliefs and practice. *Journal of Research in Childhood Education*, 21 (1): 65–78.

Pramling Samuelsson, I. and Johansson, E. (2006). Play and learning: Inseparable dimensions in preschool practice. *Early Child Development and Care*, 176 (1): 47–65.

Pyle, A. and Danniels, E. (2017). A continuum of play-based learning: The role of the teacher in play-based pedagogy and the fear of hijacking play. *Early Education and Development*, 28 (3): 274–89.

Rasmussen, T. H. (2001). *Legetøjets Virtuelle Verden: Essays om Legetøj og Leg*. Brøndby: Semi-forlaget.

Salomaa, S. and Mertala, P. (2019). An education-centred approach to digital media education. In C. Gray and I. Palaiologou (Eds.), *Early Learning in the Digital Age*. Thousand Oaks, CA: Sage. pp. 151–64.

Siljander, P. (2002). *Systemaattinen Johdatus Kasvatustieteeseen*. Helsinki: Otava.

Statista (2019). Smart toys industry revenue worldwide in 2013 to 2020 (in billion euros). Available at: www.statista.com/statistics/320941/smart-toys-revenue (accessed 24 September 2019).

Sutton-Smith, B. (1997). *The Ambiguity of Play*. Cambridge, MA: Harvard University Press.

Taguma, M., Makowiecki, K. and Litjens, I. (2013). *Quality Matters in Early Childhood Education and Care: Norway*. Paris: OECD.

Theobald, M., Danby, S., Einarsdóttir, J., Bourne, J., Jones, D., Ross, S., Knaggs, H. and Carter-Jones, C. (2015) Children's perspectives of play and learning for educational practice. *Education Science*, 5: 345–62.

UN Commission on Human Rights (1990). *Convention on the Rights of the Child.* Available at: www.refworld.org/docid/3b00f03d30.html (accessed 24 September 2019).

Vygotsky, L. (1978). *Mind in Society: The Development of Higher Psychological Processes.* Cambridge, MA: Harvard University Press.

Wong, S., Wang, Z. and Cheng, D. (2011). A play-based curriculum: Hong Kong children's perceptions of play and non-play. *The International Journal of Learning*, 17 (10): 165–80.

Wu, S.-C. (2014). Practical and conceptual aspects of children's play in Hong Kong and German kindergartens. *Early Years*, 34 (1): 49–66.

PART 4

RESEARCH RESOURCES FROM EARLY CHILDHOOD EDUCATION

INTRODUCTION TO PART 4: PRACTICAL EXAMPLES

KATE WALL AND LORNA ARNOTT

This Part is different to what has come before, but we considered that having read the more theoretical discussions and methods examples, some exemplification of the practice to which it might lead would be useful. Here we present two research projects and two proposals, each demonstrating unique real-world opportunities facilitated by inhabiting a play-based approach. In each there is a celebration of what research through play can bring as well as a pragmatic embracing of the unexpected that comes with working with young children in this way. Common themes around flexibility, voice, relationships and ethics are apparent across all the examples as the balance between the research intent and the children's play is negotiated.

We chose to include two research projects because they show the realities of carrying out research with young children and through play. They show the inherent messiness of working with young children, alongside the potential dilemmas and successes that arise. Within these projects, it is possible to see how research through play can be creative, art-based and use visual techniques to facilitate a productive space for dialogue between the adults and children, and how as a result the relationships between them emerge and develop. Issues of power dynamics, inclusivity and the adults' role as an active listener play an important part in navigating the project path.

The proposals on the other hand represent the inception of a project – the planning stage. They show the way in which the researcher/practitioner conceptualises their intent through the development of research questions, and how they lead, via an emerging line of enquiry, to the planned methods, pedagogy and analysis. In both cases, the ethics of the approach are a significant consideration as well as an embedded flexibility to ensure that the play is as child-led as possible while maintaining the intent of the project. It is useful to see how timelines for activity are thought through and how different data are planned to be collected throughout. This is particularly important if you are embarking on your first research project, or are at least new to this type of research, enabling you to see what research planning entails.

In all the examples, the way in which the intents of the adults are balanced and negotiated with the children through the medium of play is foregrounded with the understandings that emerge being both process- and outcome-orientated. The creativity of the process and the outcomes, and the extent to which they feed into answering the researchers'/practitioners' questions, demonstrate the power of play as a pedagogic and methodologic approach when working in the early years.

PROJECT 1: FACILITATING VOICE WITH OUR YOUNGEST CHILDREN

RHONA MATHESON, STARCATCHERS

Starcatchers (www.starcatchers.org.uk), Scotland's national arts and early years organisation, provides innovative arts and creative experiences for babies, toddlers and young children aged 0–5 that can be shared positively with their parents and carers. Our ethos is derived from a desire to fulfil our youngest children's right to engage with and experience arts experiences of the highest quality that provide inspiration, joy and wonder, and encourage self-expression. Starcatchers works across art forms. We work with artists who are specialists in their field and who are inspired to make work for or with very young children. We also champion work that offers positive shared experiences between very young children and the parents or carers who accompany them.

The examples shared here cover a range of our activities and highlight the positive role that the arts play in enabling our youngest children to share their thoughts and feelings. They are provided as inspiration for researchers wanting to incorporate elements of play into their research approach.

STRIPY NEST (2019) – CO-DESIGNING A PLAY INSTALLATION TO SUPPORT TRANSITION FROM NURSERY TO P1

Stripy Nest was a creative project with a primary school in Edinburgh, Scotland, focusing on supporting children with additional support needs (ASN), including those with Autistic Spectrum Disorder (ASD), as they transitioned from nursery to Primary 1.

Stripy Nest was developed by Artist Kirstin Abraham and delivered in collaboration with Starcatchers' Associate Artist Katy Wilson and playworker Max Alexander.

They co-designed the creation of an installation with 30 children aged between 4 and 5 years old, and over the course of the project delivered participatory arts activities with 70 children and 18 adults, including seven teaching staff and 11 parents/family members.

Through a series of creative research workshops that took place before, during and after the summer break, the artists worked alongside the children in small groups. During this phase, artists looked to make connections with children and be led by their ideas, interests and needs. This open-ended, play-based approach ensured that the activities delivered were fun, creative and relevant.

Central to the co-design approach was ensuring the children had time and space to communicate their feelings and needs, whether through the traditional use of verbal language or through other means of communication, such as using visual symbols. The artists were actively listening and responding, providing an attuned and appropriate reaction so the children could see action resulting from their own voices. Understanding the support needs enabled artists to design the sessions to best accommodate the children they worked with. This helped children express themselves fully during the activities.

The installation that was created and placed within a quiet woodland area of the playground encapsulated the ideas and responses of the children. Willow, plants, ribbons and wool have been woven around the metal structures, reflecting activities the children were involved in and making connections with the immediate surroundings. The domed structures that resulted provide safe spaces that children can use to play in, or have some quiet time away from others, which for some of the children was a really important outcome of the project.

The installation in the woods became a special place for children:

> Placing the installation in the woods, a space the children had not yet experienced, was very positive as it offered a 'magical' place for the children to come play. When they were leaving the session, the children asked their teachers if it would stay there. (Kirstin Abrahams, Lead Artist)

Photos from this project can be found at: www.starcatchers.org.uk/engagement/stripy-nest

SPROG ROCK (2017) – CREATING NEW MUSIC FOR AND WITH NURSERY CHILDREN IN SCOTLAND

Sprog Rock was originally developed by artist Katy Wilson during her Starcatchers Residency at Tramway, Glasgow, in 2010. Katy wanted to create a gig for young children, giving them access to music that they really liked. The band of musicians involved created covers of well-known songs and rap versions of nursery rhymes, but there was always a desire from the group to work with children to create new music that was relevant to them.

In 2017, Starcatchers and the Sprog Rock team secured support from the Youth Music Initiative that enabled us to do this. Over a number of months, members of the Sprog Rock collective visited nurseries in four communities close to local arts centres: Alloa near Macrobert Arts Centre, Craigmillar near Lyra Theatre, Greenock near The Beacon, and Easterhouse near Platform. Through a series of workshops, the musicians engaged with the children to explore what was important to them, and through this created lyrics and music that became new songs, performed at gigs in each of the arts centres for the children and their families to attend together.

The workshops were designed to be interactive, playful and creative sessions. The musicians introduced children to different types of instruments:

> It has been great to share such a diversity of percussion, brass, woodwind, vocals and electronics. Some have loved dancing to the drums and some talking and singing about birthdays and telling us about their dreams down the end of a microphone. (Liam Chapman, Drummer)

The children were also introduced to different styles of music:

> It was fun to let them hear music from diverse artists such as David Byrne & St Vincent, Battles, and PJ Harvey. Dancing to Battles with 4-year-olds is probably one of the most joyful experiences ... (Greg Sinclair, Cellist)

These experiences encouraged the children to share their thoughts and their feelings which became the lyrics for new songs. Moffat Early Years Centre in Craigmillar's song was all about being dizzy, whereas Greengables Nursery's song was about the things the children did to comfort themselves when they were scared or upset.

The process the musicians undertook with the children was what facilitated their voices to be heard. The musicians had a genuine interest in engaging with what was important to the 3- and 4-year-olds in the settings. They wanted to create music that was for them and inspired by them. The children's hopes, dreams, fears and favourite things were reflected in the music created.

The children shared their perspectives openly and honestly. *Same but Different* was created by Kelly Street Nursery in Greenock after discussions with the children about what it might be like when they got older. Pete Lannon, guitarist in Sprog Rock, reflected that it

> came from some beautiful and interesting conversations with the children about how they felt about getting older and all of the things that might be different. These ranged from 'being in a different gymnastics class' to 'going to the big school and doing homework' and a huuuuge list of all of the different things we wanted to be (Spiderman, Wonder Woman, a reindeer, a mermaid ...). It was funny listening to 3- and 4-year-olds

be nostalgic about how they were getting older but also really nice hearing what they were hopeful for...

Videos from this project can be found at: www.starcatchers.org.uk/engagement/sprog-rock-2017

BLUE BLOCK STUDIO (2014) – A PLAY INSTALLATION FOR BABIES AGED 0–24 MONTHS AND THEIR PARENTS/CARERS

Blue Block Studio was a tourable play installation for babies aged 0–24 months and their parents/carers that was created by Katy Wilson and a team of artists and musicians in response to a lack of beautiful spaces for babies to 'be', play or connect with their parents.

The installation space and the activities that took place within it were developed over a 9-month research period involving the creative team and groups of babies and their parents who tested some of the materials. The way the babies engaged during these development sessions shaped the design and content of the final installation space and ensured that the content was relevant, interesting and appropriate for babies across the 0–24-month age range. From reflective mirrored walls and sections of flooring, to black and white patterned music boxes, light boxes and projection, to a ball run and fans that blew ribbons and giant confetti – everything in the space was designed and tested with babies.

This rigorous creative process was essential to the creation of a play space that was inviting and stimulating for the babies and where the parents/carers would be able to relax, switch off from the outside world and connect with their baby for the 40-minute session.

The multi-sensory approach where the space, materials and soundscape combined in a holistic environment supported the very young audience to engage and play. Their responses were often enlightening to their parents, where they were acknowledging their babies' abilities, sometimes for the first time. The experience enabled these very young infants to be seen and heard.

Videos from this project can be found at: www.starcatchers.org.uk/production/blue-block-studio-2016

PROJECT 2: BEING AN INVESTIGATOR IN OUR LEARNING ENVIRONMENT

HEIDI SAIRANEN

In this project, I introduce a playful and participatory approach where children act as investigators of their own learning environment. I will exemplify a pedagogical tool with which children can multimodally make meaning of their learning environment. The approach is grounded in our research (Sairanen and Kumpulainen, 2014) where children are supported in discussing their sense of agency through visual-narrative inquiry (Pink, 2013). This method encourages children to discover and present their thoughts and aspirations about the learning environment where they act. The method stems from the sociocultural studies of agency (see e.g. Vygotsky, 1978) and understands agency as relational activity which develops between people and environment. The method was originally developed to investigate how different social settings – including material, social and cultural resources – can offer possibilities and challenges for children's experiences and meaning-making, and how their relational agency can be constructed in social and cultural spaces (see Sairanen and Kumpulainen, 2014).

The approach which I developed as a tool for teachers offers a pedagogically appropriate way to discuss with young children their aspirations, beliefs and hopes towards the learning environment around them. With this approach, teachers can involve children in the pedagogical design of their mutual learning environment. The approach encourages teachers to engage in meaningful dialogue with children and support children's agency. This chapter asks:

1. How can young children make meaning through a pedagogical approach called 'Being an Investigator of Our Learning Environment'?

2.   How can teachers using this specific approach encourage children to act as producers and designers in their mutual learning environment?

THEORY BEHIND THE METHOD

The play-based method used in this project is based on children's right to express their opinions and influence their lifeworlds where they act. Drawing from the United Nations Convention on the Rights of the Child (UN Commission on Human Rights, 1990), children have the right to be heard, and their voices should be taken into account in decisions concerning them. Especially in educational contexts, understanding children's agency and promoting it enables children to engage in learning and to develop an attitude and understanding that they can affect their lives, surroundings and learning (Lipponen and Kumpulainen, 2011; Stetsenko, 2013). Pramling Samuelsson and Asplund Carlsson (2008) argued that through play-based methods, young children can more broadly express their thoughts and ideas.

According to sociocultural theory (Vygotsky, 1978) and the relational nature of agency (see e.g. Edwards, 2005), in which this approach is grounded, children's sense of agency develops across time and space as agency is constantly developing between children and the environment. Children face and experience different social settings in their every-day life and use different material, social and cultural resources when interacting with others (see Sairanen and Kumpulainen, 2014). By discovering children's sense of agency and the sociocultural conditions which mediate them, we are able to ensure children's meaningful educational engagement (Sairanen and Kumpulainen, 2014). The notion of socio-cultural (Vygotsky, 1978) theory understands learning as a social process between children and the environment, and which is mediated by cultural tools such as language. This project aims to develop that idea.

The play-based method I have developed following our study (Sairanen and Kumpulainen, 2014) encourages children to make meaning of their lifeworlds and share their sense of agency with the people around them. The approach emphasises children's voices (see e.g. Lundy, 2007), experiences and viewpoints within their learning environment (Christensen and James, 2017) and adopts playful pedagogy, which is pedagogically appropriate for young children (e.g. Pramling Samuelsson and Asplund Carlsson, 2008). Playfulness is thus a state of mind which enables children to take new roles and be creative (Sefton-Green et al., 2015). This pedagogical approach is aimed at revealing the possibilities and challenges offered by different social settings for children's experiences and meaning-making.

DESCRIPTION OF THE METHOD

The approach used in this project was developed following visual-narrative inquiry (Pink, 2013), based on visual ethnography, the narrative studies of identity

(McAdams et al., 2006) and narrative semiotics in general (Greimas and Porter, 1977), in which children use photos to narrate their meaning-making using visual elements. The core of this approach is that children have opportunities to explore their learning environment. This approach offers a dialogical tool for teachers to understand how children experience their learning environment and acknowledge the cultural and social meanings embedded within it. This approach is practicable with children aged from 6 to 7. However, research shows that multimodal methods are suitable for children across age and development stages (Pink, 2013; Blaisdell et al., 2018) because of their variety and multifariousness. The approach requires teachers to work with children in a group (between five and seven children) or as individuals.

Wall (2017) argues that visual methods are ethically more appropriate for children. They offer a multimodal way for children to make meaning (Pink, 2013), so children with various development and maturity stages can participate. However, ethical considerations regarding process and outcomes are important. For example, it is important to consider how and where to store children's photos, and when the photos are in digital form they must be stored to meet the ethical rules of the specific community (Flewitt, 2020). Representing the photos taken by children is an issue which has to be discussed with children throughout the project, with their consent or prohibition about showing the photos to other people respected.

The following description is provided to exemplify this approach for teachers working with children in the transition from pre-primary to primary education.

CHILDREN AS PRODUCERS AND DESIGNERS OF THEIR LEARNING ENVIRONMENT

This playful activity begins with an orientation phase. The main idea for the orientation is to familiarise the children with the devices they will use. This phase requires digital devices with a camera tool, and the aim is for children to learn how to switch on the device, how to take photos and how to delete them. This knowledge about how to use the devices is important as a basis for the approach, so that children can take photos independently (see Thomson, 2008). However, the knowledge of using the device very likely evolves during the photo-taking (for the project), and to ensure that every child can take part in the activity children are shadowed by the teacher throughout (although this has additional advantages, outlined below). By shadowing, I mean helping children when needed so the children can concentrate on the main objective of the project, which is exploring the environment with a camera. The orientation phase lasts around half an hour, depending on how familiar the children are with the devices they will be using.

(Continued)

The second phase involves taking photos following verbal instruction. The first instruction for the children is to take photos of things which they like to do. The second instruction is to take photos of things they are allowed to do, and the third instruction is to take photos of things they wish to do. Focusing on each subject at a time, individually or in a group, children are asked to look at both sides of the subject (see Table IV.1). The children are allowed to take as many photos as they want, and decisions not to take any photos should also be appreciated. The researcher or early years practitioner (or any adult working with the children) should shadow the children to ensure that they understand the photos the children are taking.

Table IV.1   The second phase: The subject of the photo and the instruction

The subject of the photo	The instruction
I/we like to do	Take a photo/photos of things you like and do not like to do.
I am/we are allowed to do	Take a photo/photos of things you are allowed and not allowed to do.
I/we wish to do	Take a photo/photos of things that you do and do not wish to do.

The children and the teacher agree on the place where the children take the photos. In this example, the children were discovering their sense of agency in an ECE centre and in primary school, so the site of photography was the ECE centre or the school and the yard. The teacher can choose to shadow the children to support them in taking the photos and to have some sense of the photos they are taking already in this phase of the activity. When shadowing, the adults should not give any advice or hints about where to take photos. Shadowing, as explained previously, helps the adults later connect the photos and their intentions if the children have a hard time remembering all the photos they have taken. When children have been shadowed, the researcher is able to match the photos and the children after the photographing phase if the child is uncertain which photo was taken after which instruction.

After the photographing, the researcher or ECE practitioner gathers the children to discuss the photos individually. The discussions can also be arranged in a group, but concerning the meaning of the individual photos, individual discussions are advisable. The discussion phase aims at a proper dialogue between the teacher and the child, with the child leading the conversation. First, a child chooses the photos she/he wants to involve in the discussion. Children may reject any photo they want, if it was mistakenly taken, or they simply do not feel like involving it in their photos. Then, the children present their photos and talk about the object of the photo and why she/he has taken the photo. Using photos and words gives the children more opportunities to express themselves, as words are not the only means of expression (see Wall, 2017).

The discussions may last from half an hour to an hour, depending on how many photos the child has taken and wants to involve in the discussion. It is advisable to arrange the discussions quite soon after the second phase so children still remember their photos. Ultimately, the aim of the discussion is for the child to describe which elements influenced her/his sense of agency and how the environment might be developed. The child creates a folder – analogue with printed photos or digital with, for example, a tablet – where she/he includes all the photos and narratives they feel are worth saving. During the semester, the children can take photographs multiple times (at least twice a semester) and build up their folder. Further, if the approach is conducted multiple times during the semester, it is more likely the learning environment will be acted upon by the teachers listening to the children's perspectives. This means it may increasingly meet children's hopes and wishes, or their thinking will move forward with the environment.

Discovering children's thoughts and aspirations across time and school transition requires sessions in pre-primary and primary education environments. If this method is to be used during a transition phase (e.g. from pre-primary education to primary education), then the children should be given the exact same instructions in both contexts. The results can then be compared, taking account of the fact that the physical environment may have been changed, affecting the resulting dialogue.

DISCUSSION AND CONCLUSIONS

This method focuses on children (6–7 years old) with the aim of making meaning of their environment. Through visual and vocal meaning-making, children have an opportunity to explore and introduce their ideas, thoughts and wishes about the environment. The method encourages teachers to design pedagogy and to develop the learning environment in collaboration with the children. Through the method, children are not only users but also producers of the learning environment. In addition, visual narrative inquiry offers a multimodal and dialogical way to use image and narration to make meaning between the visual and the vocal.

This pedagogically designed method enables children to develop their sense of belonging and civics. Visual narrative inquiry in which children act as co-researchers offers possibilities for children to have a say and for teachers and other adults and children to listen and involve their thinking and aspirations in pedagogical design. The methodology is also intended to allow children to have a voice in transition situations (e.g. from pre-primary education to primary education) in which they can take their previous experiences to their new environments, although the method can be transferred to younger and older children in different formal and informal contexts. Doing research with children in this way positions them at the centre of the study and shows they can take part as active participants in the research process, offering insights into their lifeworlds to researchers and

ECE practitioners without gatekeepers (Wall, 2017). Instead of being 'used' for researchers' own purposes, children gain learning experiences while collecting and discussing photos. Although one aim of the method is to strengthen children's voices, the ultimate objective is to develop the learning environment as a result of the dialogue between the children and the teacher. This project aims to show how this is possible.

REFERENCES

Blaisdell, C., Arnott, L., Wall, K. and Robinson, C. (2018). Look Who's Talking: Using creative, playful arts-based methods in research with young children. *Journal of Early Childhood Research*, 17 (1): 14–31.

Christensen, P. and James, A. (2017). Researching children and childhood: Cultures of communication. In P. Christensen and A. James (Eds.), *Research with Children: Perspectives and Practices*. London: Routledge.

Edwards, A. (2005). Relational agency: Learning to be a resourceful practitioner. *International Journal of Educational Research*, 43 (3): 168–82.

Flewitt, R. (2020). Ethics and researching young children's digital literacy practices. In O. Erstad, R. Flewitt, B. Kümmerling-Meibauer and Í. S. Pires Pereira (Eds.), *The Routledge Handbook of Digital Literacies in Early Childhood*. London: Routledge.

Greimas, A. J. and Porter, C. (1977). Elements of a narrative grammar. *Diacritics*, 7 (1): 23–40.

Lipponen, L. and Kumpulainen, K. (2011). Acting as accountable authors: Creating interactional spaces for agency work in teacher education. *Teaching and Teacher Education*, 27: 812–19.

Lundy, L. (2007). 'Voice' is not enough: Conceptualising Article 12 of the United Nations Convention on the Rights of the Child. *British Educational Research Journal*, 33 (6): 927–42.

McAdams, D. P., Josselson, R. and Lieblich, A. (Eds.) (2006). *Identity and Story: Creating Self in Narrative*. Washington, DC: American Psychological Association. pp. 15–35.

Pink, S. (2013). *Doing Visual Ethnography*. London: Sage.

Pramling Samuelsson, I. and Asplund Carlsson, M. (2008). The playing learning child: Towards a pedagogy of early childhood. *Scandinavian Journal of Educational Research*, 52 (6): 623–41.

Sairanen, H. and Kumpulainen, K. (2014). A visual narrative inquiry into children's sense of agency in preschool and first grade. *International Journal of Educational Psychology*, 3 (2): 141–74.

Sefton-Green, J., Kumpulainen, K., Lipponen, L., Sintonen, S., Rajala, A. and Hilppö, J. (2015). *Manifesto by the Playful Learning Center: Playing with Learning*. Helsinki: University of Helsinki.

Stetsenko, A. (2013). Theorizing personhood for the world in transition and change: Reflections from a transformative activist stance. In J. Martin and M. H. Bickhard (Eds.), *The Psychology of Personhood: Philosophical, Historical, Social-Developmental, and Narrative Perspectives.* Cambridge: Cambridge University Press. pp. 181–203.

Thomson, P. (2008). Children and young people: Voices in visual research. In P. Thompson (Ed.), *Doing Visual Research with Children and Young People.* London: Routledge.

UN Commission on Human Rights (1990). *Convention on the Rights of the Child* (E/CN.4/RES/1990/74), 7 March. Available at: www.refworld.org/docid/3b00f03d30. html (accessed 5 September 2020).

Vygotsky, L. (1978). *Mind in Society: The Development of Higher Mental Processes.* Cambridge, MA: Harvard University Press.

Wall, K. (2017). Exploring the ethical issues related to visual methodology when including young children's voice in wider research samples. *International Journal of Inclusive Education*, 21 (3): 316–31.

RESEARCH PROPOSAL 1: INVESTIGATING THE PERCEPTIONS OF YOUNG CHILDREN IN SCHOOL-BASED PRETEND PLAY

TRÍONA STOKES

OUTCOME OF THE RESEARCH PROPOSAL

A similar proposal to that which follows was submitted to the School of Education, Queen's University, Belfast. Further to obtaining institutional ethical clearance, the research project was undertaken to fulfil the requirements of the Education Doctorate (EdD). The data were collected in January–February 2015. Following analysis and write-up, the doctoral thesis was successfully defended at 'viva voce' in April 2016.

RATIONALE

This study is set in the Irish educational context and the fast-changing government-led policy landscape of early years childcare and education. *Aistear: The Early Childhood Curricular Framework* (referred to as *Aistear*), introduced in 2009, straddles educational provisions of childcare and early childhood education. *Aistear* (NCCA, 2009), meaning journey, represents a thematic approach to young children's play and learning, linking home, school and community.

The principal aim of this study is to investigate the perception of children and other key stakeholders of how pretend play is conceived and enacted within Irish primary school contexts.

The primary objective is to examine children's agency in terms of their choice and control of school-based pretend play, as determined through pretend play themes, resources and environments, and the identification of factors enabling or hindering children's choice and control of play therein. The associated research questions and italicised sub-question are contained in Figure IV.1 below.

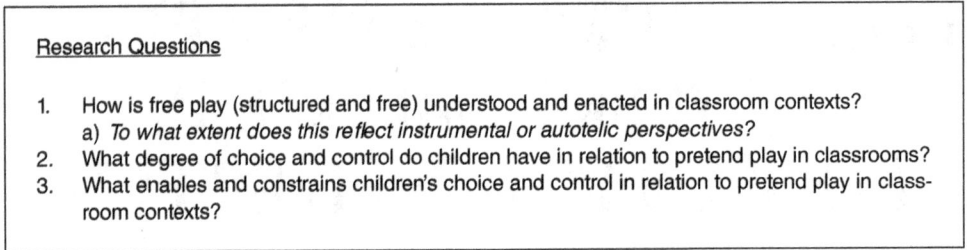

Research Questions

1. How is free play (structured and free) understood and enacted in classroom contexts?
   a) *To what extent does this reflect instrumental or autotelic perspectives?*
2. What degree of choice and control do children have in relation to pretend play in classrooms?
3. What enables and constrains children's choice and control in relation to pretend play in classroom contexts?

Figure IV.1   Research questions

REVIEW OF THE LITERATURE

Play definitions and categorisation introduce the review of the literature. In *Aistear* (NCCA, 2009: 54), the term pretend play describes dramatic, make-believe, role and fantasy play, socio-dramatic play, small-world play, and early literacy and numeracy play. Free play is play free of adult involvement, whereby children choose the theme, location and resourcing of their play texts. Play is, therefore, defined by a process, rather than as a product or outcome, which would compromise its free-flowing status (Bruce, 2001).

Lester and Russell's (2008) binary framework is used to categorise play as instrumental or autotelic, and employed as an organisational structure throughout. Play definitions broadly categorised as instrumental focus on learning and development, or autotelic, play as important for its own sake (Lester and Russell, 2008).

Claims for an instrumental view of play and pretend play cite its multiple benefits for child development, from cognitive to physical, social, emotional and linguistic development. The reported benefits extend from physical play behaviours to construction play, rough-and-tumble play and co-operative play which can assist with identifying sequence and pattern in narrative, problem-solving and social learning (Forman, 2006; Tannock, 2011).

In terms of cognitive development, independent investigation in pretend play may develop scientific thinking as children engage in experimental testing, exploring cause and effect (Dodds, 2009). Manipulation of materials may develop mathematical thinking as children explore the numerical aspects of narrative play, such as time and temperature (Stafford, 2012). Pretending is essential to children mastering their emotions, thinking and behaviour (Berk et al., 2006). In terms of social development, socio-dramatic play has been linked to creativity, tolerance and turn-taking (Smilansky,

1968), and the demonstration of advances in divergent thinking and problem-solving capacities (French, 2012).

The articulation of meaning and language development share similar processes to play, and have been shown to benefit oral language, emergent literacy and meta-linguistic awareness (Bordrova and Leong, 2015; Prendiville and Toye, 2007). In negotiating the rules of play, self-regulation can be developed, as well as 'learning to learn' behaviours in terms of metacognition (Whitebread, 2010, 2014). Persistence and determination can increase through playing regularly (Tovey, 2013).

In autotelic terms, pretend play is viewed as an expression of free play, aligning it with the writing of Friedrich Froebel (1782–1852), and the tenets of Froebel's (1826) philosophy are afforded precedence in examining the autotelic nature of play, or its intrinsic value. The Froebelian principles of *unity, connectedness, a nurturing environment* and *respect* are central with regards to pretend play.

METHODOLOGY

A total of 75 children aged 4–6 from three infant classrooms will participate in the project, with a small group (five–eight children) in each school assisting with research design and analysis as part of a Children's Research Advisory Group (CRAG). The remit of the CRAG is to advise on how best to engage children with the research subject and provide insights thereon, assisting with the interpretation and analysis of child interview data (Emerson, 2013).

A qualitative methodology and participatory approach is proposed, using multiple data-gathering methods, akin to the Mosaic Approach (Clark and Moss, 2001). Planned research instruments for use with stakeholders are outlined in Figure IV.2 and aligned with the research questions listed in Figure IV.1.

Weekly 'focal child observations' are planned for each group to focus on collaboratively created play texts (Jarvis, 2009). Observations are structured by statements relating to free-flow behaviours derived from 12 quality play indicators (Bruce, 1996).

Research Question (RQ)	Observation of pretend play	Pretend play resource audit	Arts-based research methods (pretend play catalogues)	Small-group, semi-structured child interviews	Teacher interviews	Principal teacher/ senior teacher with responsibility for play
RQ1		x	x	x	x	x
RQ2	x	x	x	x	x	x
RQ3	x	x	x	x	x	x

Figure IV.2 Planned research instruments

Catalogues of children's preferred pretend play items will be prepared with the CRAG, and child participants will be invited to engage in catalogue voting. Catalogues will serve the interview process as both a grouping mechanism and a discussion stimulus.

Due to the flexibility offered by the absence of the requirement for equivalence among all interviews, small-group, semi-structured interviews are best suited to engage young children (Basit, 2010). The purpose of the interviews is to give children more time and space to talk about their views and to explain their data. Children's interview protocol poses questions about the extent to which they get to decide the pretend play content, where their ideas come from, and the role of the teacher and other players in it.

Semi-structured interviews will be conducted with seven adult stakeholders, including school principals and a senior teacher with responsibility for play. Interviews with adults are used to garner their interpretations of children's perceptions of pretend play. Adult interview protocol addresses questions about the construction of understandings of free play, custom and practice within the school regarding play and pretend play, and how children can exercise agency therein.

DATA ANALYSIS

Audio-recorded interview data will be transcribed, enabling increased researcher famili- arity and pattern identification within and across settings. Data retrieval codes will be adopted for ease of access and management of large data volumes (Miles and Huberman, 1994). These will be employed for effective data organisation under potential themes and sub-themes and for data analysis. Due to the importance of proximity of conversations to play episodes, observations will be clarified in discussion with participants directly afterwards (Bruce, 1996). While researcher interpretation will be primary, insights will be invited from all participants in the study.

ETHICAL CONSIDERATIONS AND TRUSTWORTHINESS OF THE STUDY

The BERA Ethical Guidelines for Educational Research (2011) inform the establishment and negotiation of each stage of the research process. While ethical tensions are inevita- ble in educational research, some tensions can be anticipated, such as renewing ongoing consent (Dockett et al., 2009). Thus, processes for renewing consent with junior classes will be in built into the research methodology.

The multiple research methods used to explore play create a layering effect which ought to add richness and depth to the research findings. The choice of participatory methods with young children may also serve to increase the trustworthiness of the research, or the

credibility or 'perceived truth' of its findings (Lincoln and Guba, 1985). Adult interpretations of children's play worlds alone cannot be considered trustworthy (Rogers and Evans,
2008). However, through a commitment to check and re-check adult interpretations with
children through the CRAGs, it will be argued that trustworthiness can be increased.

POTENTIAL CONTRIBUTION TO SCHOLARLY RESEARCH AND EDUCATION PRACTICE

This qualitative study aims to add to the evidence base of Irish pretend play practice,
further to national policy developments, through offering insight into school-based play
in three settings. The conceptual contribution of the study lies in the determination of
play as autotelic, or of its own inherent value. The methodological contribution lies in its
adoption of the Mosaic Approach (Clark and Moss, 2001) and its creative adaptation of
multiple participatory methods in sharing views effectively and to suit the strengths of its
participant children and co-researchers.

REFERENCES

Basit, T. M. (2010). *Conducting Research in Educational Contexts*. London: Continuum.

BERA (2011). *Ethical Guidelines for Educational Research*. London: British Educational
Research Association. Available at: www.bera.ac.uk/wp-content/uploads/2014/02/
BERA-Ethical-Guidelines-2011.pdf?noredirect=1 (accessed 15 November 2020).

Berk, L. D, Mann, T. D. and Ogan, A. T. (2006). Make believe play: Well-being for development
of self-regulation. *Make Believe Play and Self-Regulation*. Illinois State University. Available
at: http://udel.edu/~roberta/play/BerkMannOgan.pdf (accessed 15 November 2020).

Bordrova, E. and Leong, D. (2015). Assessing and scaffolding make believe play. In NAEYC
(Ed.), *Spotlight on Young Children: Exploring Play*. Washington, DC: National Association
for the Education of Young Children.

Bruce, T. (1996). *Helping Young Children to Play*. London: Hodder & Stoughton Educational.

Bruce, T. (2001). *Learning through Play: For Babies, Toddlers and Young Children*. London:
Hodder Education.

Clark, A. and Moss, P. (2001). *Listening to Young Children: The Mosaic Approach*. London:
National Children's Bureau Enterprises.

Dockett, S., Einarsdottir, J. and Perry, B. (2009). Researching with children: Ethical tensions. *Journal of Early Childhood Research*, 7 (3): 283–98.

Dodds, S. (2009). 'We want to play': Primary children at play in the classroom. In A.
Brock, S. Dodds, J. Jarvis and Y. Olusoga (Eds.), *Perspectives on Play: Learning for Life*.
Harlow: Longman Pearson. pp. 146–72.

Emerson, L. (2013). *An Introduction to a Rights-Based Approach with Children and Young People*. Seminar at Queen's University, Belfast, November.

Forman, G. (2006). Constructive play. In D. P. Fromberg and D. Bergen (Eds.), *Play from Birth to Twelve: Contexts, Perspectives and Meanings* (2nd edn). New York: Routledge. pp. 103–10.

French, G. (2012) *Early Literacy and Numeracy Matters: Enriching Literacy and Numeracy Experiences in Early Childhood*. Dublin: Barnardos' Training and Resources Service.

Froebel, F. (1826). *Die Menschenerziehung*. Translated and annotated by W. N. Hailmann (Ed.) (2005), *The Education of Man*. New York: Dover Publications.

Jarvis, P. (2009). Building 'social hardiness' for life: Rough-and-tumble play in the early years of primary school. In A. Brock, S. Dodds, P. Jarvis and Y. Olusoga (Eds.), *Perspectives on Play: Learning for Life*. Harlow: Pearson Education. pp. 175–89.

Lester, S. and Russell, W. (2008). *Play for a Change: Play, Policy and Practice – A Review of Contemporary Perspectives*. London: National Children's Bureau, Play England.

Lincoln, Y. S. and Guba, E. G. (1985). *Naturalistic Inquiry*. London: Sage.

Miles, M. B. and Huberman, A. M. (1994). *Qualitative Data Analysis: An Expanded Sourcebook* (2nd edn). Thousand Oaks, CA: Sage.

NCCA (2009). *Aistear: The Early Childhood Curricular Framework*. Dublin: National Council for Curriculum and Assessment.

Prendiville, F. and Toye, N. (2007). *Speaking and Listening through Drama 7–11*. London: Paul Chapman Publishers.

Rogers, S. and Evans, J. (2008). *Inside Role-Play in Early Childhood Education: Researching Young Children's Perspectives*. Abingdon: Routledge.

Smilansky, S. (1968). *The Effects of Socio-Dramatic Play on Disadvantaged Preschool Children*. New York: John Wiley and Sons.

Stafford, P. (2012). Numeracy through play and real-life experiences. In M. Mhic Mhathúna and M. Taylor (Eds.), *Early Childhood Education and Care: An Introduction for Students in Ireland*. Dublin: Gill and Macmillan. pp. 141–6.

Tannock, M. (2011). Observing young children's rough-and-tumble play. *The Australasian Journal of Early Childhood*, 36 (2): 13–20.

Tovey, H. (2013). *Bringing the Froebel Approach to Your Early Years Practice*. London: David Fulton.

Whitebread, D. (2010). Play, metacognition and self-regulation. In P. Broadhead, J. Howard and E. Wood (Eds.), *Play and Learning in the Early Years: From Research to Practice*. London: Sage. pp. 161–76.

Whitebread, D. (2014). The importance of self-regulation for learning from birth. In H. Moylett (Ed.), *Characteristics of Effective Learning: Helping Young Children Become Learners for Life*. Maidenhead: Open University Press. pp. 15–35.

RESEARCH PROPOSAL 2: PLAYING AND BEING, HERE AND NOW – ADULTS USING IMPROVISATION TO JOIN CHILDREN AGED 0–5 IN FREE PLAY

MADDIE BROAD

The proposed research follows the experiences of myself and other adults as we join children in play through improvisation. The research will generate knowledge that emerges in our own playful encounters with children. Play sessions will be recorded using a small microphone, and recordings later combined with participants' sketches and notes. Data will be explored through reflective conversation and an intuitive, artist-led process.

When we sing or move or laugh together with someone else, it seems to convey the message 'I see you, I like you and as you are *you are ok*' (Kinsky, 2019). The need for that universal message is the rationale for this research. As adults who spend time with children, we have abundant opportunity to share that vital message through play. This research explores what the art of improvisation could offer adults and children in early years environments; when improvising adults are fully committed and enabled to join in. Beyond the narrative of child- or adult-led pedagogies, where might improvising adults and children lead each other?

An early years practitioner crawls beside a toddler; they are playing with a pebble on the ground. I wonder what will happen, and what won't. I wonder how far the adult will go to join in. Play is vital; in the UK, we recognise play as a child's right (UN Commission on Human Rights, 1990; DfE, 2017). What may seem a mess of noisy beings in a cheerfully chaotic early years environment can also be described as 'the highest expression of human development' (Froebel, 1826, in Early Education, 2019), 'essential' (DfE, 2017: 9), an 'entanglement of all human and non-human phenomena' (Barad, 2007; Murris, 2016: 12), and a fertile ground of encounter. However, some adults need reassurance of 'the strength of improvisation and play, a force that very young children have' (Sicat, 2018).

Too often, play is considered important only for (some of) what it stimulates: in early years education, this may be evidence of children's learning and development. The way we track and analyse children in line with EYFS[1] guidance can put adults under pressure, and the wider importance of play can be sadly neglected. When we feel under pressure, it becomes harder to play. It can seem 'as if the purpose of education is to make children into adults as quickly as possible' (Arculus, in press), and as if play in adulthood is unnecessary. This research radically counters that narrative by encouraging adults to *be with* children in play, and trust that the present moment can be everything they need.

WHAT DO I MEAN BY IMPROVISATION?

Improvisation is a way into play. It takes play beyond the question of adult or child leadership, where instead artists follow each other's lead on shared ground. With no fixed outcome in mind, improvisors are receptive and responsive through 'empathetic adjustment to others' (Young, 2011: 191). Can adults in free play with children allow themselves to be guided more by the present moment, and if so, what can their experiences suggest for early years pedagogy?

My understanding of improvisation comes from my experience as an artist who makes 'things that happen'; I 'go with the flow' in the living moment, responsive to provocations of space, time, material or other beings – 'I am in this room', 'I have this Play-Doh', 'let's see what happens'. Young children improvise in this very responsive way.

Play might feel good or perhaps challenging, and it is both motivated by and nurturing of 'the human need to engage with others' (Young, 2011: 183). Improvisation requires us to 'say yes' to possibility; to *go with* whatever is there. To make opportunities to 'say yes' with each other is crucial, in classrooms and conflict zones (Perrin, 2019), and 'particularly in a world of increasing diversity' (Young, 2011: 191). Regardless of who we are, I suggest we can come together in play.

While on EYTS[2] placement in nursery, I was encouraged to try *planning in the moment* (Ephgrave, 2018), and to use *sustained shared thinking* (Sylva et al., 2004), both of which require improvisation. However, it struck me that adults were more likely to improvise

---

[1]Early Years Foundation Stage
[2]Early Years Foundation Stage

with what is spoken and seen in play, shying away from taking part in children's physical or non-verbal activity. My definition of improvisation however includes responsiveness across sensory modes, for example between adults and children improvising together in non-verbal musical interactions (Arculus, 2013; Broad, 2018; Burke, 2018; Young, 2002, 2005, 2011), but I felt these modes of interaction were perceived as less valuable for the children.

It wasn't until my dissertation research that I experienced what felt more like *free* play in nursery. Arculus (2013) celebrates 2-year-olds as spontaneous improvisors, who 'move about a great deal, expressing themselves and making meaning through bodily engagement' (pp. 7–8); inspired by this, my research explored doing music with young children in their way, through multi-modal improvised free play. As artist/researcher, I felt relatively unbounded and more able to flow with children's ideas, with authentic fascination and presence; I was able to listen more closely and play more on shared ground. Those vivid encounters of deep immersion with children in play continue even now to shape my pedagogy.

When we improvise, it is undeniable that the present moment is plentiful of possibility; young children sense this, and I suggest that adults who may have forgotten can soon remember.

RESEARCH QUESTIONS

The project's design responds to these research questions:

- **What seems to happen when improvising adults join children in free play?** What is the nature of play, for and between individual participants, and in the intra-active environment? How do encounters of improvisation emerge and unfold during play sessions? Where does the play 'go', and where are participants 'taken' by improvised play? What seems to cultivate or stifle the possibility for improvisation in play?
- **How can improvisation in play be remembered, retold and represented?** What advantages and critical problems emerge through the processes of generating and representing data? How is it possible to listen to children through the research processes and assemblages of data?
- **What might the art of improvisation offer in practice between adults and early years children?** What do the participants and I think and feel about this question? How does improvisation feel for participants? What might knowledge, generated through the research, offer adults joining children in play?

INFLUENCES FROM LITERATURE AND IMPROVISATION PRACTICES

Elements of improvisation are shared between many disciplines, so the proposed research design invites the involvement of participants with various understandings of improvisation.

Early years music research (Young, 2002, 2005, 2011) shows that when adults improvise with children through musical mimicry and synchrony, it can extend children's creative ideas. Theories of *communicative musicality* (Malloch and Trevarthen, 2009) draw on the 'call and response' found between infant and carer, a sustained interaction of close listening and responsiveness which seems akin to the back-and-forth technique of *'yes, and'* which is integral to comedy improvisation and the art of clown play.

Intensive interaction is a technique also based on bodily and emotional mimicry and synchrony between people, which leads to a communication of empathy beyond spoken language; there are parallels to the dynamic responsiveness generated in the movement practice *contact improvisation.*

It is important for participants to be deeply involved in play sessions and then to reflect in various ways, together and alone. This was apparent when I took part in a piece of early years theatre with Emma Hutchinson, Director of Music House for Children. After almost total immersion in the present moment of performance, our troupe found post-performance conversations integral to sharing our reflections. Commitment to being in the moment and then reflecting together afterwards was extremely valuable to the quality of our practice.

Hutchinson's musical play spaces are creatively propelled by the spontaneous offerings of children, facilitated by adults' readiness to respond. This was a refreshing change from the 'one-way' arts experiences often mis-marketed as being appropriate for very young audiences. Babies and young children are now widely acknowledged as an audience demographic for early years theatre (Young, 2004: 24–6), but theatre-makers' attunement to young audiences often reveals a need for better integration of practice with available research about the approaches that strengthen ethics and accessibility (Fletcher-Watson, 2015; Fletcher-Watson et al., 2014).

The proposed study makes strong reference to the SALTMusic (Pitt and Arculus, 2018) project, which used an interdisciplinary approach and emphasised time for reflection in addressing its aim to 'create a transformative pedagogy' (p. 10). The involvement of music specialists and artists with speech and language professionals and children formed a community of practice (Wenger, 1998) through adult engagement in play with children. SALTMusic holds a strong belief in 'young children's enhanced ability to improvise across modes' (Pitt and Arculus, 2018: 17), and creates possibilities for adults to develop their practice along *with children*; this attitude is adopted within the present study.

Here are some ways of thinking that frame the ideas and approaches in the research. I start from a postmodern understanding of the child as being 'rich in potential, strong, powerful and competent' (Malaguzzi, 1993, cited in Dahlberg et al., 1999: 50) and 'resilient and resourceful in relationships' (Murris, 2016: 151). In line with 'methodological immaturity' (Gallacher and Gallagher, 2008), my researcher's identity is 'fallible, imperfect and naïve' (p. 511) because in the moment of improvisation there is no expert, and no 'truth-seeking' (Dahlberg et al., 1999: 35). The research questions call for 'meaning making, not fact finding' (Clark, 2010: 30), possibility rather than certainty. This view of reality in research means there is no singular truth, only multiplicity; knowledge might be thought of as 'knowledges', leading towards depth and further questions rather than absolute results.

METHODOLOGY

This research does not travel in a straight line towards certain outcomes but dances with the notion of a 'pedagogy of improvisation' (Lines, 2017). The research design, described in Table IV.2 and Figure IV.3, prepares the ground for this dance to take place: it holds space for immersion in as-yet-unknown improvised experiences and invites the re-configuration of 'space-time-matter' (Barad, 2007: 179) through playing with the data generated.

RESEARCH DESIGN

Table IV.2　Overview of research design

Phase one	Gather participants – early years practitioners, academics, artists and specialists working with young children in playful ways in the UK. Engage some of these practitioners as participants in recorded play sessions and involve others as critical friends of the project. Establish research locations that allow adults to join children in their naturalistic play environment.
Phase two	Visit each adult participant in turn to spend time with children in recorded play sessions and to reflect on the play sessions. This could be thought of as a series of short ethnographic adventures; while each visit is too short to be an ethnographic study, the characteristics of ethnography could inform the process of generating interpretivist data across a short period.
Phase three	Invite participants to come together to play with and reflect on the data.

Figure IV.3　Illustration of proposed research design, expressing its fluidity rather than discreet phases

RESEARCH METHODS

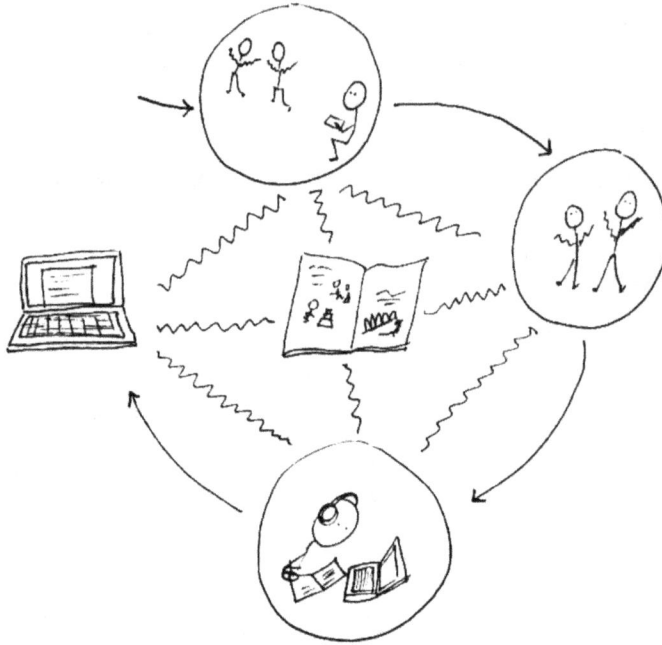

Figure IV.4   Diagram showing the proposed relationships between data

The research methods, shown in Figure IV.4 and Table IV.3, are chosen to explore 'the possible' rather than locate 'the certain'; they will generate data that allows for interpretations bound to context, not generalisations of findings.

Table IV.3   Matching research questions to methods

Research Questions	Research Methods	Discussion
What seems to happen when improvising adults join children in free play?	**Documenting play sessions**: The adult participant wears a lapel microphone and joins children in their naturalistic free-play environment using techniques of improvisation. Sketches and field notes are made to help the participant express, and remember later, significant moments and thoughts that stick out (see also below).	The microphone should give a good impression of the original play event through participants' voice, intonation, timing and energy. Because it does not capture visual information, the adult participant uses sketching and note-making from memory shortly after the event. Cameras are considered more obtrusive, impractical and ethically problematic.

Research Questions	Research Methods	Discussion
How can improvisation in play be remembered, retold and represented?	**Listening back and playing with the documentation**: The adult participant makes reflective written notes, sketches and transcriptions based on the sound recordings and memories of play sessions. They have reflective conversations with others. They live with the documentation and rework it in various written, embodied and creative ways. **Hearing children's voices**: Spending time with the participating children, inviting their reflection in appropriate ways and discussing with others who know them could give insight into the children's knowledge, thoughts and experiences of the research. Data in visual and sound form is more accessible to child participants and this should be considered throughout; perhaps a sharing of data can be inclusive of and of benefit to all participants.	Moments that glow (MacLure, 2013) emerge through spending time living with the data in mind. In previous research (Broad, 2018), I combined recorded sound with sketches and field notes to create video-like impressions of play events without the need for a camera, which generated different knowledge by playing with the documentation. These 'videos' were shareable beyond the study and with the research location, allowing for positive impact beyond the initial project.
What might the art of improvisation have to offer in practice between adults and early years children?	**Participants reflecting on the research activities**: Organised opportunities to reflect immediately after play sessions. Continued informal opportunities for adult participants to share thoughts and experiences in person and via messages. Respectful and appropriate involvement of participant children in research processes. **Researcher's impression**: The researcher takes responsibility for forming an overall interpretation of the research activity and documentation in relation to theory and literature.	Moments that glow (MacLure, 2013) emerge through expressing your experiences and relating to others. It is important that as the researcher I take responsibility to bring it all together in my thesis, but I also claim not to be the all-knowing expert, because no one person can see it all. This is an interpretive study, and my position will be highly informed while also incomplete, following 'methodological immaturity' (Gallacher and Gallagher, 2008).

These qualitative, interpretive methods are flexible, mobile, immersive and able to acknowledge – never entirely capture – the complexity of play sessions. Sound recording, sketching, reflective writing and conversations, and playing with the data, allow knowledge to unfold with time.

The proposed methods reflect the fluidity of improvisation itself. There is an emerging, relatively under-documented movement toward similar approaches to data generation, particularly in new materialist research. Donna Carlyle makes sketches 'to sharpen [her] ethnographer's gaze and attune [her] to the sensory and tactile nature of child-dog encounters' (2019: 200). Christina MacRae's use of drawing from slowed-down film data makes it 'possible to read an event in terms of its complexities' by paying 'attention to children's intra-actions' (MacRae, 2019: 6). The term intra-action (Barad, 2007; Davies, 2014; Murris, 2016) describes how everything in space and time 'affects, and is open to being affected by, the other' (Davies, 2014: 6); through intra-action, all human and non-human things are connected in a place of play.

ETHICS

> It is not sufficient to carry out research on or about childhood; childhood researchers must research for and with children. (Gallacher and Gallagher, 2008: 500)

Ethical approaches in research with young children go hand-in-hand with improvisation. Going *with* others' cues in improvisation uses the same skills as listening and responding to children's non-verbal consent.

Consent must be sought not as a one-off but as an ongoing achievement (Albon and Mukherji, 2010). The ongoing, informed, voluntary consent of participants is a central ethical challenge in any research, especially with young children. While adults can give consent through verbal and written agreement, it is the researcher's responsibility to continually communicate with children in ways they can understand, with sensitivity to children's multiple languages (Clark and Moss, 2001). Babies may demonstrate consent more bodily by 'refusing to engage, becoming abnormally quiet, turning away or crying' (Langston et al., 2004, cited in Arculus, 2013: 26); such indications translate as consent withdrawal. Researchers can use objects of data collection, such as a microphone, to stimulate conversation with children towards developing their understanding of participation in research processes.

The safety of children and other participants is protected by following BERA guidance (2011), working with the research locations' own policies and conducting risk assessments, maintaining the anonymity of children and research locations, and ensuring the safe storage and consented sharing of data.

CONCLUSION

The proposed research would generate emergent understandings *of* improvisation *through* improvisation and its practitioners, at once highlighting how and why to *be with*, rather than *do to*, other beings. The project would meet a need for connection between children, adults, practice and research, in the arts and early years, inviting their interplay more on shared ground. Perhaps, despite our adult-world strategies and struggles, *being with* one another is child's play.

REFERENCES

Albon, D. and Mukherji, P. (2010). *Research Methods in Early Childhood: An Introductory Guide*. London: Sage.

Arculus, C. (2013). *What is the Nature of Communication between Two Year Olds in a Musical Free Play Environment?* MA research module, Birmingham City University. Available at: www.crec.co.uk/research-paper-archive/2013-011.pdf (accessed 15 September 2019).

Arculus, C. (in press). What is the potential of music as emergent knowledge? *International Journal of Music in Early Childhood*.

Barad, K. (2007). *Meeting the Universe Halfway: Quantum Physics and the Entanglement of Matter and Meaning*. Durham, NC: Duke University Press.

BERA (British Educational Research Association) (2011). *Ethical Guidelines for Educational Research*. Available at: www.bera.ac.uk/wp-content/uploads/2014/02/BERA-Ethical-Guidelines-2011.pdf?noredirect=1 (accessed 15 September 2019).

Broad, M. (2018). *Musical Encounters on Shared Ground: Possibilities of Intra-Active Encounters in Nursery between an Adult and 2.5–4.5-Year-Old Children*. Brighton: University of Sussex.

Burke, N. (2018). *Musical Development Matters*. Watford: The British Association for Early Childhood Education.

Carlyle, D. (2019). Walking in rhythm with Deleuze and a dog inside the classroom: Being and becoming well and happy together. *Medical Humanities*, 45: 199–210.

Clark, A. (2010). *Transforming Children's Spaces: Children's and Adults' Participation in Designing Learning Environments*. London: Routledge.

Clark, A. and Moss, P. (2001). *Listening to Young Children: The Mosaic Approach*. London: National Children's Bureau Enterprises.

Dahlberg, G., Moss, P. and Pence, A. (1999). *Beyond Quality in Early Childhood Education and Care: Postmodern Perspectives*. London: Falmer Press.

Davies, B. (2014). *Listening to Children: Being and Becoming*. Abingdon: Routledge.

DfE (Department for Education) (2017). *Statutory Framework for the Early Years Foundation Stage*. Available at: https://assets.publishing.service.gov.uk/government/uploads/system/uploads/attachment_data/file/596629/EYFS_STATUTORY_FRAMEWORK_2017.pdf (accessed 15 September 2019).

Early Education (2019). *About Froebel*. Available at: www.early-education.org.uk/about-froebel (accessed 15 September 2019).

Ephgrave, A. (2018). *Planning in the Moment with Young Children: A Practical Guide for Early Years Practitioners and Parents*. Abingdon: Routledge.

Fletcher-Watson, B. (2015). Seen and not heard: Participation as tyranny in theatre for early years. *Research in Drama Education: The Journal of Applied Theatre and Performance*, 20 (1): 24–38.

Fletcher-Watson, B., Fletcher-Watson, S., McNaughton, M. J. and Birch, A. (2014). From cradle to stage: How early years performing arts experiences are tailored to the developmental capabilities of babies and toddlers. *Youth Theatre Journal*, 28 (2): 130–46.

Gallacher, L. and Gallagher, M. (2008). Methodological immaturity in childhood research? Thinking through 'participatory methods'. *Childhood*, 15 (4): 499–516.

Kinsky, V. (2019). A dialog between music and movement: About the art of musical accompaniment of movement. Paper presented at EuNet MERYC 2019, Counterpoints of the Senses, Ghent, Belgium, 29 March.

Lines, D. (2017). Jazz departures: Sustaining a pedagogy of improvisation. In C. Naughton, G. Biesta and D. Cole (Eds.), *Art, Artists and Pedagogy: Philosophy and the Arts in Education*. Milton: Routledge.

MacLure, M. (2013). The wonder of data. *Cultural Studies ó Critical Methodologies*, 13 (4): 228–32.

MacRae, C. (2019). The red blanket: A dance of animacy. *Global Studies of Childhood*. DOI: 10.1177/2043610619832899.

Malloch, S. and Trevarthen, C. (2009). *Communicative Musicality*. Oxford: Oxford University Press.

Murris, K. (2016). *The Posthuman Child: Educational Transformation through Philosophy with Picturebooks*. London: Routledge.

Perrin, A. (2019). *The Real Play Revolution*. London: Watkins.

Pitt, J. and Arculus, C. (2018). *SALTmusic Research Report*. Available at: https://issuu.com/gyct/docs/SALTmusic-research-report (accessed 15 September 2019).

Sicat, B. (2018). 'Icilà', *Benoît Sicat, an indisciplinary artist*. Available at: http://benoitsicat.blogspot.com/index.html#2802366569624402917 (accessed 15 September 2019) [translated from French to English using Google's 'Translate this page'].

Sylva, K., Siraj-Blatchford, I., Taggert, B., Sammons, P., Elliot, K. and Melhuish, E. (2004). *The Effective Provision of Preschool Education (EPPE) Project Technical Paper 12 – The Final Report: Effective Preschool Education*. London: DfES and Institute of Education, University of London.

UN Commission on Human Rights (1990). *Convention on the Rights of the Child* (E/CN.4/RES/1990/74), 7 March. Available at: www.refworld.org/docid/3b00f03d30.html (accessed 5 September 2020).

Wenger, E. (1998). *Communities of Practice*. Cambridge: Cambridge University Press.

Young, S. (2002). Young children's spontaneous vocalizations in free play: Observations of two- to three-year-olds in a day-care setting. *Bulletin of the Council for Research in Music Education,* 152 (Spring): 43–53.

Young, S. (2004). 'It's a bit like flying': Developing participatory theatre with the under-twos: A case study of Oily Cart. *Research in Drama Education,* 9 (1): 13–28.

Young, S. (2005). Changing tune: Reconceptualizing music with under three year olds. *International Journal of Early Years Education,* 13 (3): 289–303.

Young, S. (2011). Children's creativity with time, space and intensity: Foundations for the temporal arts. In E. Coates and D. Faulkner (Eds.), *Exploring Children's Creative Narratives.* Abingdon: Routledge. pp. 177–99.

INDEX

www.ingramcontent.com/pod-product-compliance
Lightning Source LLC
Chambersburg PA
CBHW080556030426
42336CB00019B/3212

9 781526 493545